CW00525871

How to Be the Grown-Up

www.penguin.co.uk

How to Be the Grown-Up

Why good parenting starts with you

DR MARTHA DEIROS COLLADO

bantam

TRANSWORLD PUBLISHERS
Penguin Random House, One Embassy Gardens,
8 Viaduct Gardens, London SW11 7BW
www.penguin.co.uk

Transworld is part of the Penguin Random House group of companies
whose addresses can be found at global.penguinrandomhouse.com

First published in Great Britain in 2024 by Bantam
an imprint of Transworld Publishers

A CIP catalogue record for this book
is available from the British Library.

ISBN 9781787636880

Typeset in 10.5/16pt FS Benjamin by Jouve (UK), Milton Keynes.
Printed and bound in Great Britain by Clays Ltd, Elcograf S.p.A.

The authorized representative in the EEA is Penguin Random House Ireland,
Morrison Chambers, 32 Nassau Street, Dublin DO2 YH68.

Penguin Random House is committed to a sustainable future
for our business, our readers and our planet. This book is made
from Forest Stewardship Council® certified paper.

To my daughters, because being your Mama has made me a better grown-up. And to C, for willingly choosing to keep growing up with me.

Contents

Contents

5: Skills for Living

6: Big Topics

7: Family Life

Where to Begin . . .

Parenting is not for the season of childhood, it is for a lifetime. I believe that becoming a parent unfolds alongside your child. As your child grows, develops and learns, you too will learn, change and evolve. One of the hardest truths is that parenting is not about finding strategies to control a child's behaviour. At its core, parenting is about how adults learn to control their *own* behaviour, to find effective tools to appropriately respond and relate to children.

This book contains no new knowledge.

Yes, you read that right! None of what I share here is new; I am not trying to sell you a 'new model' or a revolutionary parenting framework no one has ever heard of. Yet everything in this book is unique because it has been shaped by my professional learnings, clinical experience and, fundamentally, my experiences of becoming a mother.

Having a child has taught me what it really means to be a 'grown-up' and how the words, actions and interactions we choose can impact so deeply on the relationships we create with our children. I have the privilege of getting to know children and their families' stories every week, through therapeutic encounters that have taught me more about children than any scientific paper or theory ever could. In this book, I want to offer you some insights into how things might sound or look in practice. All the information on infant and child behaviour and development, neuroscience, attachment and parenting research has been well documented over the last ten to thirty years. I have embedded this alongside my clinical learnings over eighteen years of professional practice and shared some of my own experiences of parenting to illustrate some of the ideas I offer. I hope that this combination will give you a sense of what this means for you and your relationship with your child.

I take a systemic approach to the clinical work I do with children and their families. This isn't a model, it's more like a philosophy, a way of seeing children and what they do as deeply interrelated to language and being in relationships with others. So rather than focusing on behaviour at face value alone, I focus on how behaviours create or rupture relationships, what leads children and parents to pull closer together or further apart, and the way language can be used to either cement ways of relating or plant small seeds of change. My work often means exploring children's personal stories, their ideas about themselves and the world, and how these are similar or different to the ones their caregivers carry. I always work with the whole family: adults, children and any systems or networks that influence and impact them (e.g. school, friends, extended family members). This has given me a broad understanding of children's and young people's lives, and rich, creative and impactful strategies to support them and the adults around them.

My clinical career in paediatric settings with children and their families has helped me understand the needs and concerns of parents, and I get how children see the world. It is this multiple-view perspective I hope to bring to this book – a new lens through which you can look at your child so you at times see the world as if you were in their shoes and can make sense of where your choices come from. This book is a summary of psychological ideas and clinical frameworks shaped in a way that translates science and practice into your everyday family life. A snapshot of ideas that I hope will stimulate your curiosity to explore them further and try them out yourself and with your child.

I won't promise this will be the 'only book' you'll ever need, because there are no easy routes to parenting and no 'parenting hacks'. You are unique, and so is your child. There is no such thing as a 'manual' for how to be with your child – being a parent means shifting and changing alongside your child's developing needs and their life transitions. You are the expert on your child, and they are the expert on themselves and their experiences of the world. I want you to trust yourself in making the right choices for you and your family. My hope is that one of the biggest takeaways you have from reading this book is a sense of empowerment – that you have the authority to parent your child in a way that allows you to recognize that this power already exists within the relationship you are developing every day with them.

Parenting will push you to grow into a better version of yourself, often in ways you never expected. Parenting relies on us, the adults of today, to be the change we want to witness in our children. We have to work on our self-regulation before we can teach our children to do the same for themselves. We have to show respect, kindness and warmth, and use our words appropriately, if we want our children to show up in this way with us and with others. We are the ones who have to shower our children with love and warmth, even when they don't 'pay it back', so they know what love feels like and can love another the way they were loved by us. Because children learn most through what they see adults around them do, I want you to see this book as an opportunity to bring you greater self-awareness that will help you to make conscious choices about the way you relate to children, how you understand their behaviours and choices, and the responses you recognize as most useful to guide them.

I hope this book opens up your curiosity and offers practical tools that you can use in order to recognize:

- Children as whole people in their own right, and how you can support and safeguard this first season of life we call 'childhood'
- The essential and unique role emotions play in our lives, and ways you can meet your own needs so that you can then support your child's
- Why we work so hard as a society to control kids, and the truth about what happens when we stop

3

- The power of being firm and loving with the help of boundaries
- Why having honest and open conversations matters and what talking about topics such as sex, consent and death can also teach you
- The most important person, the one that matters most in this work – YOU.

Each chapter weaves in stories around research, theory and scientific knowledge, with clinical examples from my therapy room and points of reflection to invite you to experience some of this for yourself. I have taken care to modify the content so that no one family or child can fully recognize themselves in these stories. I have used the names of children I have worked with across my many paediatric settings in ways that don't make a child or family recognizable. It is a small nod to all the children whose lives have touched mine, more than I will ever be able to share back.

As you read this book you may discover new stories and/or get a sense of who you are from a different perspective. If you find yourself sparked by intense emotion as you read, I want to invite you to perform a simple action:

- Place a hand on your heart
- Breathe normally for five or six breaths
- Notice the feeling and give it a label (e.g. sadness, disappointment, calm)
- Greet the feeling (e.g. 'Oh, hello there, sadness.')
- Remind yourself that emotions are temporary; they are just visitors, and will pass
- Then let it go. Do not hold on to the emotion.

Come back to this whenever you feel the need to ground yourself.

Successful parenting is not about raising children who meet all their 'milestones' on time, are well behaved, polite and compliant at all times, eat everything off their plate, rarely complain or protest and get top grades. Successful parenting is about how you choose to show up in your relationship with your child, how you regulate your emotions, how you model the lessons you want children to learn, and how willing you are to reflect on your mistakes – and to apologize, repair and accept that, sometimes, your child might be right.

If you are ready to begin, let's go.

It starts with you – and I am here to walk you through this.

1

Foundations

CHAPTER 1

How They Develop

As a parent juggling the many practical tasks of your day, it is easy to miss the incredible things your child is doing just by the simple act of growing. Development tends to happen so gradually that you might not see it. And yet when you slow down just enough to notice the complexities of your child's development, it can help you adjust your expectations and allow you to respond in ways that align with who your child is in this moment rather than your adult vision of what they 'should' be doing. I want to invite you to be in awe of your child's social and emotional development, because it is breathtaking when you understand it. And when you see your child in this new light it will make you realize how your parenting choices can have a powerful impact on your child's brain, identity and their sense of self.

Human brains are born under construction; they are built from the ground up, and just like a house, they need strong foundations. By the age of three a child has over 1,000 trillion brain connections, the most they will ever have in their life. These get 'pruned' depending on the experiences they have – they are either consolidated and strengthened or shrunk and lost. The 'triune' model of the brain that is so widely spoken about and divides brain function into three areas – the 'reptilian brain', the limbic brain and the cerebral cortex – has been strongly discredited by neuroscience (Cesario, Johnson & Eisthen, 2020). The human brain is not compartmentalized into different sections for different actions or emotions – it's far more complex and interconnected than that. It is important to understand this because we have to rid ourselves of the common belief that emotions such as fear and other behaviours for survival (e.g. the 'fight-flight-freeze' response) are hardwired into us from our evolutionary past. We now know that these are concepts we learn through our relationships with others, and this means that how we treat children and the words we use with them are vitally important: they become blueprints for how they understand themselves and the world. Parents and caregivers play a vital role in either supporting or blocking brain development and the patterns of behaviour that emerge in relationships.

In our society we have a very poor understanding of child development. For example, adults often ask children to 'wait a moment' before listening to what they have to say or giving in to their request, and yet adults expect children to stop playing or running around immediately when asked to put their shoes on in order to leave the house or leave the park when it's time to go. We tend to overestimate children's capabilities while underestimating the pressure of the demands we place on them, and of course these change throughout their development.

Typically, the development of a child's brain, along with their social and emotional development, has a certain trajectory. However, there is a lot of fluidity around this. Some children will develop a little faster in certain areas than others, depending on their abilities and individual interests. For example, some children may enjoy language and using words and may be more likely to talk sooner; those who prefer movement, climbing and pulling themselves up may walk a little earlier. Some children take longer to master skills; perhaps they have a neurodivergent brain, or benefit from more practice than others in learning and developing skills.

Many of us in society carry an idea that babies and children 'manipulate' adults with their cries and their behaviour. How many times have you heard an adult say that when a child starts crying it's because they can't get what they want, or if they cry out at bedtime it's because they are 'trying to get their own way'? It's an easy assumption to make. The truth is that manipulation is a high-order brain function. In order to manipulate someone you have to be able to understand that multiple outcomes are possible and be able to analyse the pros and cons of a course of action in order to choose the 'best' option – the one that will lead someone to respond in the way you want them to. Manipulation involves understanding how another person may respond to and feel about your actions and requires good impulse control, the ability to pull back on certain behaviours while prioritizing others. When we break down what 'manipulation' is, it becomes easier to understand why children cannot begin to carry this out until they are closer to adolescence. Their brain development simply has not reached the capability to manipulate others with intent.

Once you understand that a baby's or a child's brain is nothing like an adult brain, you might start getting curious about their behaviour rather than applying adult assumptions about what is going on. You may wonder, 'If this isn't a manipulation, what could it be?' So, when you see a child screaming or protesting, can you start to see this as an expression of disappointment in a moment when they cannot get what they want? When a child cries at bedtime and begs you to not leave them, can you see this as the best way they know how to ask for comfort before the longest period of separation they have from you? This may seem like a tiny shift in adult perspective, but it can create powerful changes in the responses adults choose to make towards a child's behaviour, and this in turn has an impact on how their overall development progresses.

Similarly, when a child begins to talk, that doesn't mean they are developmentally ready to comply with what we ask of them, or even understand complex social concepts such as showing empathy, sharing, having 'good manners' or expressing gratitude. Up to the age of twenty-five, our human bodies haven't fully matured (including body shape, bone density and structure, and even hormonal changes), and our brains are not fully developed either. As the adults in our child's life we need to bring an awareness of the adult expectations we are imposing on them, the hopes we have for the skills and abilities they will carry into adulthood, and instead try to focus on seeing where our child is now in their developmental trajectory – what they can already do, the skills they have yet to learn, and how we as adults can be the powerful leaders that help our child practise, develop and learn skills for living.

Developmental milestones

We call the developmental trajectory by which children reach stages of growth 'milestones'. There are no set ages at which children develop or move through these developmental milestones, but we do know there are certain age ranges in which most children typically reach them. The best way to think of developmental milestones is that they are the beginning of a skill being formed, with the full picture still needing time to be completed. For example, a child who takes their first steps at around twelve months isn't yet fully mobile. They cannot jump until they are around twenty-four months old, won't be skipping until around three and a half years of age and won't have the strength, coordination or balance to ride a bike until closer to four years old. The first steps are the milestone for walking, but the work has only just begun. This is true for most developmental milestones but in particular for those we consider to be emotional, social and behavioural skills, which need time and lots of practice to learn – alongside full brain maturation at around twenty-five years of age – to be consolidated and fully formed as 'completed skills'. And this trajectory isn't a simple upwards path. Sometimes it can look as if a child is taking a step backwards. For example, when a child begins to walk, they also begin to ask for more physical closeness. As they understand that walking can take them further away from you, they need to be more physically attached to you than they did before. They are learning that your legs can take you places away from them too.

Often, when adults witness a 'regression' in an area of skill it is because the brain has decided that other skills will take precedence in that moment, and skills in that area can take a back seat, momentarily. Rather than thinking of this as a 'step backwards', reframe it as a leap forward in a slightly different direction. I remember when my child started to want to get dressed by herself. I would lay out her clothes and she would put them on, with loud cries of 'I can do it,' no matter how tricky it was. As she grew in confidence in this area she began to stop using her cutlery at the table. Instead, she started to eat with her hands, or more passively sit staring at her plate and say, 'I am tired . . . help me,' and we would spoonfeed her. Don't get me wrong – this was highly frustrating, particularly when I thought that the messy-eating phase was nearly over. Yet I was not worried by this temporary 'step backwards' because I knew she was making a big leap forward in other areas. Whenever this happens to your child, don't worry. Your child is still developing.

And if what you see is that your child is lagging behind their peers in reaching certain areas of development, focus on whether you are offering them appropriate experiences and opportunities to develop skills. Are you giving them lots of opportunities to experience language, physical movement, play and social interaction? If your answer is yes, then rest assured that your child is still learning and developing skills – they are just doing it at their own pace. Some children will show patterns in their behaviour that may lead you to consider whether they have a brain that is different from what we think of as 'typical'. Perhaps your child is neurodivergent. If this is the case and your child meets a diagnosis for Autism Spectrum Condition (ASC), a learning difficulty (e.g. dyslexia, dyspraxia) or an Attention Deficit Disorder (ADD or ADHD), you will inevitably adapt how you approach teaching your child skills. You will place your focus on their unique strengths and abilities, and this focus may be different to that of parents of a 'neurotypically' developing child. This difference is unique but that doesn't make it better or worse than for any other child.

Nurturing brain development

One of the questions I am asked most frequently by parents with young children is 'Will I spoil my baby if I hold them too much?' I strongly dislike the word 'spoil'; it conjures up visions of what happens to fruit when it is left too long and becomes bruised and rotten. Babies don't 'rot' when we meet them with warmth and love, they grow and develop in ways that have a huge impact lasting into their childhood and adulthood.

I recall a recent consultation with a mother who asked me whether she was at fault for her child's 'clinginess'. She explained that her family had come to visit and noticed that her child cried every time she left the room and only appeared to settle in her arms, not when being held by a loving grandparent or other family member. Some members of the family started to express concerns that her child had 'separation anxiety' and that it was the mother's reactions of staying close, holding her child and returning to soothe them when they cried that was creating this 'problem'. This story is not unique – I have heard many parents expressing similar concerns. The little one in this story was ten weeks old, and to me this speaks volumes about the stories of independence we privilege in our society.

It is so hard as a parent to know what is 'right' rather than 'wrong' when you are surrounded by conflicting messages coming from all sides. I remember when I became a mother being told that I was 'creating a rod for my own back' when I carried my baby in a sling, and that my child would 'never learn to self-soothe' if I didn't stop holding her before she fell asleep. The opinions and stories of others made me doubt my own professional knowledge and understandings during my early motherhood. It takes courage and confidence to stand up to the persistent and loud voices of our society that push for individuation and want babies and children to be 'independent' as soon as possible, regardless of the cost to the foundations of brain development.

I want you to rest safe in the knowledge that holding, carrying and cuddling babies and children will never, ever harm them. Holding babies and offering skin-to-skin contact is not only important for parent–child bonding, it supports brain growth and emotional development. Babies are not born able to 'self-soothe'; when they feel physical or emotional pain they cannot do anything to help themselves feel better. They can't wriggle out the wind in their tummies without your help, or know how and when to stretch when they have pins and needles, and they definitely cannot put on music, run themselves a bath, or talk about how they are feeling when they are upset. They need help and physical comfort from a safe, loving adult, the same way they need to be fed, dressed and cleaned.

Picking up and holding a baby when they cry meets their need for safety and security, and the effects can be profound. Feldman, Rosenthal & Eidelman (2014) randomly assigned premature babies to receive two weeks of skin-to-skin contact from their mothers in neonatal intensive care; others were randomly assigned to remain in incubators. All the babies were followed up seven times across their first ten years of life with physiological tests that looked at measures of stress, cognitive assessments of their abilities, and mother–child measure of interaction. Those babies who received skin-to-skin contact showed healthier stress responses, better sleep patterns and appeared to develop cognitive abilities sooner than babies who did not. Importantly, these effects were still evident ten years later. Touching and holding babies boosts oxytocin, which in turn switches off the impact of the stress hormone cortisol, which lowers the heart rate and allows the brain to grow and develop more rapidly and healthily. The long-lasting effects of holding and nurturing babies means that even if your child was in neonatal intensive care and needed to stay in an incubator, the skin-to-skin and holding you offer when you can will have a long-term impact.

Luby et al. (2012) carried out a study with ninety-one children aged between three and six who either had symptoms of depression or were psychologically well. Initially, all the children were observed and recorded interacting with a parent, usually the mother, who was completing a task while the child had to wait to open a gift. This task was set up to be an approximation of a daily parenting stressor – when a child wants something they cannot immediately have and a parent is busy with another task. The researchers conducted brain scans, and these revealed that those children whose parents empathized with their situation and offered them nurturing words and actions, such as holding them for comfort, had a hippocampus almost 10 per cent larger than those children whose parents showed less nurturing behaviour. This remained true whether the child had symptoms of depression or not. The hippocampus is the area of the brain involved in storing memories, learning and responding to stress. While many studies have shown how physical touch and closeness can decrease the stress response in children, this is one of the first human studies to link the impact of emotional nurturing on anatomical brain development.

So whenever someone questions 'how much' you hold your baby, you can come back to the knowledge that when they cry out for you, the impact of cuddling, carrying and the experience of warmth you offer your baby or child with words and calming sounds such as humming and singing is always positive. You are helping them develop the ability to soothe their emotions, have healthier sleep patterns, and have a greater capacity for learning and developing skills. In adulthood, early experiences of parental warmth have been found to protect from the risk of coronary artery disease (Caroll et al., 2013). Nurturing a child with warmth supports and protects their brain and physical health for life.

The art of attunement – reading a baby's cues and following through to meet their needs – begins as soon as babies are born. But it's not a straightforward process. All parents move in and out of attunement as they navigate their relationship with their child. You get pulled into tuning into your own body, your own mind and the world that surrounds you. It's a new relationship for both of you, and this means there will be times when you will naturally get it wrong. But a baby still needs you to scaffold what is happening in that gap between their cries and you attempting to meet their need. A lot of the time this will look like you tolerating their frustration, pain and disappointment, empathizing with their unmet need while compassionately giving yourself the space to understand that you can't get it right every time. This authentic and messy tuning in and out of being in a relationship with your child, the process of mismatch, rupture and repair, is where the brain begins to grow and wire itself for resilience. Holding and offering loving touch is part of this scaffolding for children. However, all babies are different, and they don't all like being held all the time. What matters most is that a baby's cries are met with warmth and a consistent effort to soothe and support, even when you don't know what they need. Standing beside them through this struggle communicates, 'I am here for you. You are not alone. You are safe.'

Crying is communication

The brain is born with two abilities: to feel sensation and to communicate. In terms of sensation, it may help to know that a baby's brain is like a sponge, absorbing everything from their environment and interactions with you. A baby benefits from warm, loving, sensory experiences, including hearing your voice in gentle intonations of speech, humming and singing, receiving loving strokes and massage, welcoming facial expressions and close eye contact. You can help a baby feel comfortable in a new environment by describing what is going on around you and what you are doing with them. For example, when you give them a bath, this may sound like, 'Oh, the water is so warm and lovely. Let's take this white sponge and sprinkle some water over your tummy. Ooooh. Is it tickly? How nice.' Your baby takes in your vocal tone, facial expressions and the way your touch feels on their body. Joining touch with soothing vocal tones helps your baby know they are safe with you. In the critical time period of the first three years of life, a baby's brain is especially sensitive to anger, fear and aggression. Frequent shouting, loud arguments and sudden bangs can affect their mental health and the development of the brain, even if it doesn't seem that they are noticing it.

A baby's cry is always a communication, a resounding alarm that something isn't right. Feeling lost with a crying baby is part of the process of beginning a new relationship with this little being who has arrived in your world. Rather than diving into a book to understand your child's cries, I want to invite you to see your baby as your map and trust that your internal compass can guide you to do what is best if you lean into it and trust it. Just as you know how to be and respond when your best friend calls you sobbing on the phone, you know how to be with a baby that is crying in distress. This may mean holding them, rocking them, using soothing sounds, singing or shushing and meeting their needs, which in babies are usually primary and immediate: sleep, food, warmth and dryness, and avoiding pain and discomfort (sometimes physical and sometimes environmental).

There will be times when you can understand your baby's needs and meet them with soothing comfort. And there will be many times when your baby's cries will be confusing and, no matter what you try, they continue to cry. You are not a bad parent when your baby's cries are a mystery to you. A newborn's sense of threat is huge because they only feel sensation, without understanding what is and isn't safe. So the first time they hear a loud bang, they cannot make sense of whether this is a door shutting, a balloon popping, a motorbike backfiring or a gunshot. Little ones' brains go quickly into high-threat mode because they register any sensation or sound as frightening, and their body tenses and their cries get louder as a signal for help. But they don't know whether what they feel in their bodies is anxiety, a wound, heartburn or reflux. Babies only receive sensory information, and to make meaning of what is happening they need an adult to create meaning for them – by holding them, giving them medicine, taking them to a doctor or protecting them from danger.

The crying upsets me too

A crying baby is a stressor on an adult. It heightens our senses for danger and it can be physically painful and distressing to witness a baby cry when they will not be soothed no matter what you do. If you become stressed and overwhelmed in the care of a crying baby, you are not alone. It is very common. It's okay to take a break, put the baby down in a safe place (such as their cot) and let them cry with you by their side. Allow yourself to cry or release your own emotions and take this as a sign that you may benefit from reaching out for help from a partner, friends, family or a health professional. This isn't a sign that you are a bad parent, it's a sign that you are not getting the right type of support, and meeting your needs is essential for you to be able to soothe your baby.

Crying doesn't make a child 'good' or 'bad'

In our society we have labelled crying as 'bad'. Nothing makes this more obvious than calling one of the critical periods of infant development 'The Terrible Twos'. Children begin to learn about emotions from six months, and at around eighteen months their awareness of the world expands and you are more likely to witness them lose control of their emotions. Science has clearly shown that this is a critical stage, a tremendous leap in development, and adults need to see it as full of teachable moments and opportunities to shape a child's brain in emotionally healthy ways. Because of all the changes children go through in this phase of development it is also one of the most challenging periods for a parent. Learning to give yourself grace, finding ways to meet your needs and remembering that it will pass is key to getting through with your sanity as intact as possible.

Remember that, due to temperament, some babies may cry a lot whereas others appear more content. Neither makes a child 'good' or 'bad'. They are simply individual differences in how they experience sensory input and what they need to bring soothing and regulation to their bodies. Our job as adults is to respond to a baby's individual needs as sensitively as possible. Some may need more holding and physical closeness whereas others may need more space. Sensitive care does not mean you will always get it right. Your response may not always calm their tears or dampen their cries, and this does not mean you have got it wrong or that you are harming their brain. It simply means their body has not yet finished releasing the emotion fully and the baby needs that bit longer to stay in your warm and caring embrace. For children who cry for long periods of time and cannot be soothed, it can be helpful to look out for signs of physical discomfort that may not be visible to the naked eye (e.g. allergies, pain, aches, etc.). Seeking support from medical professionals can be useful. Always remember you are the expert in your baby and if something does not feel right to you, you have the right to speak up about it.

Language is communication

As children become more able to interact with others and the world they begin communicating through babbling and start to develop a rudimentary idea of what socializing looks like by copying you and interacting with your verbal responses. Although they may not be able to articulate words yet, little ones benefit from you narrating or 'sportscasting' and describing what is going on around you. When my little one was this age I used to narrate my actions when I was doing chores, imagining that she knew nothing about the world (which of course she didn't) and so over-explaining things as if we were having a conversation. For example, 'Ah, look, it's that pink top I love. Ugh, yeah, I spilt tomato sauce on it the other day. I am going to have to soak it before I wash it. Here is the washing powder. I am going to put a little bit on and rub it like this – mmm, smells yummy. Can you smell it?' If you have never done this before, it can feel really odd, like talking to yourself, but you are doing so much more than that. By naming objects around you and narrating what you do, you expand your little one's curiosity about the world and invite them to explore their surroundings. It can help to remember that, for little ones, everything you say and do is likely to be 'a first'. And the more you talk about what you do in the world and name the things around them, the more they build vocabulary and a sense of safety that those things around them that make noises, move or look strange (washing machine, vacuum cleaner, etc.) are just part of your everyday home life.

There is good evidence that language development (i.e. vocabulary) and speech (i.e. articulation) is a predictor of children's long-term performance at school and academic outcomes (Eadie et al., 2021). Current guidelines for speech and language development suggest that by the age of two a child typically speaks fifty single words fluently enough for a stranger to understand them, and can put two or three words into sentences ('More water', 'Bye bye, Papa'); they may start asking 'why' questions, which are not real questions as such but a way to begin an interaction with you. By the age of three, a child's vocabulary typically expands to two hundred words and they can say short sentences ('He took my ball', 'I want a snack, Mama'); their questions have evolved into curiosities about 'who', 'what' and 'where'. By the age of four, a child will be speaking in longer sentences, using words such as 'because' and asking lots of questions starting with 'what', 'where' and 'why'.

Children are keen to share their perception and experience of the world with others. It is one of the ways they check that what they see, hear and feel is 'real' – in other words, that they are real individuals in this world of adults. Children do this through asking, telling, ordering and requesting, and adults can find it overwhelming when the same questions or statements are repeated over and over again. See this as the beginning of a child's socialization, a small start towards making sense of how they can interact with others. For example, you may witness your child asking 'Why?' repeatedly around the age of eighteen months. Whenever you answer logically, they go on to ask, 'But why?' When this happens frequently, stop seeing the 'why' (or the 'what' or the 'how') as a question – see it as a rudimentary way for your child to start a conversation. Answer their question willingly and extend it to asking them what they think the answer is and talking around the topic that prompted their question. See it as a game of turn-taking with words that is helping your child expand their vocabulary and make sense of how to interact in conversation with you.

There are going to be times when you will witness your child 'lose' their words. Instead of articulating how they feel or saying what you expect them to, they might use behaviour instead or explode in outbursts of emotion. Sensory experiences develop first, so it's normal for children to be unable to articulate something they feel, want or need when big emotions are flooding their bodies and brains; for example, saying 'Thank you' when receiving a gift can be difficult when a child is flooded with big feelings such as excitement, anticipatory anxiety, embarrassment and/or awe. In these intense experiences, let your child borrow your words and learn through the way you model language with others.

Concrete and abstract experiences

What is key is an understanding that no matter how articulate your child is, how much vocabulary they have or how well they are able to construct sentences (or even begin to read words), up to the age of between six and eight years they can still only make sense of the world through concrete experiences (i.e. they have a literal understanding of what they can see and touch as real; what they cannot see or touch doesn't exist or becomes 'magical' to them). As language helps us co-construct our understandings of the world, the words you use with a child at these early ages can make a big difference to what they understand or misunderstand. For example, children don't understand metaphors, so saying, 'It's raining cats and dogs,' can confuse them and prompt them to look out for cats and dogs falling out of the sky. Similarly, children don't tend to understand sarcasm and may feel sad, upset or ashamed when someone says something sarcastic to them or someone they love. For example, saying, 'That is so funny,' sarcastically may prompt a small child to jump in and say, 'No, it isn't'; they may even burst out crying. This is because sarcasm involves two conflicting ideas, usually a positive one and a negative one, and holding two ideas in mind begins to develop only around the age of eight. Saying what you don't mean is confusing to children and it can frighten and upset them to think you are being unkind or mean.

Being mindful of language and using clear, simple communication can greatly help your child. So, for example, saying, 'I won't let you hit,' is a much better instruction to a small child than 'You don't hit.' The first sets out a clear boundary that you, the capable adult, can ensure stays true. The second is giving a child an instruction that they may want to 'test' out, wondering, 'Hmmm . . . can I hit? Let me try . . .'

Of course, making sense of abstract concepts is a skill set that takes years to complete. Ideas such as time (i.e. the sense that five minutes is different to one hour), the permanence of death (i.e. that when we die we don't come back in physical form), basic geographical distances (e.g. to a country, a city, a town), abstract numerical concepts such as the value of money, and ideas such as truth, fairness, collaboration and faith are all abstract.

Imagination and play

At around eighteen months, many children exhibit 'imaginary play'. This is the ability to see objects for something that they are not. Children may use objects to represent something else. For example, using a plastic cup as a hat for a doll or pretending a plastic brick is a slice of cake. They may also assign certain properties to an object, for example pretending a teddy is crying and comforting it with hugs, kisses and soothing sounds. Children may also refer to invisible objects, perhaps pretending to grip an invisible steering wheel to drive a car or pouring from an invisible kettle to make a cup of tea. Play is a cognitive skill and an important marker for language development. When a child begins to engage in imaginary and pretend play we know their brain is beginning to understand symbolic representations, the idea that objects can represent something else – and that is exactly what words are: a representation of objects, people and abstract concepts (emotions such as 'happy', 'angry' and 'sad', and physical needs such as 'hungry', 'hot' and 'tired'). Some toddlers do not do imaginary play, and for some this is a part of their unique differences, for others a possible sign that they are falling behind and/or that they may have a neurodivergent brain. Children don't tend to show one difference in isolation, but if you are concerned about this talk with a health professional, who can carry out a full assessment and offer reassurance and guidance to meet your child's needs.

Imagination remains a key part in a child's development and they have trouble separating reality from fantasy up to around the age of six, living for a large part of their early years in a 'dreamlike state'. How many times have you witnessed a small child breaking into a little bop and a jiggle in a shop or a restaurant? Or asked your child a simple question like 'Hey, want an apple?' and received the reply 'Beep bop boop boop I am a robot.' A child's imagination flows into their reality. It is this ability that lets them find joy in the smallest of things, that makes children's play full of life and why they delight in what seem to adults like mundane events, like the breeze in the trees, finding a stick or watching their construction of blocks tumble to the floor again and again. If you have ever seen a child's happiness at seeing a butterfly flutter past or witnessed their joy when you blow on the white puffball of a dandelion and the stalks disperse into the wind, you will know exactly what I am talking about.

Abstract ideas land in the realm of imagination, which is why you may witness children asking, 'Are we there yet?' a few minutes after you have told them you are an hour away from your destination. To help little ones make sense of things such as time it is best to offer concrete information they can understand ('When you see the big red C sign on the road signs you will know we are coming into London and are nearly there').

A child's vivid imagination helps them to experience moments fully but it also leads them to fear everyday things (a dog's loud bark, the sound of fireworks or lightning) and imaginary dangers (a monster under the bed). These experiences often show up at around three to five years of age, and while they may feel like a problem, they are actually a sign that your child is beginning to reach 'milestones' where abstract and concrete thinking are developing. Children need safe adults to believe their fears are real but also to support them to make sense of these experiences by focusing on concrete information.

Between the ages of six and eight, children begin to make sense of fantasy as 'make-believe', and this is a big shift from how they perceived the world before. This can lead to a witnessing of more worries, fears and anxiety around everyday things such as separating from you, because they now understand that you are doing something else without them; asking questions about death and dying; and playing in ways that appear more 'real' in terms of the world (e.g. a toy might be put in a car to travel but it won't sprout wings to fly). This is also the age at which certain stories we tell children begin to lose their reality to the child. Children are able to understand that Father Christmas is not real and that their presents are the ones they saw with you at the shop. Many children may still choose to 'believe' that Father Christmas exists – and I know many adults who do this too. There is something magically innocent about believing in fantasy and continuing to dive into 'imaginary worlds' that go beyond logic.

The good behaviours we want to see

One of the most important markers for parents of whether they have a 'good' child or not is how they behave with others. Are they good at sharing? Do they 'play nicely' with others? Do they show kind and polite manners towards others? But these behaviours are rooted in development. It is the prefrontal cortex in the brain that is responsible for these emerging skills at the age of seven or eight, and this doesn't mature and consolidate until the age of twenty-five. Babies and toddlers don't have access to a well-formed prefrontal cortex, and this makes complex skills such as empathy and impulse-control difficult. We know little ones can show sympathy towards someone else (e.g. they may reach out when they see that someone is crying or hurt), but this is different to the concept of empathy, the ability to have a 'theory of mind' and make sense of someone else's perspective and understand that they might have different feelings and emotions to yours. So when a child is having fun on a swing they won't understand what it is like to be the child waiting to have a go. As an adult, you may try and remind your child that 'someone else is waiting', but this is likely to be met with a protest that they are having fun and don't want to stop. This isn't a child being selfish, it's a sign of an immature brain that as yet lacks capacity for empathy.

Adults tend to misunderstand this developmental readiness and place unrealistic expectations on children when it comes to saying 'thank you', 'sorry', 'please', and/or sharing with others. These expectations are flawed and put adults in a tug of war, using strategies that force, push, bribe or threaten children to behave as is expected. How many times have you heard an adult say to a child, 'Say sorry,' when they have pushed past others to grab a snack or food at a party? When the child says sorry but continues to push ahead to grab the yummy popcorn, does it look like they have understood what they have done wrong or why apologizing is important? Children will repeat the words you ask them to say, but it doesn't mean they are capable of empathy in the early years. Their brains are self-focused for survival and this allows the focus to be on learning skills for themselves rather than looking outwards at others.

When we begin to understand that children's brains need adult support to grow and develop we can begin to shift some of our expectations and focus our time and effort on teaching skills in ways that make developmental sense and help children learn more effectively. When we do this, we wire a child's brain for deep emotional understanding of what it means to have empathy, gratitude, remorse and compassion towards another.

If we could physically see the neural connections that are being created and strengthened every time we make a parenting choice that supports a child's brain, I believe it would change our outlook on the value and role we ascribe to parenting. All those hours spent holding a baby while they cry are not wasted hours in your day. They are building a brain that is beginning to create neurological connections for soothing and regulation. Every time your body becomes a place of rest, support, safety, comfort and warmth it creates stronger attachment bonds between you and your child that bring them inner safety, resilience and soothing. Whenever your hands reach out to carry, hold, connect or play with your child, it helps them gain a sense of being seen and wires them for self-esteem, confidence and belonging. And whenever you meet your child with words of validation and affirmation that their experiences are real, they link emotion with language, inner bodily signals with external experience, and grow confidence in their own instincts, their capabilities and their connection with you.

CHAPTER 2

It Starts with You

In this book, I want to help you understand the *why* behind your child's behaviour and share some ideas and inspiration that I hope may help you find your own way to meet your child's needs. This begins with respect for you as an adult who is navigating the tricky journey of parenting and respecting your child as a whole person in their own right.

Becoming a parent is a process. It begins with a child, the one you were in your childhood, and it continues when you have a child of your own and call yourself 'a parent'. We tend to learn how to parent our children by the way we were parented ourselves. A lot of parenting is talked about as though it's 'natural' or 'instinctive', but in reality parenting is both a learning and an unlearning of stories, ideas and concepts for both you and your child. Parenting is bidirectional: you are both shaping and being shaped by the child in front of you. No two children are the same, and the ways in which you interact with each of your children will be different, depending on how they respond and interact with you and how your individual temperaments and personalities complement each other.

Some of what I share in this book is going to make sense to you and so it may feel comfortable to try it out. However, some may seem uncomfortable or even alien to you. How what I offer lands with you is going to depend on the scripts and stories that you carry and your experiences. It's also going to come from the context of your culture, the societal norms and expectations you live with as a parent and the ones you lived with when you were growing up as a child. When you were raised in a society that is different to the one you are parenting in, this can bring additional layers of complexity and influence. Try to notice what it feels like when you read ideas and concepts that are new or unfamiliar to you and catch those times when you feel a little sting that says, 'No. That's wrong.' I want you to try and pause and meet this feeling with a curiosity that asks, 'Why do I find this idea difficult?' See it as a small flag that this is an area that perhaps needs further exploration, perhaps an indication to unlearn something you held as a truth for a long time, or an opportunity to learn something new.

So much of parenting our children starts with us: the stories we bring to our parenting relationship, the moments that spark big emotions in us, and the ways in which we choose to respond and communicate to set boundaries as a parenting team or co-parents. In this chapter I want to think about you and to help you develop some self-reflexivity in moments of challenge with your child, allowing you to see what you bring into the dynamic and giving you options for how to move things forward.

Blindly following the script

How you interact with your child has partly been shaped by the experiences and the stories you learned in your family of origin. We call these 'family scripts', templates of how to behave and be in relation to ourselves and others that we learned in our childhood and over time. Some of these scripts will be experienced as positive, and you may wish to hold on to them as you create your own family. These may be around traditions, rituals, ceremonies and unique stories that are part of your family and bring a sense of connection about 'who you are' as a family. For example, baking a Christmas cake with all the children in the family, mixing in the batter while singing Christmas carols, or wearing red pants on New Year's Day to bring good luck in the year to come.

Other scripts may seem automatic and unconscious – things you fall into doing or words that roll off the tongue without you thinking about or planning them. They may seem familiar, as if it's a 'natural instinct' to do them. These are the scripts that you know as 'rules for living' – stories and ideas that have been absorbed as facts rather than thought about or questioned as to whether they are still useful to you now. Many of these scripts don't show up until parenthood, which is the first time you will be back in a parent–child relationship since your own childhood.

Think about the thoughts and ideas you have when you see a small child having a big tantrum in public. You may think, 'That child is so dramatic,' or even 'How naughty!' You might assume the parent is not doing 'enough' to control their child or is not meeting their needs appropriately. In these moments, you bring your own experiences and scripts to the situation, and this creates expectations about how children 'should' behave and how adults 'should' respond. Some 'traditional' scripts may sound like:

'A good baby sleeps through the night.'
'Good children don't cry or play up in public.'
'Children should play nicely with others.'
'Children should have good table manners and not get up until they
    have finished all the food on their plate.'

We often do not realize the strength of the scripts we carry until we witness our own child behaving in a way that brings out an immediate reaction from us, one that either teaches them the same story we carry or offers them a different experience.

Rewriting scripts is challenging: it takes conscious awareness of the scripts you hold, the capacity to meet them with curiosity and then be able to find a 'new script' you wish to carry. So, for example, if you carry a script that says, 'A parent's job is to keep their child's behaviour under control,' you may need to break this down and consider:

- Where did you learn that?
- What experiences confirm or deny this as a fact?
- What does 'keeping behaviour under control' look like in practice? What strategies or techniques does it make parents more likely to use?
- How does trying to keep a child's behaviour 'under control' help or get in the way of building a relationship with them?
- Is there another script that you could rewrite from this place of greater openness and curiosity?

As a parent, I used to hold this script about 'keeping my child's behaviour under control'. It was such a contrast to my professional belief as a clinical psychologist that we cannot control another's behaviour, we can only learn to manage our own, that I found myself in conflict. I was following a script I grew up with and it was going against the script I have learned professionally and worked with. Any time my child had a tantrum in public I noticed anger flare up in my body and a real need to shut my child's screams down. When I first noticed this in myself I was in a busy supermarket and I picked up my child and ran to the car, feeling the weight of judgement from others. Once in the car, with a calm child, I started to rethink my reaction. We went back into the shop and carried on shopping. I haven't reacted in that way since then, despite still having these strong feelings in my body when my child has a tantrum in public. It took conscious awareness and practice to re-write this script and be the parent I want to be, with and for my child. Nowadays, when my child has a tantrum in a shop I stop and I breathe deeply. I will often sit down beside her on the floor and wait until she is calm. Recently, this has meant sitting in a large shopping centre outside a coffee shop as people came and went. As long as it is safe and we are not in the way, I focus on my child and I ignore the stares. I know for some parents this would be really hard to do, and doing what works for you in the moment is often good enough. For me, it has to do with coping in public. I know the tantrum shrinks faster when I remain calm and bring her safety and comfort. My script now sounds a lot more like 'A parent's job is to learn to control their own behaviour [aka regulate their emotions] so they can guide and support their child's needs.' We'll talk about how to regulate your own emotions in Chapter 3. I know it's something I definitely needed to learn.

Learn to meet your past so you can live in the here and now

When you become clearer and more conscious about the scripts you carry, you can begin to see them as windows into your past. A moment that triggers strong emotions in you is sometimes about what is happening in the moment (i.e. loud shrieks from a child can be very overwhelming and anxiety-inducing); at others, the strong feelings you experience may be 'ghosts' from your past. Rather than being about what your child does or doesn't do, they are rooted in parts of yourself that were shut down in your childhood or the social norms you learned about your culture growing up.

Moments that activate big emotions in you don't need to be avoided; they are points of reference that can give you a clue about what *you* need in these moments, which will then enable you to support your child with *their* needs more effectively. For example, if you hold a script that 'Anger should be kept under control,' it is likely that when your child is protesting loudly you may escalate your behaviour in an attempt to shut their anger down, to communicate to your child that anger is not acceptable. Your reaction may show up rapidly and automatically, making it hard for you to stop yelling at your child in that moment and unwillingly teaching your child that shouting is acceptable. Becoming aware of how your child's anger makes you react won't stop strong feelings being sparked in you, but it can slow you down enough to make a more conscious choice of how you want to speak or react in that moment.

Self-reflection is a skill you can practise

Self-reflection is hard to find in the moment you notice an intense emotion inside you, so looking at situations in hindsight, when you are calm and able to process your thoughts and ideas, can be useful. Here are some steps to guide you in looking at a moment when strong feelings were activated in you.

Event: Think of a time when your child did something that led you to shout or escalate your behaviour. What were they doing (e.g. saying no to the meal you have lovingly prepared)?

Script: What story does your child's behaviour bring up for you? Does it say something about you as a person, or bring up words in your mind? Words such as 'My child is ungrateful,' 'I worry they are spoilt,' 'I have to get them to eat something,' or 'It's not okay for them to say no to me.'

Look at your 'ghosts': Take a moment to consider what would have happened if you had done this same thing in your home as a child. Would your 'no' have been met with understanding and connection? Would you have been dismissed, shamed or isolated? What would you have done in that moment?

Acceptance: Try and meet your child's behaviour with curiosity and acceptance. What is going on for your child in this moment? Is it okay to not want to eat sometimes or to not like every type of food? Would you find it more acceptable if their 'no' was expressed differently? If so, what do you need to teach your child? Are there other needs your child has that may be getting in the way of their appetite, for example tiredness, anxiety, stress or any changes in their life or within the family?

Self-reflection: How do you want to parent your child through these moments, and what will help you get there? Do you need to learn coping skills? Do you have unmet needs that compound how you feel at these times, for example a need for rest, nourishment, movement, creativity, intimacy, or to feel seen and understood and valued by other adults? Are there things you might be able to change, boundaries you can set, people who may be able to help, or resources you might be able to tap into to support you?

Repair: When your behaviour escalates, you need to recognize this and be accountable for your actions, no matter what your child did in that moment. This is key to healing the relationship with them and with yourself. What good repair looks like is something we'll talk more about later.

If you have ever shouted at your child in a moment of overwhelm and later realized that the anger you let out on them was not to do with what your child was doing but instead related to something that happened to you that day (stress, lack of sleep, an argument with your partner), then welcome, you're a normal human. It has happened to everyone (including me).

When you are able to bring curiosity to these moments of intense emotion in you and begin to accept the stories and unmet needs you carry in that moment, it can stop you from replaying old scripts and bringing back 'ghosts' from the past. Instead, it will bring you to the here and now to consider with more openness how you can be most useful in this moment to your child. The more you make sense of these moments and meet them with curiosity and acceptance, the better you will be able to tune in to the 'ghosts' of your past and recognize that your feelings are not always switched on because of what your child is doing in the moment, they are sometimes about a script that you learned or an unmet need that you carry. This will allow you to connect more meaningfully with your child in the here and now.

Parenting styles: what is yours?

Once we are more self-aware, we can begin to look at how we were parented and the parenting style our parents used with us – often unconsciously – and how this created our own parenting scripts of what 'good parenting' looks like.

It is likely that you experienced different styles from different carers in your life – the people who come to my therapy room tell me that this is very common – but there is often a pattern of one style being more over-arching and present than another. See if the three questions below help you make sense of the style of parenting that may have influenced your life growing up as a child:

- How did you learn the family rules in your home growing up? What words and/or actions did the adults in your home use?
- Were you allowed to protest and say no to your parents and/or adults when things did not feel right to you? How was your 'no' responded to (in words and/or actions)?

- What were the consequences (in words and/or actions) when you made a mistake and/or did not do as you had been asked to do?

Modern parenting research has defined four accepted styles of parenting: authoritative, permissive, authoritarian and uninvolved parenting (sometimes called neglectful). Parents who have an uninvolved style of parenting respond to a child's basic needs of food, clothing and shelter but tend to be emotionally distant and provide little or no supervision or boundaries. The definition of these styles has been refined and shaped by cross-cultural studies into parenting that look at how parents influence children through specific practices such as encouraging them to play outdoors, socializing them with their peers, or helping them with their homework. A parenting style is about more than specific practices around a child. It is about an overall 'attitude' of how to be with a child and the atmosphere you create in the language you use, the approach you take and the way you relate to your child.

Authoritative parenting has been shown to be the most effective parenting style to raise emotionally intelligent, securely attached, confident and responsible children with better, more long-lasting relationships with their parents and others across their lifespan. This has been found to be true not only in Western society but across many cultures, including in China (Zhang et al., 2017) and in African American and Latino communities (Dixon et al., 2008). This style is punctuated with warmth and empathy alongside clear, fair and firm boundaries towards a child, which allows parents to hold a position of leadership in the household while respecting and considering a child's emotions and needs within the context of their developmental stage. An authoritative parent is always playing 'detective' and leaning into curiosity to make sense of a child's behaviour and what they might be communicating. They value a child's opinion even when they maintain the authority to make the best decision for them.

Without knowing it, you are likely to have heard of authoritative parenting by its 'rebranded' name 'gentle parenting'. This was an attempt to differentiate it more clearly from authoritarian parenting, which sounds very similar but is vastly different. Authoritarian parenting places high demands and expectations on children without valuing their voice and tends to use harsh punishments to control behaviour. Authoritarian parents may show warmth to a child, but this is conditional on their behaviour and makes no acknowledgement of a child's developmental stage. Authoritarian parents see children as 'mini adults' who need to follow the rules they are set without questioning them.

The main issue with the 'gentle parenting' label is that it has confused parents into thinking that this parenting style is 'soft' and devoid of rules, limits or adult guidance. Many confuse 'gentle parenting' with 'permissive parenting', which often communicates to children: 'You can do what you like. I don't want to be mean or upset you.' So in a scenario where a child is protesting about not being able to watch more TV and deliberately throws a cushion across the room, a permissive parent would ignore the behaviour and, when the shouting and screaming get louder, agree to let the child watch more TV. Giving greater autonomy to a child and not setting boundaries disempowers the authority of the adult and leaves a child without a scaffold to manage anger. An authoritative parent would set a clear boundary on a child's behaviour and hold the authority about what happens next, while empathizing with the child's disappointment about not getting what they want (i.e. 'I get that you are angry and you want to watch more TV. I won't let you throw things, but you can say, "I don't like it," and I will listen. You can watch more TV tomorrow. For today it's over').

Parenting styles set up a particular atmosphere in a family home. Think of a time when your child wanted to play a song over and over again . . . It might have driven you a little loopy and perhaps you wanted to shout something like 'Not this again. Stop it right now!' I don't blame you. That would be an authoritarian way of communicating how annoyed you are by their choice of music. If, instead, you respect your child's delight in the song while communicating that you feel differently about it, perhaps you would say, 'Please can we change the music? I am bored of this song. What could we listen to instead?' This is what an authoritative parent, who has the confidence to know they are in charge while respecting their child as a separate individual, sounds like. If you lean into permissive parenting, you are more likely to simply sigh audibly and allow your child to play the same song for the 254th time even if it means you get a headache and later become snappy and irritable towards your child without explaining why.

When a parent has not learned to communicate their emotional needs, wants and wishes in appropriate ways, it can make them use behaviour and language that includes sarcasm, criticism or humour, which are often received as passive aggressive by a child. Authoritarian and permissive communications clearly express displeasure to a child, but they both fail to explain what a child can do next. Children may know an adult is unhappy, but they don't understand why, and this leads children to see themselves as the cause of an adult's displeasure. Authoritative parents try to communicate clearly what is bothering them (i.e. a song on repeat is getting irritating) and separate this from their relationship with their child. When a child understands that it's not them that is the problem – it's the song – and that your taste in music has nothing to do with how you feel about them, they find it reassuring and grounding.

In the authoritative parenting style there are no 'invisible rules' placed upon children. Adults deliver a message that is clear and has explicit boundaries, and the adult takes ownership and is accountable for their own emotions, wants and wishes. To embody this, you have to accept that your child will have feelings, thoughts and ideas that are separate and different to yours. For example, when a child accidentally topples over a tower they have been building and starts to cry and you are able to hold your adult perspective ('It's no big deal, we can build it again') alongside your child's experience ('It's fallen down and it's the end of the world'), you might be more likely to reach out to your child in a way that says, 'Aw, no . . . It fell. You didn't want that to happen. It is sad, you worked hard on that tower. I am here.' However, if you only hold an adult perspective, you are more likely to land in authoritarian mode, saying something like 'It's just a tower. Stop crying,' or in permissive mode, dismissing their experience, and try to fix it for them: 'Chin up, love, we can build it again.'

Boundaries are a big part of what sets the atmosphere of a home. Don't be fooled into thinking that children push the boundaries because they don't want them. They push to get independence and see how far they are allowed to go. But all children benefit from having clear rules and limits, as this creates predictability and safety. When boundaries are healthy and appropriate, they teach children how to take responsibility for their own feelings and actions. When boundaries are fuzzy, unclear or broken without explanation this can make children try to make things better for their parents or fix their problems. This can lead to co-dependency and people-pleasing tendencies in an attempt not to upset others. For example, if a child throws a glass of milk on to the floor as a form of protest, a boundary may be to calmly ask the child to wipe up the spillage and then talk about how they can show anger more appropriately (e.g. 'You are allowed to be angry and say it or stomp your feet, but I won't let you throw drinks around'). In contrast, authoritarian control would not acknowledge that a child is learning 'how' to show anger and would go straight into punishment: 'What did I say about throwing things? You make me so angry. No books at bedtime tonight.' Permissive, fuzzy boundaries are likely to attempt to appease a child while making them feel responsible for how an adult feels, not their own behaviour: 'Aw, no, you spilt that. That's not very nice. I now have to clean that up. Do you think that's fair?'

There's only a small chance that you will stay in 'authoritative parenting mode' at all times – it's really hard and takes a lot of conscious work. Yes, it is something to aim for, but there will be times when you jump into a more controlling way of approaching your child, perhaps when you feel scared or think they are at risk ('NO. That's dangerous. How many times have I said not to touch the stove? Why don't you listen?'). Other times, you might be a little softer, allowing your child's wants and wishes to take precedence, for example when your child is unwell and wants comfort foods, or when you just think, 'Yes, I will give you an extra five minutes of screentime so I can finish my cup of tea.' Of course, this will not harm your child. Finding your parenting style is about getting a balance that edges towards authoritative parenting, where healthy boundaries, respectful communication, empathy and warmth are bountiful, so that when the other 'parenting modes' show up, your child has built the resilience to cope and adjust to this. At the end of the day, the approach you take and the atmosphere you build in your home is about trying to teach children the skills they need for life and offers them the greatest long-term benefits to their emotional wellbeing. If calling it authoritative sounds too much like authoritarian, give it another label that makes sense to you. My preference is to think of it as 'developmentally appropriate' parenting, because we all have our unique style that is shaped alongside our child's needs, with some needing more boundaries and others more flex. Just remember that effective parenting is not soft; you don't just drop the boundaries and let your child rule the roost, because embodying an attitude of love sometimes means that, as a parent, you have to make the harder choice and sit with the difficult feelings this brings up for you and your child. There isn't always a solution, there are moments that are just hard, and you can move through this with your child by remembering that you are doing your best, even when you're in 'survival mode'.

Assertive communication versus aggressive communication

Do you know the difference between assertive and aggressive communication? It's subtle but important in your relationships with others, including with children.

Assertive communication expresses your needs to someone else and offers a balanced view of what is happening. It empowers. Aggressive communication takes the form of criticism and prioritizes your voice over someone else's. It frightens.

Both types of communication are learned in relationship with others and through how others model disagreements and conflicts. This is why it's so important to give a child opportunities for their voice to be heard, so they can learn that they are allowed to protest and we can guide them to understand how to do it most appropriately.

ASSERTIVE In control	AGGRESSIVE Out of control
Respectful 'I respect your ideas. Here are mine . . .'	**Disrespectful** 'This is happening. Because I say so . . .'
Firm and gentle 'We are allowed to have different views. There is no "right" or "wrong".'	**Loud and menacing** 'Stop crying and listen to ME.'
Clearly states needs 'I need to take a breather, I'm starting to get angry . . .'	**Criticizes or attacks** 'You never stop shouting. Give me a break!'

Requests with 'I' or 'we' statements	Demands with 'you' statements
'Maybe we need to find a different strategy that works for both of us . . .'	'You are wrong. That won't work.'
Listens to the other person and validates	**Interrupts**
'I can hear that you find this scary . . .'	'It's always about you, isn't it? Have you thought about me?'

Assertive communication is hard to put into action, and it may feel even harder if you were never given space to be assertive as a child. If your feelings were denied, dismissed or belittled, and if you were told your 'protest' was rude, inappropriate or simply wrong, you may find that an 'aggressive tone' shows up when your capacity to tolerate things has been surpassed.

It is never too late to work on:

- Learning to express your emotions, naming them so you can share with others how an experience makes you feel
- Learning assertive language to get your needs met, including using boundaries when you need to
- Finding your voice separate to what others want, wish or find pleasing.

It's okay to disagree and have a different opinion. Often there is no right or wrong, just something that is more or less useful in the moment. If you are able to listen and understand your child's experience, new possibilities you have never before thought of may open up to you.

Cooperative conversations: build the 'we' over 'me'

What do you do when the person you are raising a child with doesn't agree with your parenting style? If your partner feels more control is needed to guide your child in the right direction and you want to approach your child with connection and warmth, how do you find a middle ground (and does one even exist)?

One of the greatest sources of conflict between co-parents, whether you live under the same roof or not, is the idea of 'how' to parent a child. Many parents judge 'how well' they parent by comparing their style to their partner's. When your words and actions are too dissimilar it can make you question some of the ways you were brought up or lead you to question the way your partner was raised. There can be discomfort in witnessing difference.

Imagine your child is running in the park, stumbles over and starts to cry.

Parent 1: Leans into the child, looks at their knee and says:
   'Aw, you are hurt. Let it out, just let it out. I am here, my love.'
Parent 2: Shares a story about what has happened and offers a choice:
   'You fell. Ouch! Can you get up, or do you want to sit down for a while?'
Parent 3: Picks the child up and takes them away from the park to a safe place.

In these scenarios, all the parents are being responsive and showing attunement to their child; however, the words and actions they choose are different. A child is likely to feel seen, safe and understood in all three cases. The one you choose to take is both a personal preference and what you know will help your child in that moment. However, because every child is different, what works for your child may not work for another. Only you know what the best fit is, and this may be different to what works for your partner with your child, because your parent–child relationships are unique to each of you.

Children benefit from having parents who have different skills; it means they can learn different things. There will inevitably be times when you witness something happening between your partner and your child that you do not agree with and you may wish to bring your partner's attention towards finding a different approach. When we think of a team, we accept and look out for differences in the various members' roles. Good teams have a range of players with different skills that complement and support each other. I want to invite you to think of your co-parenting in this way, whether you are still in a relationship with the other parent of your child or not. Being a 'team' and presenting a united front is not about having a romantic relationship, it's about sharing the common goal of raising a child. The way you do this as individuals may look different on the surface, but your common goal is the same. If you learn to communicate collaboratively, taking on actions you can both support will feel easier.

Here are some steps to take if you notice a behaviour or difference of parenting styles that you'd like to discuss with your co-parent. Begin by considering what setting will feel safe and be most beneficial to your conversation. Would it feel safe to talk in a particular room in your home? At a particular time of day? In the car? Over the phone or by email? While you're walking somewhere? How you position yourself in the conversation physically (e.g. side by side rather than face to face) and the location you choose can make a difference to you feeling able to begin and to open up to talk about it. So, although this may seem like an extra step in the process, don't skip it.

1. Open up the conversation
Inviting a co-parent to talk about something they have done with your child that to you felt inappropriate or wrong can raise your partner's

defensive hackles. You want them to listen and understand your concerns, and for that you need to engage in collaborative ways of talking. Consider beginning with:

'Can we talk about . . .'
'Would you be open to feedback on . . .'
'I noticed the other day when . . .'

2. Focus on objective behaviour

This may sound like 'I noticed the other day when Nieve didn't want to put her shoes on that you shouted at her.' This is better than 'It was really bad when you shouted at Nieve the other day.'

3. Actively listen and validate

Validation does not say, 'You are right.' Validation says, 'I hear you. I understand your experience.' When you validate your partner, you show them that you are paying attention, you are willing to listen to their feelings and to understand. Rather than getting stuck in problem solving ('You should . . .'), minimizing ('It could be worse . . .'), denying ('That didn't happen') or avoidance ('Focus on the positives . . .'), validation calms our nervous system, which then allows us to listen, connect and engage in a conversation. Validation may sound like 'I am listening,' 'It makes sense that you feel like this,' 'I see that you are upset/angry/nervous.' When you want someone else to consider your point of view, be open to considering theirs first.

4. Share your concern

State clearly and simply what your concern is. Make sure you accept your feelings and your concerns and don't layer assumptions on the other person. This might sound something like 'I am concerned that when you shout at Nieve she learns that you can be scary. I worry that it's affecting her relationship with you.' This is better than 'I am concerned that you have an anger problem.'

5. Find a shared action

The best resolution is for both of you to find an agreed next step. This may be an action you can take in that moment, a different strategy you are both going to try, or something else. Consider asking questions such as 'What can we do differently next time?', 'I wonder if there is a way that we can . . .', 'How can I best help you when . . .?'

No matter what parenting styles you and your co-parent have inherited, you are bonded by one powerful thing – your love for your child and the values you share in wanting to raise them into the best person they can be.

Approach your child with 'unconditional love'

Your parenting style needs to be imbued with the commitment of wanting to grow alongside your child, intertwining your growth with theirs, like branches on a tree. You may have a million reasons to love your child – their contagious giggle, their funny turns of phrase, the way they reach out to hold your hand when they are scared – but it is loving them whether or not they're doing those things that is most powerful.

The power of this love isn't just an intangible, feel-good theory. Fifty years ago, the psychologist Carl Rogers suggested that loving our children wasn't enough. 'We have to love them unconditionally' for who they are, not for what they do. Love is powerful, and it has ripple effects on our brains, our bodies and our sense of self. This isn't just a 'Pollyanna' idea about how nice 'love' feels, it's hard science on the mental and physical impact love has on the critical phase of child development, where the brain is like a sponge, learning and absorbing information for growth, developing and strengthening synaptic wiring and brain–body connections.

Even knowing this, the biggest parenting test your child will throw at you is your answer to the question 'Do you love me, no matter what?' Most of the time, and while things are going smoothly, your answer may unwaveringly be 'Yes, of course, always and for ever. Never doubt it.' But this won't be asked of you when things are going well; it's when your child is protesting, saying mean words and pushing the boundaries that the strength of your love will be put to the test. It can be easy to think in these moments that you do not like your child at all. And yet it is in these moments that challenge you to your core that your child needs to know that you are with them for the pretty parts and the happy days but also for the rough days and the bad times. No matter what, your love is unshakeable.

I know that the idea of unconditional love can feel controversial to some, particularly if you hold the belief that love is a weakness or that children need to be 'toughened up' in order to overcome the challenges life throws at them. As humans, we have an innate drive to bond with others, and our first attachments are with our caregivers and members of our family. To be securely attached means to have a sense of belonging, to feel cared for and supported and to receive predictable comfort and protection. These experiences in the early years give children an understanding of what a healthy relationship looks like, and this enables them to easily identify 'red flags' in their relationships with others. However, without conscious intent, often parents dial up affection when a child is 'good'. This might be when they are doing as they are told, they are playing nicely with a friend, or they haven't had a tantrum all day. And when behaviours become annoying or less likeable, parents withhold affection, through ignoring, punishing or reprimanding a child. This way of 'toughening up' children by dismissing, ignoring or belittling their words, emotions or struggles doesn't build up their capacity to face life's challenges, it simply turns you into their first bully. When adults place 'conditions' on affection, it teaches children that their worth is dependent on how others feel about them. This means that children come to associate love with care and warmth, and the withholding of love with abandonment and rejection.

A recent study followed the progress of 170 children for 30 years with the aim of understanding the impact of secure attachment on quality of life (Young et al., 2019). The first assessment took place at the age of between twelve and eighteen months of age and uses Mary Ainsworth's 'Strange Situation', where a child is separated from a parent for a short period of time and observed interacting with a complete stranger. Secure attachment is observed when children show distress at the separation, minimal interaction with the stranger, and are rapidly comforted when the parent returns. At the age of thirty-two, the participants were reassessed, this time on the 'Big 5' measures of personality. The differences were striking: the children who had been rated as securely attached early in life scored highly on the construct of agreeableness, which means that they showed greater warmth, kindness, cooperation and consideration towards others. They also scored low on scales of neuroticism, a personality trait that has been linked to clinical disorders that are associated with the experience of emotional distress, such as anxiety disorder, mood disorder, substance abuse, eating disorders, and conduct and behavioural problems (Watson, 2001). Those children who were rated as insecure in early life scored significantly lower on agreeableness and higher on neuroticism.

So if secure attachment in early life is so positive for their future, why wouldn't we offer children the right foundations to equip them as best we possibly can? Why try to 'toughen them up' by removing our love or warmth as a tool to control their behaviour? Why try and teach them to shut down their emotions, be 'less sensitive' or not to cry when life is tough on them? We know that 'toughening up' children fails to build the skills for resilience and offers no healthy template for what a good relationship looks like. So when a child has been 'toughened up' and someone acts in ways that hurt them, cause them pain or threaten them, children are more likely to dismiss the impact it has on them because it feels familiar to what adults once called 'love' when they were growing up.

To be 'tough' in the world, your child does not have to wear an armour that closes off their emotions and vulnerabilities and keeps others at bay. What children need is an internal scaffolding that helps them show strength in the face of adversity, be able to cope with whatever challenges come up by problem solving or seeking social support, and have an unshakeable sense of being capable of moving through the challenge. We call this resilience, and a secure attachment formed with unconditional love, warmth and respect is the greatest building block for this.

Lead with warmth and hold on to your boundaries

When you maintain a position of warmth, compassion and understanding towards your child, it helps them rest in the comfort of your love and brings them a deep sense of security. Holding unconditional positive feelings towards your child helps them develop positive self-worth, and this in turn shapes behaviour in positive ways, because when we feel good about ourselves we want to be good towards others too.

What children mostly want to understand through their behaviour is:

- Am I good enough?
- Do you love me even when I get things wrong?
- Will you always protect me, even when my words and actions are out of control?
- Can you love me just as I am, even when my choices/interests/ experiences are different to yours?

An adult's job is to show children that it is possible to feel disappointed, upset or angry with someone and still love them deeply. So if your child talks back, does something you have asked them not to do (e.g. draw all over the wall), lies to you or says mean words, your response can carry two important truths: 'I love you AND this behaviour is not okay.' You can lead with warmth while setting firm boundaries.

Children don't need to eliminate any parts of themselves in order to be loved or cared for; they need to learn they are good enough just as they are. So when they are struggling and at their worst, your unconditional love will remind them that you see their struggle and you love them and will support them through it. It says to a child, 'I will help you through the tough times. Your struggle will not change how I feel about you.'

Having unconditional positive feelings towards your child means perceiving them deeply and empathetically for who they are, separate to their behaviour. You can offer this in the way you reframe moments of tension and conflict with your child:

Instead of: 'Why are you so naughty? You do this every night before bathtime.'
It sounds like: 'We get into a daily struggle before bathtime, don't we? Shall we think about what might make this easier for both of us?'

Instead of: 'Don't you dare embarrass me like you did last time we went out.'
It sounds like: 'Last time we went out you got really overwhelmed in the restaurant. Before we go out today, shall we have a think about what might help you? Is there a sign or a word you could say to me if things start to get a bit much? I will keep an eye on you, and if I notice your signal we will go for a little break outside the restaurant and away from the meal. How does that sound?'

Responding in ways that communicate that you are seeing more than just their external behaviour is what gives children a 'felt sense' of being held by you. These 'mindsight' connections also help children understand their own mind and make sense of how others experience them in the world. They build a sense of being both 'me', an authentic individual who is loved, and part of a 'we', belonging to a family community that doesn't require a loss of individuality.

Protecting children physically, emotionally and relationally is your primary job as a parent. For a secure attachment, children need to have an internal template that parents and adults who care for them have their best interests at heart and are going to keep them safe, always.

This looks like setting boundaries that protect your child physically:

Instead of: 'Come back! How many times have I told you not to run off?'
It sounds like: 'This is a busy road, and I know you will want to run off. To keep you safe, I will have to carry you or strap you into the buggy until we get to the park. Which do you prefer?'

With their personal boundaries:

Instead of: 'What was that? No? How dare you say no to me!'
It sounds like: 'If you don't want a kiss, that's okay, I still love you. Want to give me a high five instead?'

Ensuring physical contact with your child is not harmful, abusive or frightening:

Instead of: 'I don't care if it hurts, I have to pick you up, okay?'
It sounds like: 'I need to pick you up. I know you don't want me to, but my job is to keep you safe.'

49

And meeting a child's feelings with validation and empathy:

> **Instead of:** 'You are fine. Stop crying like a baby. That didn't hurt.'
> **It sounds like:** 'Oh, you fell. Did that hurt? Was falling over a little scary? Yeah, it happened so fast. I am here.'

Unconditional love is necessary for you too

Attachment, and the close bond between you and your child, begins with you taking care of yourself. Children know when adults meet them half-heartedly because they are tired, or have so much going on that they are half present emotionally, misattuned to them in the moment. When you show up with a full heart and willingness to be with your child, children feel it and are more likely to get that feel-good boost of connection after a few moments of togetherness that give them the capacity to let go. To do this, you first must fill yourself with goodness, and that will allow you to pass it on to your child. Some of this comes from meeting your own needs, as a radical act of love. It also comes from acknowledging your mistakes with compassion and unconditional love so you can remember that you are doing a good enough job as a parent, and that continuing to learn and grow is part of the process and not a sign of failing.

For many parents I have met in the therapy room, meeting their own needs is a challenge. This may be the same for you. So often this may not have been something you witnessed growing up. Perhaps you never saw your parent rest, or they explicitly said that they had 'no time' to watch a film, have fun, or simply just be together because there was always something more important to do, a household chore or paid work that cannot be put off. Or perhaps you never witnessed your parent doing something for themselves, or protecting their time as a couple if you grew up in a two-parent household. I worked with Ms Taylor for a while, a mother of two boys who felt anxious, irritable and guilty whenever she went on holiday with her family because she was incapable of switching off. She reported how, when she was growing up, her parents had never taken her and her brothers on holiday. She remembered her father saying that 'to take time off work is a frivolous luxury that serves no purpose'. Understanding her childhood experiences and the values that had been modelled by her parents about what was most important helped her connect with her own wishes as a child, which were not always about being 'productive'. This opened up space for her to see the need and worth of spending time playing, having fun and simply enjoying being with her children, away from chores or any thoughts of productivity.

Take a moment to think about the person your child sees when they are with you. Are you the kind of person you want to be around your child? If you could witness your child as an adult caring for their needs the way you care for yourself now, would you feel proud, pleased or disappointed? At first it may seem like a short-term plaster for a greater, societal problem – the lack of value and support we offer parents. This is a huge difficulty, but if you turn this into a daily practice for yourself, you will notice a difference in your overall wellbeing and your capacity to regulate, which in turn will have a ripple effect on your interactions with your child. This may look like:

- Setting your child up with a screen or some play in a safe space so you can take five minutes to close your eyes and perhaps lie on the floor with your legs up against the wall
- Going for a ten-minute walk or jog after dropping your child into nursery or school and before starting work
- Having a nourishing snack and a cup of tea or coffee just for you, in the quiet, before collecting your child

- Going food shopping alone (This may seem a tiny thing, but it can be so nurturing simply to go to the shop on your own. Take. Your. Time. Breathe in that space)
- Call a friend in a room away from your child so you can properly listen to and talk with them
- Get enough sleep. This may mean a 'reverse lie-in', taking an earlier bedtime and putting adult social time aside (temporarily) so you can give yourself the indulgence of rest. (I know social contact is also essential, but when it comes to our hierarchy of needs, sleep comes first. Get sleep, then you will socialize better)
- Do some stretches or gentle movement when your child is asleep
- Do something that gives you meaning, purpose or connection. This could be something like drawing, knitting/crochet, reading/watching something you enjoy.

Parenting is not about self-sacrifice, and the way you take care of yourself gives your child permission to take care of themselves too when they become adults, and perhaps parents. Unconditional love towards yourself is not selfish – it's necessary so you can have a purposeful relationship with your child.

As parents, we want to preserve as much of our influence as possible for as long as possible. Cultivating unconditional love in the relationship with your child is a daily practice of respect while maintaining boundaries to guide behaviour, with a large sprinkling of acceptance and compassion for you, the parent who tries their very best. Don't be fooled into thinking this is easy – there will be times when the idea of 'unconditional love' will be a distant ideal. You are only human, and you will get it wrong sometimes. Unconditional love means accepting when you mess up and get it wrong too. Reframe these moments by remembering that your worth as a parent is not determined by the way your child behaves; your love is unconditional, whoever they are and however they behave.

Setting boundaries around your parenting

To protect our mental health and self-worth as parents, we need to learn how to set boundaries respectfully with others. I know how it can sting when someone makes a judgement about your parenting, particularly when you are working so hard in the moment to do something that may be unfamiliar to you. If your child is playing in the park and you notice an adult huffing and puffing at them when they skip the badly formed queue of little ones going up the slide, you can set a boundary that supports your child in that moment ('Hey, I think you missed the queue. Look, these kids were here first. Come. I will wait with you') and empowers you to remember that, despite someone else's judgement, you are doing a good enough job as it is. Yes, you can parent your child with warmth and respect and model to other adults what this looks like – and doing so may teach someone else to be more conscious of their 'huffs and puffs' next time.

I invite you to meet those who judge with curiosity. It can be hard to witness adults connecting with children in empathetic and meaningful ways because this can bring up shame and, perhaps, the idea that 'I was a bad child and that's why no one cared enough to treat me like that.' If you receive an unkind or judgemental comment from a stranger on the street, you might not have the energy or desire to do this. A simple, respectful boundary in that case may be to say 'Thank you for your opinion' and walk away. For those who are in a relationship with you, whether it's extended family members or friends, it can help to let go of being defensive and become vulnerable. This may feel uncomfortable, and you will have to judge whether or not you know the other person well enough to go through these steps.

1. Acknowledge the feeling the other person is expressing. It's theirs, they are allowed to feel it and it's okay for you not to make it your responsibility to change it.
2. Set your boundary and follow through with meaningful action that protects you and your child as necessary.

When someone says something to you that sounds like:

'In my day, children didn't have tantrums. I wonder why children are allowed to do this now.'
Acknowledge their feelings: 'I cannot imagine how hard it must be to witness something so different to what you experienced.'
Set a boundary: 'I am parenting the way I think will support my child best.'

When someone says to your child something like:

'How rude. Children should not say no to an adult. Your child needs to learn respect.'
Acknowledge their feelings: 'I can hear that you found our child's choice rude. That must be painful.'
Set a boundary: 'We want our child to say no when things do not feel right to them. We are working to teach them how to say no respectfully, but this takes time. We ask that you show our child respect in the way you wish them to respect you.'

I am aware how uncomfortable it can be to do this, and the scripts above are not to be learned by rote, they are just examples to put in your own words. And yet . . . in the same way that your empathy and compassion are powerful tools in supporting your child's development, offering them to others is a powerful way of both modelling what you wish to witness more of and an opportunity to practise setting respectful boundaries. You have no control over someone else's response, and they may get upset or angry or sad at your words. If you have shared them with respect and empathy, this may be the time to end the conversation, to stop it from escalating into a conflict. It's always okay to create a break and come back to it another day. Not everyone will understand or agree with your parenting approach, and it isn't your job to convince others that your way is the only way. Trust yourself to make the right choices for your child and focus on how you want them to see you as a parent.

Shame and guilt

Parenting is the hardest and most important job you will ever have. So, of course, when you think you might have got it wrong, you will inevitably experience feelings of guilt and shame. These are normal human emotions, and they tend to show up at times that are important to you. Don't be surprised to see them appear around your parenting; it only says that you care deeply about the job you do with your child.

- Guilt says, 'I did something bad.' It allows you to take responsibility, repair and learn from your mistakes.
- Shame says, 'I am bad.' It tells you that you are not good enough to be loved or to belong.

Your inner critic is likely to echo the words and expressions you heard adults say to you when you were a child and made a mistake or did something perceived as 'wrong' and/or when they commented on your looks, actions and overall person. This may not have come just from your parents but from others around you such as family members, teachers, friends, ex-partners, in patterns of behaviour that reinforced ideas about yourself. If your inner critic is harsh and makes you turn against yourself, bringing up shame more than guilt, try to notice what it is saying to you. Don't push it away. Listen and respond as you would to a friend who might say this out loud to you. We know shame tends to sit in our bodies and make our brains ruminate over and over again about our wrong-doings. Put it on paper and write down the response. It may sound something like:

Shame: 'I shouted at my child again. I am a monster. They are going to hate me for ever. I hate myself for it too.'
What you might say to a friend: 'You are human. We all shout sometimes. It sounds like you were running on empty and next time maybe you have to protect a few minutes to rest before bathtime. For now, maybe what you and your child need is repair. Have you apologized to them? Can you acknowledge you got it wrong and didn't mean to scare them? It's good for children to learn that you are imperfect and still learning.'

Shame: 'I left my children sobbing at Grandma's house. They really didn't want me to go and I left anyway. I am such a selfish parent.'
What you might say to a friend: 'You are allowed to have some time away from your children. It's good for you to fill your cup so when you go back to be with them you are in a better place to enjoy their company. Those tears are a sign of your bond. Think of the stories they will tell you when you pick them up.'

Giving you a new perspective away from shame not only offers you a different way of looking at things, it also wires neural pathways that link your experiences to a grounded reality away from negative self-talk and shame. This is the practice of self-compassion. You can take small steps to practise this, like writing down three things a day that you can reframe as you would for a dear friend. This can change the way you speak to yourself into a voice that sounds closer to a friend that is looking out for the best in you.

And when you lose your sh*t . . .

There are going to be times when you don't parent the way you want to. This may look like shouting, threatening, saying the unthinkable . . . My daughter is a headstrong, wilful, determined, bright toddler. She knows her mind and she speaks up when she needs to. I love her strong voice and I see myself in her a lot – and therein lies the problem. We sometimes end up in a tug of war about little things, times when I need her to do something and she point-blank refuses, or she is demanding something of me and I cannot meet her request. And sometimes, when it's the end of the day and I have run out of patience and I need to just vent out my frustration, I will shout and she will stop what she is doing, not because she is listening to me but because she feels scared of me. If something like this also happens to you and your child, I want you to know that it does not make you a bad parent. Good parents are not the ones that never shout at their child or don't ever get it wrong. Good parents get it wrong AND they meaningfully repair when they slip up – this means that they are accountable for their actions and they learn something from them.

I like to reframe ruptures, times when the nurturing connection between you and your child momentarily breaks, into opportunities for growth that can strengthen the relationship you have with your child. They can help you look at what led you to shout in the first place, which often won't be your child (although that might be the first thing that comes to mind) but a trigger from your past or current unmet need. It can help you to learn something about yourself that you need to work on more consciously, and something about your child that can help you adapt your approach towards them the next time a similar situation arises.

To repair means to apologize for your wrongdoings in a way that is meaningful, genuine and shows accountability for your actions. As a parent this might feel like eating humble pie, especially if, as a child, no one ever apologized to you. One thing that helps me is letting go of the idea that my power as a parent is about being the one who is 'right' and my child is the one who is 'wrong'. 'Right' and 'wrong' aren't useful in this context. When adults shout and communicate aggression rather than assertiveness, no matter what a child has done, the responsibility of the harm lies with the adult. So the first step is to let go of the story that your child 'did this' or 'said that' and focus on YOUR story. What happened that meant you were unable to remain as the grounded, safe adult your child needs and spiralled into a shouty, yelling mess? What story are these big feelings that showed up in your body telling you about your unmet needs in this moment? And what can help you get back into a grounded 'adult' state that can reach out to your child more meaningfully?

When it comes to parents and children, repair is always an adult's responsibility. It tells a story that we do not want to intentionally do harm to a child, but sometimes, despite our best intentions, we get it wrong. Repairing in a timely way after a rupture teaches your child:

- That even when conflict shows up, love and connection can remain
- That to mess up is human and you can learn from mistakes and do better
- That repair needs to follow conflict or when harm has happened.

If the idea that repair is an adult's job brings up discomfort for you, it is likely that when you were a child, no adult ever apologized to you. Now, when you are the parent who shouts at your child, you may experience mirror emotions to when adults treated you this way in your childhood, which in turn trigger guilt and/or shame. Repair is the way to heal this for yourself and the relationship you wish to have with your child. A simple breakdown of the steps needed for repair includes:

- Telling yourself the story of what happened
- Using words to label your emotions and bring context to this. Use the word 'because' if it feels helpful to bring perspective. That may sound like 'I shouted at my child when they wouldn't listen *because* I am tired and haven't had a minute to myself.'
- Accepting your feelings
- Putting a label on your emotion and accepting that it is yours. For example, 'I felt so stressed by the mess they created during play that it brought up my shouty side. It is normal that it triggered me; I feel a complete sensory overload on top of my exhaustion.'

Take responsibility

Once you have put perspective on to the situation and given yourself compassion, accept your responsibility to be accountable for your behaviour and repair with your child. Apologizing is not a weakness. It takes courage and strength to admit to our faults. This communicates to your child that they are worthy of an apology for the hurt, fear or upset you may have caused them. This helps children learn that your emotions are not their responsibility to fix and that even when you mess up, your love and acceptance can shine through.

Make the repair

Offer your child a meaningful apology which communicates clearly that they are not at fault for how you behaved, that you care for how they were left feeling and want to make amends.

How to meaningfully apologize

The quicker you offer repair to your child, the faster your child's nervous system begins to settle down.

There are no 'but's', 'if's' or conditions that your child must meet in order for your behaviour to be appropriate towards them. Saying, 'I am sorry I shouted at you earlier but you two were making a lot of noise and I had already asked you twice to bring the volume down. When I am tired at the end of the day I need you to listen to me, okay?' is not a meaningful apology.

Meaningful apologies clearly communicate that someone else is not at fault for how you behaved in that moment and that you will take active steps to do better next time. This might sound more like 'I am sorry that I shouted at you earlier and it made you feel scared. I had big feelings in my body that I threw out at you in a shouty voice. Those are my feelings; it is my job to learn how to manage them better. It is never your fault when I shout, and it is never your job to find ways to keep me calm or make it better. I am sorry.'

As adults, we all need to practise repair and get better at apologizing meaningfully. It always starts with a simple, yet hard-to-say at times, 'I am sorry,' alongside the acknowledgement of a wrongdoing. For example:

'I am sorry I shouted/said mean words/picked you up too fast and it . . .
. . . hurt you.'
. . . scared you.'
. . . made you sad.'

You then need to bring accountability for your actions, which for children means spelling out clearly that your behaviour is not their responsibility. That sounds something like 'It was wrong. It was not your fault. I am going to work very hard not to do that again.' A meaningful apology means getting vulnerable and putting your pride aside. This is why meaningful apologies are often rare: it can be hard to access the courage to seek forgiveness.

Repair needs to hold a separate and protected space from conversations about what your child was doing in that moment that sparked an intense emotion in you. This moment is about healing the relationship with your child. Any teaching you want to give your child about their behaviour needs to happen in a different space at a different time.

What if it's too late?

It's never too late to offer a sincere apology that makes you accountable for your behaviour.

Repair is for everyday moments and also that thing that happened two weeks ago that you cannot forget.

Children do not process experiences the way adults do. The same way they need lots and lots of repetition to learn a skill, when something has ruptured their connection with you they often need extra doses of repair to feel safe and secure with you. Every child is unique, and it doesn't mean you have traumatized them or harmed them if the repair you have offered is not enough. It simply means they need you to keep showing up for them and demonstrating that your relationship with them is safe.

If after a rupture with your child you notice they show signs of irritability, anger, tears or greater defiance and avoidance of your requests, see this as a communication that your connection is frazzled. Take a moment to pause and think, 'What has happened to rupture our connection?' If you can remember something that may have upset them, reach out to your child and repair. Name what you have noticed and why you think it may be important to revisit it. This may sound something like 'I have noticed you are getting very shouty at me whenever I ask you to do something. I was thinking that the other day when I shouted at you that must have felt really scary. Am I right? . . . Hmmm . . . I am so sorry I did that to you. My shouting was not your fault and I am going to keep working at being less of a "shouty parent" so I don't make you feel scared again. Is there anything I can do to make this better? Are there any feelings you want to share with me? I am here. I am listening. It's okay. Nothing you say will make me love you any less.'

Repair is a process, not a performance

Repair is more than an apology, it needs a conscious action to follow it through. Conflict is an opportunity to learn a new rhythm as a parent, to understand something about yourself you need to work on and/or something about your child you need to help them with. Repairing with words alone is meaningless if you don't take conscious action to avoid repeating the same thing. You will know if there are certain moments in the day or particular behaviours from your child that make conflict more likely. When this happens, pause and ask yourself, 'What is one thing I can do that will stop me from losing it next time?'

- Can you commit to doing one thing a day to support your capacity to manage the emotions and behaviours your child brings up (e.g. prioritizing rest, exercising, taking 'time out' for yourself when emotions start to escalate . . .)?
- Is there a certain time of day when everything seems to fall apart? What small shift can help give you and your child more support at that time of day?
- What needs do you have that are unmet? How can you meet them sooner so they don't escalate into outbursts of emotion?

Forgive yourself. This parenting gig is hard, and no one is perfect. You cannot avoid or run away from conflict if what you want is a healthy relationship with someone else, and this includes your child. Instead, put your focus on the process of repair – name what has happened, take responsibility for your actions, acknowledge the impact this has on your child and commit to taking steps that show you want to avoid causing the same rupture in the relationship again. When you genuinely engage in this process you will begin to change, as a person and as a parent. It takes courage to be vulnerable in front of your child, to show that although you may be an adult, you still have lots of room left to grow. Repairing with your child teaches what repair looks like and feels like, making it much more likely that your child will initiate repair with you and others in the future. It also teaches them that regaining trust and safety is part of being in healthy relationships with others, so that even when they break, they don't have to fall apart.

2

Feelings

CHAPTER 3

Emotions Are Your Superpower

Having emotions is not a choice, it's part of what makes us living, experiencing human beings. Emotions are immediate bodily reactions to our experiences of the world. They provide raw data to our body that is essential to our understanding of our in-the-moment experiences. Feelings are stories about how we interpret our emotions. Feelings lead us to react, depending on how we have learned to respond to a perceived threat or an opportunity. To use an analogy, emotions are like the engine of a car and feelings are the frame. So, for example, noticing an emotion that gives you butterflies in your tummy, makes your body feel a little jittery, shaky and hot could be interpreted as feeling nervous about something . . . or it could also be that you are feeling excited, depending on how you interpret the situation you are about to face.

Think for a moment about how emotions and feelings were discussed with you growing up. Did anyone ever explain what emotions are? What they do and what purpose they serve? Or did you only learn about emotion through experience, by having them overwhelm you, frighten you? Did you learn what to do with them by how others responded, by either embracing and welcoming the emotion positively, or shouting and shaming you for showing it?

Children's emotions often look wild, and they can feel like a threat to adults, sparking emotions of fear, anxiety or anger. Rather than connecting with the need a child's emotions are trying communicate in that moment, adults may instead try and shut down a child's emotions by telling them to 'stop crying' or 'get over it', or attempt to calm the child with distraction, humour or fun. Some of these tactics are used with the intention of helping a child feel better, but in reality it is often a sign that an adult struggles to tolerate the intensity of a child's emotions.

Emotions are not something you or your child need fear. Emotions do your body no harm, even when they feel uncomfortable. They are our human 'superpower', an energy we carry inside of our bodies that gives us important information that drives our responses and motivations for what we choose to do next. I like to think of emotions as visitors that bring you information from the moment you wake up until the moment you fall asleep, and they pass through your body as needed. There are no 'good' or 'bad' emotions; most of our experiences are tinged with more than one. For example, you may feel deep frustration (and even some anger . . .) when your child isn't falling asleep at bedtime, but once they are fast asleep, you may begin to miss them, watching them on the monitor to feel a little closer to them. Mixed emotions are a key ingredient to parenting.

Emotions should not be pushed away; they need to be met with curiosity so you can hear the important messages they are communicating. That is what we call 'emotional regulation'. When you begin to get more curious about the relationship you have with different emotions and learn to accept them as part of your experience of being alive, it can help you to stop dismissing or avoiding them. You can then embrace them as the superpower they are, to guide your next steps for you and for your child.

Emotional regulation

Regulating emotions means creating a pause between the moment you notice a feeling and the moment you choose how to respond to it. It is both a skill and a capacity that is inbuilt. How you interpret your emotions determines how you will respond. For example, if your manager shouts at you in a meeting, you might feel anger and embarrassment and yet you may respond calmly. However, if after you have done all the family laundry your partner shouts at you for leaving some socks on the floor, you may respond much less calmly. These situations have happened to the same 'you', so what is different? With your manager, you may be able to regulate your emotions just enough to remain professional because, given the context, you won't want to bring greater attention to yourself and your feelings. At home, however, you may interpret your partner's criticism as a sign of how much of your work is invisible, and snapping back may be a way for you to be seen or heard in that moment (even if it's in a way that is unhelpful . . . but I will come back to that in a moment). When you think about your reactions towards others, including your child, it can be useful to understand that emotional regulation may vary depending on the context and who we are in a relationship with.

There is no age at which emotional regulation stops developing. Studies show that the prefrontal cortex continues to develop well into adulthood, both structurally and functionally (Durston et al., 2006), so even in adulthood, there is room to learn and develop emotional regulation skills. Unlike adults, babies and children cannot regulate their emotions because the prefrontal cortex, which is the home of regulation in the brain, has not fully formed and won't mature until they are in their mid-twenties. This makes emotions qualitatively different in childhood. Without an internal buffer, emotions have no 'dimmer switch', which is why children's feelings look so big, often taking over their whole bodies and leading them to say and do things that seem wildly out of control and over the top. Even in adolescence, when the prefrontal cortex begins to switch on, studies show that emotions are only partially 'dimmed' by the prefrontal cortex in intensity and reactivity (Silvers et al., 2016).

So, in childhood, adults and parents have to act as an external 'dimmer switch' to help support, contain and manage emotion. This is what psychologists call 'co-regulation' – being in the presence of a child to act as a buffer for their wild and impulsive emotions. You can think of this like 'exercising' a child's brain to strengthen the circuitry between the prefrontal cortex (for regulation) and the amygdala (for emotion). Like any form of exercise, it takes many repetitions to build strength, and the impact of co-regulation is often witnessed most significantly during adolescence. Children who have experienced their parent as a safe buffer and regulated presence during childhood tend to have better-modulated emotions and lower reactions to distress, fear and anxiety. What this means is that until they reach adolescence (and really, beyond . . .) you need to be a buffer for your child's emotions because they do not have the capacity to do this. And that is why emotional regulation is not so much about 'teaching' our children, it's about adults doing the work to remain a safe presence when children's big feelings explode.

Regulation starts with you

Children absorb how to regulate their emotions when they are in the presence of a regulated adult. How you regulate your emotions is the most important and often the most challenging work of being a parent. It takes conscious effort and practice to notice emotions in your body, to accept them as valid and important and to learn to let them move through you so you can take appropriate, healthy actions.

Emotions are contagious, and when we feel something strongly those around us feel it too and may even at times mirror it. Think of what happens when a stranger in the street smiles at you. The instinctive response is to smile back without even thinking about it. When children are screaming and shouting, often adults respond by behaving in exactly the same way towards them, not necessarily because they are angry themselves, but simply because they mirror their child's tone of voice. This mirroring often escalates the situation and teaches children that to be heard you must shout louder, which is the opposite of what adults are wanting to teach them. The good news is that calm is just as contagious as chaos. When emotions show up in your body, your child is able to join you in whatever emotional state you are in without conscious awareness. Focusing on pausing to regulate your emotions is key if you want to support your child to find their calm.

The goal isn't to 'stay calm' and 'get it perfect' every time, the goal is about offering you more capacity for regulation so you can support your child's brain in developing this capacity alongside you. So if as a child you learned that it isn't okay to show anger, you may not have learned to effectively communicate your anger with words that sound like 'I am starting to feel angry right now' and taking steps to regulate. Instead, you might be more likely to use passive-aggressive behaviours such as banging doors, snapping at others, or huffing and grunting to communicate your emotional state. The simple act of allowing yourself to notice emotion when it shows up and consciously taking a moment to pause so you can listen to what your body needs is a powerful first step.

Begin the practice of taking an 'observer' position to your thoughts and feelings. Increasing your self-awareness of what is going on inside you and with your emotions is important, because when you know how you feel and you understand why, you can better channel emotional energy towards a better response.

How to regulate your emotions

Step 1: Notice what is happening in your body
Put words to any sensations you feel in your body. Notice where these sensations are if you can. For example, 'My chest feels tight and heavy. I can feel my hands are shaking and my arms are tensing up.'

Step 2: Put a label on these sensations

What emotion is this? Is it anger? Is it anxiety? Is it sadness? Remember that we all show emotion differently. Whatever label is a good fit for you is right. This may mean the words that emerge for you are not 'standard emotion' words, they might be more like 'wobbly', 'shaky', 'squidgy', 'hard', 'spiky' . . . these are all emotion words children have gifted me and they all accurately describe an emotion for them. Lean into what words may fit for you.

Step 3: Stay with the emotion

Rather than escape into thinking, intellectualizing or using words that dismiss and avoid the sensations in your body, just try and let them sit there. It doesn't need fixing or changing. Your brain and body can experience discomfort without anything catastrophic happening. Emotion is energy – let it flow. Just breathe as you would normally, or slightly more deeply, placing a hand on your chest to ground you while you breathe. This isn't to bring relaxation to your body, it's to allow you to simply sit with the emotion. If you need to step away from your child for a moment to let emotion flow, state it: 'I can feel my body tensing up. I need a moment to bring my body to calm. I am coming back.'

Step 4: Soothe yourself the way a nurturing parent would soothe a child

As an adult, you have a mature brain, but this doesn't mean your emotions were nurtured in the way they deserved to be when you were a child. You can bring a new voice and context to emotion by bringing the compassion you offer outwards to yourself. This may sound like simply having a conversation with your emotion, a way of accepting that it is there and has a function for you: 'Hey there, anxiety. I feel you. I know you are trying to protect me. This screaming is a threat to my body. When I was small, adults screamed at me and frightened me, so of course I now find these loud screeching sounds scary too. This is my child. I am the adult now. I am safe now.'

Step 5: Let the emotion flow through

Emotions need to pass through your body fully in order for regulation to happen. Try not to fight it, and find some tools that may help you through it. Remember that emotion is energy and you can help it flow. It may help to drink a glass of cold water, walk it out, climb up stairs, lie on the floor with your feet up against the wall (changing position shifts the body's energy), go for a jog, do star jumps or dance to music.

Step 6: Notice when your nervous system has come back to calm

Once the emotion passes, you will feel your nervous system settle. Notice the difference. This feeling can only be accessed when emotion is accepted and allowed to flow through.

Step 7: Make sense of your emotion through talking

Once you are in a rested state, perhaps later that evening or the next day, spend some time making sense of what it meant for you. This is key in order for you to make sense of your own experience of emotions. When you switch on the thinking part of the brain when your nervous system is resting, it allows the connections in your brain to strengthen. Some questions that may be more or less useful to you include:

- What are my emotions trying to tell me? Can I listen to their story and accept it doesn't make me a bad person or a bad parent? Can I tolerate my own pain?
- Is the feeling in my body linked to something that is happening right now or is it remembering something that happened in the past and alerting me about a perceived threat?

- Will it help me to share this experience with someone? If so, who? (For support, to bring further understanding and awareness in my relationships, for connection so I don't feel alone with my emotions like I may have in the past?)
- If sharing this isn't going to be of service to me, what self-care can I access to bring soothing and comfort to myself?

For some adults, it can help to do this work with a professional, either through therapy, yoga therapy or a guided practice of mindfulness. It can help to know you are not alone in this – most adults need support in strengthening emotional regulation skills and building a healthy nervous system.

Remember that it takes practice to rewire the brain and, at first, just like a muscle, it may feel uncomfortable or not seem to be working very well. Don't give up. You may need to do this daily for a few months, even years, before you truly begin to notice that how you think, feel and respond to the emotions in your body is shifting. And if you feel that this is too much effort, remember that this is no different to training for a 10k or learning a new language or musical instrument. Yes, it is effortful, and it takes time and regular practice. But if you are a parent, know that working on your self-regulation is one of the greatest gifts you can offer yourself, and your child.

Regulating in front of your child

When you practise the steps towards self-regulation you may begin to notice that instead of just reacting (e.g. snapping and yelling at your child) you are starting to slow down your reactions, moderating your emotions by communicating what is happening in your body.

In practice this may look different depending on the context and the emotions you experience.

- Name what is happening to your body
- Label the emotion
- Reassure your child that the emotion is safe
- Share your coping strategy or tool for how you will let the emotion pass through.

For times when anger shows up (e.g. your child is not listening):

Instead of: Huffing, puffing, grunting and getting snappy
Try: 'I am starting to feel angry. I need a break. I am going to go outside for a breather and then I will come back. You are safe here. Don't be scared. I will be back.'

For times when fear shows up (e.g. you have a fear of something, such as flying):

Instead of: Trying to appear cool as a cucumber when in the airport and on the flight while feeling nervous on the inside
Try: Openly prepare your child for the reality of how they may witness your fears and what you will do about them. This may sound like 'We are going on holiday tomorrow and getting on a flight. I am excited to go on holiday, but my body feels scared to be on a plane. I know the flight is safe but my body gets shaky, so you may see me go a little quiet, focus on listening to my music or playing on my tablet. Don't worry, I am safe and I am okay. These are things that help my body feel more comfortable when I am on a plane. You do not need to worry about me.'

For times when anxiety shows up (e.g. before a job interview):

Instead of: Being quiet and acting like everything is fine
Try: 'Today is a big day for me and I can feel my heart racing fast. I always get nervous before an interview. I can only do my best and show up with my skills and knowledge. I am going to take some deep breaths and review my notes. I don't think I can eat breakfast right now, but I will eat later once calm is back in my body. I am going to be okay.'

For times when sadness shows up (e.g. becoming tearful during a film):

Instead of: 'Aw, silly me, blubbering tears over a cartoon. Ha ha ha!'
Try: 'Oof, that has made my chest feel heavy. This film is moving me to tears, it's so sad. Thanks for passing me a tissue, my love. I am okay, just going to let my eyes cry it out. Such a poignant cartoon. It's amazing how realistic they are these days.'

Compassionately accept times when you feel strong emotions such as anger, sadness, anxiety, and so on. Instead of bottling up or hiding these emotions, use them as opportunities to teach your child that being human means feeling things AND learning how to manage them.

Feelings need to be seen and heard

One of the greatest long-standing myths is that we need to 'fix' feelings that bring discomfort. That letting them hang around for 'too long' is bad, perhaps even harmful. The reality is that when we try and take away our children's distress through our words or actions, children learn that difficult feelings are not allowed to be felt, and this takes away the opportunity for them to learn the skills of coping with and managing uncomfortable feelings.

Your child's feelings don't need to be 'fixed'. They need to be understood. Emotional regulation is the first step in this process. When you approach feelings with the focus on curiosity and validation, the feelings shrink down of their own accord and rational thinking returns more easily. The more you tolerate and give space to your child's emotions, the more you wire your child's brain for resilience.

Reframe emotion

As adults, it can sometimes feel like we are 'leading' children towards an emotion rather than leaning in to hear their experience. When we name a feeling we position our experience and the role we take in a particular way. When we talk about someone feeling 'angry with us' it can put us in a very different position towards them than if we think they are feeling 'hurt'. Similarly, thinking about a sibling feeling 'jealous' will lead you to perceive their intentions differently than if you think that a child is feeling 'left out'.

It can help to adopt an attitude of curiosity, and not assume what your child is feeling or try to find the word that is the best fit for their emotion. This may feel tricky at first because, as humans, we tend to prefer certainty. However, emotion words don't just describe an experience, they also shape the relationship we have with each other in those moments. So, for example, if what you label at times of challenge with your child is that you are 'angry' with them, it may bring up feelings of guilt or shame for you, and for your child later on. If instead you label this as 'sadness' that your relationship with your child is struggling right now, it may bring you greater compassion and open up new possibilities. What do you think would happen if you called a child 'attuned' rather than labelling them 'shy'; 'passionate' rather than 'overly emotional'; 'misunderstood' rather than 'naughty'? Don't you think these reframes give you a completely different idea about who a child is?

Putting a label on emotion shapes its experience. Being mindful of the words we use can be a small tweak that has a big impact. Here are some questions for you to reflect on when you use a label on a child:

- With this label, what relationship am I creating in this moment?
- What does naming this feeling [anger] do to my relationship with my child?
- What emotion word helps me create a preferred relationship with my child?
- What happens when I swap [anger] for [hurt]?

Check the label

Many of us have a limited range of emotional vocabulary. Studies show that most adults only automatically label five or six emotions, which tend to be happiness, sadness, anger, surprise, fear and disgust (Eckman, 1970). We have for a long time thought of these as 'core emotions', but recent research has shown we may have a lot more. Below are thirty 'feeling' words. Have a think about which you typically use to label your emotional experiences and which you rarely say:

Anger	Fear	Judgement
Anxiety	Frustration	Loneliness
Belonging	Gratitude	Love
Blame	Grief	Overwhelm
Curiosity	Guilt	Regret
Disappointment	Happiness	Sadness
Disgust	Humiliation	Shame
Embarrassment	Hurt	Surprise
Empathy	Jealousy	Vulnerability
Excitement	Joy	Worry

Plutchik (1982) came up with the theory of a 'wheel of emotions' with core emotions at the centre as building blocks for more complex, sometimes more ambiguous feelings. This is a theory with little evidence base; however, an emotion wheel can be a useful resource to expand your emotional vocabulary and help your child label their emotions with more expansiveness and nuance. Children may find it useful to refer to the emotion wheel (p. 78) once they can read in order to articulate their feelings. They might not know all the words yet, but younger children should know the inner feeling words and start to develop their understanding of the middle section and outer sections as they get older. You can also let your child create emotion words that are a good fit for them and make their own unique emotion wheel. Ask them, 'What name would you put on this feeling if you could call it anything you want?' This can be particularly helpful if you have a verbal child who is neurodivergent; it can help you make better sense of their emotional experiences. Through my therapeutic work I have heard many emotion words that are unique to describing the emotional experiences of children, including:

Scared: wobbly, shaky, dizzy, the heebie-jeebies
Angry: hot, explosive, spiky
Sad: dark, hollow, blue
Happy: fizzy, sunny, bright, chirpy
Disgusted: gross, yucky, sour

Naming an emotion is powerful. This doesn't mean you can never say, 'Oh, you are so angry with me.' Of course you can. Just be mindful of not creating an impasse in the communication with your child and not allowing their emotional experience to be seen. If you label an emotion and your child denies this is their experience, listen to them and remain curious. That may sound like 'I am sorry I told you what you were feeling. Anger didn't feel right. What name would you put on this feeling?' If your child responds with 'I don't know,' let it go. They are likely dysregulated and unable to use

Feelings

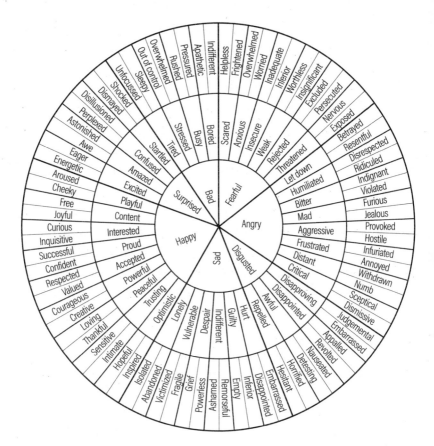

The emotion wheel

language in a way that is meaningful. Simply respond with something that sounds like 'Whatever you are feeling is okay' and set a boundary if necessary (e.g. 'I won't let you throw your toys'). Later, when the storm has passed, you can revisit this moment with curiosity and help your child develop emotional vocabulary. That may sound like 'What word would you use for how your body was feeling earlier, when I asked you to put your shoes on and you shouted? Can you describe the feeling as a word or two? Would it help to look at the emotion wheel and see if any of these words are a good fit?'

When you begin to talk about 'feeling words' you begin to create a shared language for how to talk about emotion. Emotional literacy is one of the foundations of emotional regulation. Building a common language for emotion in your home allows you to remain curious about each other's experiences and brings you greater understanding in tricky moments.

All feelings are welcome; not all behaviours are acceptable

There is a deep fear in our society that validating emotion is 'mollycoddling', that it is an indulgent overprotection that does a disservice to children. Validation doesn't mean that you agree with what your child is experiencing. It simply says to your child, 'Your experience is real.' Validation is your superpower that says:

- 'I see you.'
- 'I accept you.'
- 'I am here for you.'
- 'I can meet you where you are in this moment.'
- 'I see your feelings are not mine and you are allowed to have them.'
- 'I will not try to fix your feelings, I will hold their pain with you.'

Validating someone's experience acknowledges their feelings and wishes, even if they seem ridiculous, irrational or even wrong from your perspective. Acknowledging is not the same as agreeing; it does not reinforce a behaviour, it gives your child a powerful message about their emotions: 'Anything you feel, think and wish is acceptable, appropriate and loveable.' You can still set boundaries for behaviour, and you should always move through with a gentle action that allows your child to take a step forward in the right direction.

To give you an idea of how this might feel, think of a time when you felt scared. Perhaps going for an important interview, asking someone on a date, or taking a driving test or exam. Now imagine someone responds to you with 'Stop worrying. You'll be fine.'

How would that feel in the moment? Would it feel reassuring and supportive? Would you begin to 'should' your emotions and/or begin to dismiss and devalue them, and yourself in the process (e.g. 'I should not be scared. What is wrong with me?')?

What if instead that same person said, 'You feel scared . . . I think that's so normal. Want to talk about it?'

How would this feel? Would you feel some comfort or reassurance? Would it give you permission to feel scared in that moment and perhaps begin to process this so you can move through to thinking about what steps you need to take to feel ready to move forward, even with fear as a companion?

We often misunderstand validation as something you have to convey in words. But emotional validation comes through most powerfully in your non-verbal communication. This looks like:

- Being present. Use eye contact or share a mutual gaze. If you have a neurodiverse child and eye contact is too difficult, try gentle touch and a soft tone of voice
- Listening with compassion so you can remain attentive to your child's emotional core beneath the behaviour
- Showing understanding of your child's experience (even if it is not how you would experience the same thing).

Validation allows you to move your child through to action. So, for example, if a little one is scared of a dog barking, moving through these steps may sound like 'You are scared of the dog. I get it. The barking is so loud. I am right here. You are safe. Did you know barking is a dog's way of talking? Hmmm . . . I wonder what he is saying to his owner about that ball . . . What do you think? . . . Now, let's keep going. I am here. The dog can keep barking, we are okay.'

In my professional *and* my mothering experience, less is more when it comes to using words in the heat of the moment. What your child needs in the moment is space to feel. Staying present while holding space may look like saying very little but offers your child empathy about their emotional process. Sometimes in the moment all your child needs to hear is 'Let it out' or, simply, 'I am here.'

Winning and losing – a great way to practise emotional regulation

Practising emotional regulation is a hard thing to do, particularly with all you have to juggle as a parent. One way you can practise this, both for you and your child, is through structured activities that allow the kind of emotional responses your child (and you) might need help to channel differently.

From board games to competitive sports, winning and losing will come up many times throughout your child's life. They are a great way of practising emotional regulation skills, building empathy, and connecting and growing relationships with others. Use these situations as opportunities to develop regulation with your child so they can transfer these skills to situations when they won't have you as their coach to support them through it.

Preparation is prevention

Rather than letting your child win at every game to avoid the fallout, prepare what you foresee. Prior to a situation you know may bring out your child's competitive streak, talk about different scenarios and use role-play with toys or just your own self to bring the emotions and words to life.

Think about what might happen if they win

'So, we are going to play a board game later with your cousin. Let's take a moment to think about what might happen if you win at the game. How will that feel in your body? How will you share this with your cousin so they want to play with you again? I think I remember last time you said something like "YES! I WIN! YOU LOSE!" Do you remember what happened to your cousin? Yeah, they got a bit annoyed, didn't they? And they stopped playing. That was so disappointing to you. Maybe there is something different you could say if you win that will help your cousin want to try again? Hmmm . . . maybe something like "Wow! That was so much fun. Shall we try again and see if you can beat me?" What do you think? Worth a try?'

Think about what might happen if they lose

'And if your cousin wins, how will that feel in your body? Do you remember what happened last time you played this game and you lost? Hmmm . . . yes, I remember you shouted and ran off and didn't want to play with your cousin any more. And how did that feel afterwards? Hmmm . . . Shall we think about how you can feel sad and upset if you lose without running away shouting so you don't feel worse later? What could you say or do? I like that. Yes, you could say, "Well done. I feel sad I didn't win. I need a break from this game. Can we do something else for a bit?" And if you feel really sad, you can come and find me. I am always here for you.'

Talking through scenarios and replaying what may have happened in a similar situation helps children emotionally prepare for what is to come. Like packing a rucksack with what you need for a day out, it equips children with emotional language and behaviours that they can reach for in the moment because they are prepared for the eventuality of losing or winning rather than going in blind and only having their in-the-moment emotions to guide them. And if in-the-moment emotions escalate, they also know from your safe communication and presence that they can reach out to you to help them.

Model what gracious winning and losing looks like

Modelling to your child what graceful winning and losing looks like is one of the simplest and most effective ways for children to learn socially appropriate responses.

When you lose, let your child see how you overcome those feelings of disappointment and show them how you congratulate the winner and can still smile in defeat.

Show your child that you can be happy about winning AND show genuine appreciation for those involved in the game or activity. For example:

Instead of: 'I hate playing with you. You always win.'
Try: 'Well played, Analisse! You did some really great throws. I had some pretty good aims at those bowls too. Next time I will have better luck.'

Instead of: 'I WON! WOOOOOOP!'
Try: 'YES! That was such fun. Great game, Cameron, you really made that tough today. Have you got time for another round?'

Try as much as you can to emphasize the importance of the social side of playing together and the connection that happens while you play, rather than focusing on the outcome of who wins or loses.

Be mindful of where your place your praise

Saying, 'Well done!' or 'You clever kid' easily rolls off the tongue and can make some children feel great for winning or accomplishing something. It also only reinforces the outcome, positioning winning or getting good results as more important than the process of playing a game, connecting with others, and learning or practising skills. Try punctuating some of these moments in games or sport by placing your attention on the effort your child has put into an activity – regardless of whether they win or lose. Use descriptive words to highlight the areas in which you see learning or effort or skill.

Some simple examples of what this may sound like in practice:

Instead of: 'You won! I am SO proud of you.'
Try: 'You won! I am SO proud of how you worked with your teammates to set up that final goal.'

Instead of: 'Such a shame you lost. You'll do better next time.'
Try: 'Such a shame you lost. You did so well with your tactical move on the board when you put me behind ten spaces. I had so much fun playing with you.'

We all have the power to change the narrative around emotions. It is not just 'okay' to feel, it's an important part of being alive. Learning that emotions are our innate 'superpower' which make our experiences meaningful to us can help you focus your attention on developing skills that don't shut down emotion but help it pass through, for yourself and for your child.

As parents, we are the best coaches and role models for our children. That doesn't mean your job is to make a child 'feel happy' or stop them from feeling bad. If reading that brings up some discomfort, you're not alone – I find it hard to know I am not the agent of my child's happiness too. As a parent, the hardest part of supporting my child's feelings has been to accept that I cannot protect her from feeling disappointment, sadness, pain or hurt, and that allowing her to experience all feelings fully is what will help her grow into a well-adjusted, resilient adult. What I can do is help my child recognize feelings as they show up, hold a safe space for her to process them, and teach her skills to move through them, with playful and practical strategies to grow an emotional toolkit she can carry throughout her life.

Children don't choose what they feel, but you can teach them to make choices about how they behave when feelings take over. There is sometimes a fear that if we let children express their feelings in raw ways, we are creating adults who are not strong enough to face life's challenges. The opposite is true – shutting down feelings by saying to a child, 'Stop crying,' or 'Enough now,' bottles up distress in the body and robs children of the opportunity to learn coping strategies. When we allow feelings to exist, we give our brains and bodies the experience of what they feel like and what tools can be useful to cope with them, which is what builds emotional resilience – the ability to find the strength and tools to carry on at times of stress and difficulty.

Feelings that are difficult or uncomfortable take up a lot of our time and focus because they are often loud and impossible to ignore, but I want you to actively notice and look out for the positive feelings you and your child experience every day, too, like happiness, joy and excitement. When, as a parent, you have been working through the hard stuff, like sadness and fear, it's the happy feelings in the little moments of your everyday that will bring the balance, and that makes the hard job of holding space for feelings so much easier.

CHAPTER 4

Sadness

Sadness is a painful emotion to witness in your child. It can make you feel helpless and frustrated, and trick you into thinking you are 'failing' as a parent on some deep level if you are not able to shift your child back into 'happy mode'.

Tears are the body's natural painkillers. On the inside they trigger the release of oxytocin and endorphins – the 'feel-good hormones' in our bodies – while on the outside they communicate a signal for others to get closer for support. Crying is a part of being human that naturally supports the ability of our body to regulate. The stigma of tears as a 'loss of control' and emotions as a 'weakness' is not a belief children are born with. These beliefs are learned in relationship with others.

Bradley, a quiet eight-year-old, came to see me with his mother for help with sadness and tears. Bradley had unmissable fiery-red hair and had been diagnosed with Type 1 diabetes. However, Bradley's sadness had nothing to do with Type 1 diabetes, which he was good at managing with the help of his parents. Rather, he struggled whenever his football team lost a match and the sadness permeated every family interaction on the weekends it happened. Bradley mentioned that whenever his football team lost he would say to himself, 'I am not going to cry,' and when he couldn't hold the tears any longer he felt like he had 'failed' twice as badly.

Sadness and tears are deemed to be more acceptable for women than for men. This has a big impact on how we relate to each other in society and how we teach our children to feel and be with their emotions. A 2019 study by Thomassin & Seddon that looked at nearly 600 parents (302 mothers and 289 fathers) found that mothers respond to boys' tears differently to how they respond to girls', but fathers do not. Parents were shown images of boys and girls displaying either sadness or anger and had to make a choice about whether they found them 'pleasant' or 'unpleasant'. While fathers showed no gender bias when making their choices, mothers were more likely to call an image of a boy displaying sadness 'unpleasant' than a similar image of a girl. This study doesn't necessarily translate into parenting behaviours between mothers and fathers, given that the 'experiment' may not reflect real-life parenting styles. However, it is more acceptable in Western society for girls to be more emotionally expressive than boys, and there is also an idea that boys cry less, so when we see a boy in tears it can feel like a threat to the societal narrative that 'big boys don't cry'. It may be that the mothers invited to take part in this study showed greater awareness of cultural norms, which would lead them to react negatively to a boy crying, out of concern that they might be bullied or teased for being 'over-emotional'. What this study does is to make us question our own gender biases when it comes to tears and emotion. Have you ever fallen into the stereotype or witnessed someone else thinking that little boys need to be tough and little girls need to be vulnerable? Do you tend to dismiss or shut down more easily a little boy's tears than a girl's? Mulling this over can help you understand whether gender biases are influencing your response to a child's emotions.

When tears are responded to with empathy, compassion and support, body and brain learn that tears offer physical and social soothing through connection. When tears are responded to with ridicule, shame and dismissal or are shut down, body and brain learn that tears have negative consequences and impact on relationships. Feeling better after crying is linked to the narratives our bodies and brains hold about tears and the emotional support and comfort we receive from others. In other words, although tears release physical hormones for soothing, we only perceive those beneficial effects when we have developed those connections. These links all begin in childhood.

- Begin by noticing what tears bring up for you when you witness them.
- How do you respond to yourself when you cry?
- What words do you hear yourself say?
- Is this similar or different to what you do with your child?

Our emotional needs matter just as much as our physical needs, and shutting down tears can have harmful repercussions on our wellbeing. When you allow your child to shed tears and embrace them fully, you are helping them develop lifelong associations that soothe their body and brain in a way that is uniquely human. This means supporting them to link emotion words that align with their bodily responses to integrate their experience. That may sound like 'I can see you are sad' or 'I can see you are hurting' alongside validation that says, 'Let the tears out. It's okay. I am here,' reminding them that you are a safe space where their vulnerability can be held.

Let them feel whatever they feel

Sadness can often come with disappointment, when children begin to understand the let-down of missing out on things they are looking forward to or want. This can be a painful and heavy emotion that needs time to heal because at the core of disappointment is the processing of loss.

Witnessing your child in distress can leave you feeling helpless and trigger uncomfortable feelings within you, too. This can lead you to try to problem-solve or lessen the disappointment by focusing on 'silver linings'.

Inadvertently, this often makes things worse, escalating disappointment until your child feels you have truly, meaningfully, seen how hard this is for them.

Morris et al. (2011) invited 153 children from preschool up to Year 2 to take part in a task and be given a prize. The prize was chosen so as to intentionally disappoint the child, and the mothers' responses were recorded alongside each child's expression of sadness. The study found that when mothers used 'attention refocusing' and tried to shift a child's attention on to something else through distraction or by dismissing the experience ('It's okay, you'll get something better next time'), the sadness of the child grew. When, instead, mothers used 'cognitive reframing', so giving a story of the situation and reframing the outcome (e.g. acknowledging it was disappointing to have won a pair of baby socks and suggesting they could be a gift for their new baby cousin), the children became less sad more quickly.

Common responses to disappointment:

Distraction: 'Oh, but think of how much more fun you will have next time!'
Dismissing: 'Come on, chin up.'
Minimizing: 'It's not that bad.'
Shaming: 'Why are you so upset? You're not a baby any more.'

All these strategies send your child the message that you cannot handle their discomfort and, therefore, neither can they. This makes heavy feelings like disappointment big and scary and something to be avoided.

Bradley's father had attempted to ban football in an attempt to protect Bradley from getting upset. He also shared a fear that other boys would see Bradley as 'weak' or 'girly' and that he would be bullied for this. Bradley's mother tried to empathize with Bradley, but she also found his sadness 'over the top' and would try make things better, saying things like 'It's just a game. Sometimes you lose and sometimes you win.' No matter what his parents did, Bradley's response was always the same – to sit on the sofa sulking and crying.

Children don't want you to talk them out of their sadness. They want to know: 'Can you be with me when I am feeling this bad?' Before they can begin to get unstuck they need you to sit with them in the messy, uncomfortable place disappointment has put them in.

Listen and validate

So many disappointments that will bring up sadness for your child are unavoidable and unfixable. Not being put in the same class as their best friend, not winning a tournament, not getting the doughnut/cake/biscuit/ toy they wanted. To have someone sit with their pain and learn that it is never 'too much to bear' is one of the most comforting and self-affirming things you can do as a parent.

Encourage your child to express how they feel by validating their feelings and them as people. When you listen with empathy and validation without correcting your child or changing their story, you clearly communicate to your child, 'Your experience is real. I see you, I hear you. I am right here. You can tell me anything.'

I wondered with Bradley and his parents what it might be like to just sit with Bradley's big disappointment – not to avoid it, or change it, or fix it. Bradley's parents understandably felt confused – they had not come to see a psychologist to be told to 'do nothing'. On the other hand, Bradley was quick to say, 'Whatever they do, it won't take the sadness away.' We sat with that idea for a while . . . that sadness would stick around Bradley for a bit, no matter what anyone did or did not do. And what would 'sadness' want in that moment? Bradley said, 'To let it be. I have to feel sad because football matters to me.'

As a parent, it can feel hard to just accept that sadness is around and let it be. It can help to ground yourself in your job with a mantra that sounds something like 'I do not need to make my child happy; I don't have to fix this feeling.' Going through this process of naming the feeling and staying with your child's experience helps a child learn that whatever feeling they have is safe with you and builds a deep and intimate trust in your relationship.

Sadness needs company

Although tears are often a sign of sadness, not all children cry. A few other things to watch out for that might indicate sadness include:

- Losing interest in activities they used to enjoy
- Withdrawing from socializing (face to face or virtually)
- Struggling with everyday tasks
- Needing greater physical closeness with you
- More tiredness and sleepiness
- More frequent irritability and negative self-talk (e.g. 'I am bad at everything')
- Complaining of aches and pains (tummy aches in little ones)
- Sleeping more than usual
- Changes in appetite (either loss of appetite or eating a lot more)

Sadness can feel like a burden, and having someone show empathy without wanting to fix it or change it helps children feel less alone with the weight of carrying it. Help your child to understand that sadness is normal; give them permission to show their feelings and grow their emotional literacy.

Bradley's parents began to build a new story of what was happening for Bradley, outside of what they felt or thought as his parents. They recognized that Bradley's participation in football had remained unaffected by his diabetes, and that one of the reasons he was so good at maintaining his blood glucose levels was because he was committed to playing football and performing at his best. So when his team lost a match, it sent him into a downward spiral. They practised 'storytelling' what they now understood. That sounded something like 'You feel so sad when your team loses because you care so much about football and it is so important to you. Nothing can help you feel better when you lose. It is important for you to feel sad, it's part of the experience of caring so much about football. We get that now and we respect that your sadness needs to be around for a bit.'

To Bradley's father, it was important to build coping strategies to empower Bradley and help him see he could get through this. Bradley's father chose to remind Bradley of things that had helped him cope in the past, for example, 'I remember when you felt sad that you had not done as well as you had hoped on your spelling test and we did some kick-offs together and it helped you feel better . . . Would goofing around together with a ball help you when you feel sad about the football?' Bradley's mother practised connecting to the sadness without trying to fix it or make it better: 'I remember losing at tennis competitions and feeling devastated . . . my parents did not understand how much it meant for me to win . . . I want to understand how important football is for you . . . Do you want to sit together and talk for a while? I am here for you.'

Sadness always shrinks

Sadness can trick you into thinking it is always around. It can feel like a black cloud hovering over your entire home.

For Bradley's family, as soon as a football match was lost on Saturday morning, the entire home felt tainted by sadness. This is part of how sadness makes us feel, but there are always times when sadness is a little smaller. For Bradley and his family, this often happened around mealtimes whenever his parents made 'smiley fries' with the Sunday roast, or his sister decided to put on a 'show' and wore face paint that Bradley said made her look like 'a clown walking through a tornado'. He could not help but smile or let out a tiny giggle.

Noticing what shrinks sadness can help you do more of the things that support your child – not to distract them away from sadness, but to give them a more rounded experience of what it is to feel sad, while having other experiences too. Some examples of what may shrink sadness include:

Increasing connection: stay close, even by just sitting with them, inviting them to enjoy nature, have fun, play . . .

Creating meaning: invite them to join in with things that interest them, even if it's for a few minutes or less than they usually would

Focusing on nourishment: basics like eating well, getting a good night's sleep and movement can help to shrink sadness

Creating moments of joy: with humour, fun and silliness, not to distract from the emotion but to put more life into their experience of sadness, allowing them to witness that other emotions can coexist alongside sadness.

Some children benefit from a more physical approach. This may be more important for neurodivergent children, though I have never met a child who doesn't enjoy one or more of these activities:

- Use self-care moments such as moisturizing to slow down and intentionally offer touch as a way to soothe and calm. Try longer, slower strokes and, if the cream has a lovely soothing smell, even better
- Cuddle, hug and kiss, with your child's permission
- Invite your child to do some play with you and allow them to feel that you are fully with them in this moment

- Rocking, swinging, jumping, skipping, running, rolling, dancing, climbing and singing are useful emotion shifters. When you join in with your child, it can strengthen their connection with you.

It helps to know that finding a 'solution' will not always be possible. When it comes to sadness and disappointments, often children just need a listening ear and an open heart. The message you ultimately want to give your child is 'I know it's hard; you will get through this. I am right here beside you.'

No such thing as fake tears

When a child appears to be making the sounds and actions of crying but no tears show up, adults tend to dismiss this as 'fake crying'. Children are not actors; they are excellent communicators and will use the behaviour that will get their needs seen the quickest. Children's feelings are always real. See this behaviour for what it truly is, a 'cry for help'.

When you interpret this as 'fake crying' you may end up dismissing, mocking or threatening your child to get them to stop. What typically happens next is that distress grows, the tears become real and there is an escalation in the child's behaviour. When children feel unseen and unheard, their distress has nowhere to go but outwards.

Messages that intensify a child's emotion include:

- Denial: 'You are not sad.'
- Resistance: 'I don't see any tears,' with an eyeroll.
- Minimization: 'Crying won't help you.'

- Shame: 'Smile and the world smiles with you. Cry and you cry alone.'

Rather than dismissing their communication, meet your child with acceptance and validation. That sounds more like:

- 'I can hear you are upset. I am here.'
- 'You didn't want that to happen. It means a lot to you. I can see it.'
- A calm tone of voice and warm physical gestures.

This shows an openness to accept the experience your child is having because, in their brain, body and world, it truly does matter.

Remember that resilience is born from a place where emotions are felt, processed and worked through. As hard as it is to bear witness to sadness, allowing your child to experience it is the first step towards healing. This can take time. It's okay to go slowly, and if sadness sticks around for longer than a couple of weeks, no matter what your child's age, always seek further support and advice from a healthcare professional.

CHAPTER 5

Anger

There is a strong narrative in our society that anger is 'bad', that it should be kept 'under control', suppressed, stifled or hidden. This often comes from a fear that anger will turn into aggression and the physical harm of others and/or oneself. The truth is, anger is something we all experience at one time or another, and underneath it there are often more vulnerable feelings that need to be seen and understood, such as sadness, hurt and pain. It can be useful to see anger as a messenger that is trying to communicate something important. Anger often sounds the alarm for unmet needs. It's easy to see anger; it is often more difficult to understand the underlying feelings it may be protecting.

Anger is not the same as a tantrum or a meltdown. Tantrums are signs of distress at not being able to do, have or avoid something. They are the unavoidable physical consequence to emotional overwhelm, and we will explore them in more detail in later chapters. Anger, on the other hand, may show up as frustration and is more likely to bubble up as angry words, huffing, puffing and stomping than big outbursts of distress. For example, a child may become angry at hearing you share a story about them that makes them look silly, or they may get angry when they are trying to draw or build something and it is not taking shape in the way they had hoped. In many ways, anger and tantrums are at different points in the spectrum of emotion. When things escalate and anger keeps rising, a tantrum may follow.

Anger is an emotion adults tend to struggle to tolerate in children, and often in themselves too. If you grew up in a family where anger wasn't allowed, you may feel paralysed or triggered to action when you see it in your child. Perhaps your first instinct is to try and fix it because it looks dangerous or scary. Or perhaps it triggers rage inside you and you have an impulse to 'fight it back'. Fighting anger with anger turns this interaction with your child into a battlefield, and more: when you both have your 'shields' up, you are not connecting with what is really happening in that moment and the more vulnerable side of your child. It can help to remember that meeting your child with anger simply models to your child that it is morally appropriate to shout, scream and become scary when anger shows up. I want to invite you to help your child learn how to respond to anger so they can learn that it is an emotion that can be felt without causing harm to themselves or those around them.

Learning to notice anger in your body and connecting to the pain that may be lying underneath, such as not feeling seen or heard by your child, can help you find a more useful response that helps to bring anger to a fizzle rather than starting a bonfire. Think of the last time anger showed up around you and led you to shout. Hold that situation in mind and look at the diagram on p. 98.

What was lying underneath? Do you notice a more painful emotion that anger was protecting you from? How can you connect to this more vulnerable part of you next time to reach a different outcome? Instead of jumping to a reaction that attacks someone else and sounds like 'How dare you. You make me so angry,' can you reach a more open communication about your experience that sounds like 'I feel really hurt by what you just said to me. I can feel myself getting angry. I need a moment'?

Developing the skill to communicate your feelings and learn how to

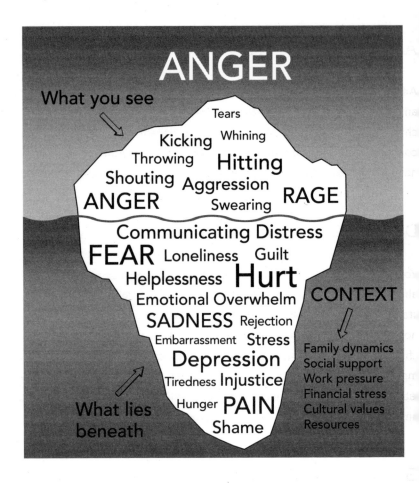

channel anger energy in a healthy way begins in childhood, but it is never too late, no matter how old you are. As you make sense of anger when it shows up for you and relate to it differently, it will open you up to seeing the more vulnerable emotions when they show up around your child too. If we are able to give it the space it needs, anger can help you understand your child in a new light, giving you a chance to see their unmet needs, their skills, vulnerabilities and fears.

Anger is not who your child is

Anger can often be internalized as blame, stigma and even shame. When anger becomes part of a child's identity it can sound like 'I am a naughty child,' 'I am an angry child,' 'I am a bad child.' When anger and identity become merged, it can be difficult to focus on the real problem, which is never anger; it's how that anger is being expressed that is the problem.

Don't take it personally

Your child's anger is not about you. It's about their feelings. Staying curious about the purpose anger is serving can lead you to discover and understand your child better. Hold on to a mantra such as 'This anger I see is not about me' and focus on what you witness during the times your child shows anger. What is happening in this moment? Is there another, more vulnerable emotion lying beneath their anger? Can you give it a label that helps you connect with your child, rather than rejecting their angry outburst?

Get on your child's side, not anger's

The goal is not to change or fix the anger but to stand with your child to bring them a sense of safety and calm when anger is around. Remember that anger can lead to out-of-control behaviours that feel frightening to your child. This is not the moment to teach or lecture your child about anger. Try to keep talking to a minimum and use short sentences and a calm tone of voice. Repetition can be helpful and invite calm. Phrases that you can say in the moment anger shows up, if your child tolerates talking, may include:

- 'I'm here with you.'
- 'I want to help you.'
- 'I will keep you safe.'
- 'It is okay that you feel angry.'

Explore their anger triggers

It is when calm returns that you can try to open up conversations about anger. There is no need to rush to talk – take your time. The learning is always most effective when your child is calm and their mind is open and receptive to what you tell them. Sometimes this happens hours later, or the next day. This conversation may begin with a simple noticing of the events without putting blame or shame on to your child: 'Earlier you started shouting really loudly. You are not in trouble, but I think it would help to talk about this. What would you call that feeling in your body?' As your child develops a better understanding of their emotions and how to describe them they will start to use words more than behaviour to express them.

You can then move on to more exploration, if your child allows it. This is also for you to think about – away from your child's presence – to make sense of what is happening.

- What moments in the day, activities or people are more likely to invite anger in?
- What is the first thing they (and you) notice when anger is around?
- Does anger show up to say they have a physical unmet need (e.g. hunger/thirst/tiredness)?

- Does anger show up when they have a skill they need to practise/learn (e.g. language skills, assertiveness, confidence, knowledge of a topic)?
- Are there environmental triggers that make it more or less likely that anger shows up (e.g. noises, visual images, movement, places, people . . .)?
- What could you do to help them before anger shows up?

Accepting that anger is like a mask that hides more vulnerable feelings and unmet needs can help you find a way through to meeting your child's pain and develop an action plan that works for you and your family.

Luca's parents came to me because their son got angry 'a lot', and despite helping him learn to release anger in healthy ways, it wasn't working.

When we teach children how to let anger pass through, it does not mean we accept or allow aggressive behaviour to happen. That is where firm, loving boundaries come in.

Luca's parents explained that when Luca started to feel angry he began to shout, and his father didn't like it, and in fact one of the goals of working together was for Luca to 'stop shouting in public'.

Shouting is one way in which children regulate their bodies. Rather than suppressing shouting, you can guide it in a way that is safe, healthy and appropriate. In the moment, this may look like getting really close and saying in a soft, calm tone of voice, 'I hear what you are saying. You don't have to shout for me to listen. Next time, come and grab my hand and I will lean close to pay attention.'

Luca's father felt that when anger showed up, Luca needed to find ways of getting calm, and he taught him to cross his arms tightly around his body and breathe out.

Before you try to invite calm, your child needs to be seen and heard, otherwise the anger will escalate. If your child tolerates you naming the emotion you see, do that. If they don't, I invite you to name what you objectively witness is happening. This may sound like 'I notice you are making fists with your hands' or 'You are shouting very loudly.' Offer them permission to release anger safely, holding a boundary if you need to. That may sound like 'Let's go outside for a moment so you can stomp the anger out' or 'You can roar like a lion, but I won't let you shout in my face.'

Children shout in public not because their parents are 'bad' or 'getting it wrong', but because they haven't learned how to modulate their voice, which takes practice and conscious effort. You cannot expect a child not to shout if they have not learned an alternative release. You can model what you want to see by making your voice softer and quieter when you speak to your child; this makes it more likely that they will listen and copy you. Outside of the public gaze, you can play a game whereby you set a timer and your child can speak in a boomingly loud voice until the alarm goes off, and then they have to speak in a tiny mouse whisper. This allows children to explore and experience their vocal range.

I helped Luca and his parents find new ways for Luca to release anger. Luca begins to use his words and say, 'I am SO angry,' and his parents learn to acknowledge and accept his anger rather than trying to shut it down, saying things like 'You are not in trouble. I get that you felt angry. You can tell me what is wrong without shouting. I am listening.'

It helps children find their calm faster when you convey that you are not going to meet their anger with your own and, instead, you are working alongside them to understand their needs. When a child feels seen and heard, the anger tends to pass because they know someone is now listening and attempting to help them. This doesn't mean you will always give in to your child, but you can empathize and acknowledge their wants before you set a boundary (e.g. 'I know you want to stay at the park, it's so much fun and I love coming with you. We will come back, but today it is time to go home'). When you leave out connecting to a child's need before setting a boundary, you become authoritarian in parenting style, and this makes children less likely to collaborate and follow your guidance because 'doing what you are told' doesn't feel good to anyone.

Your anger toolkit

If, growing up, you didn't learn strategies to soothe anger, you may not have a toolkit to pass on to your child. One of the ways we can diffuse anger is by offering our body times of calm. This is most powerful when it happens as part of a daily routine. Another powerful way to diffuse anger is having the tools to talk about the things that make us feel angry, without fear of being blamed, punished or attacked. Here are two simple ideas that are a good fit for most families, with some adaptations to suit your individual needs.

Create a 'calm kit'

This can be useful following a big anger outburst and can bring you and your child some connection. For children who are highly sensitive or have neurodivergent brains this can be particularly powerful and soothing.

You will need:

Activities that help your child feel calm and include their senses if these feel good to them.

A small box or bag to make this accessible for use and easy to take with you whenever you need them.

Many parents and children already have a sense of things that bring soothing and calm. Use these tried-and-tested items and, if you are unsure, make this an opportunity to discover these things.

Some ideas for things you may wish to include in your kit:

• Colouring-in or drawing items
• A special or preferred reading book

- Sticker books
- Maze and dot-to-dot books
- Fidget toys and sensory items to hold, pop, chew or squeeze
- A soft toy to hold or stroke
- Something comforting to eat and/or drink
- Sensory smells and items (e.g. lotion or hand cream for massage)
- Music that soothes or helps get their body moving
- Tissues – for those tears, when they come.

Draw your 'anger creature'

It can be hard to talk about emotions when we think of them as sitting inside our bodies. When we view emotions as a 'part of us', moving towards a change can seem too big a challenge. A therapeutic approach that I frequently use is the process of 'externalizing' (Michael White, 1989). It involves objectifying and personifying feelings in order to position them 'outside' of ourselves. This separates emotion from identity, and reminds you that your child is not their behaviour. I have found externalizing conversations to be one of the most useful antidotes to overcome the feelings of shame and guilt that can get in the way of openly talking about anger with children.

This can be useful from the age of two and a half onwards, and for little ones I would add in role-play, facial expression and movement to create a 'picture' of the emotion. You can invite your child to do this after an event where anger has shown up, or as an explorative exercise to make sense of how your child experiences anger and teach them emotional literacy.

Some questions that may be useful starting points to guide you, whether you invite your child to draw or role-play include:

- How does anger look to you?
- Does it have a colour?
- Does it have a face?
- What about arms/legs? What do they do?

Keep the conversation open:

- 'Tell me more about that.'
- 'Can you show me?'
- 'When does it show up?'
- 'Who notices when anger shows up?'
- 'Who never sees anger?'

Remember to listen, stay curious and leave your opinion or judgement about emotion locked away. You are offering your child the opportunity to reflect on what emotions are like for them, and the words and actions they use will give you a deep understanding of their emotional experiences. This is an exercise that builds collaboration and places you firmly beside your child.

Bonus activity:

Draw out your 'anger creature' and share this with your child too.

You might like to write up a 'Family Manifesto' that highlights:

- The anger creatures that live in your home (with their names)
- A brief list of responsibilities for each person when anger shows up (including the person whose 'anger creature' it is). For

example, Luca will name his anger with words and Daddy will listen and stay calm so he can help him.

With some small steps, you can help your child understand that it is normal and healthy to feel anger at times. It's what you do when the feeling shows up that matters the most.

CHAPTER 6

Anxiety and Fear

'Anxiety' and 'fear' are words that are often used interchangeably, but they are not the same.

Fear primes us for survival – it is the intense experience you have when faced with an immediate danger. Anxiety is the perception and often anticipation of danger when, in reality, you are completely safe. It's important to understand the difference between fear and anxiety because the way we work through these two emotions is different.

Befriending fear

Fear is natural, automatic and necessary for survival. It can be a distressing emotion for both children and adults. When you feel scared, your senses of sight, hearing, taste, smell and touch switch on to alert you to danger. This might be when you see a big, barking dog running towards you, when you are unexpectedly touched on the back, when you hear a loud bang at night, or when someone enters the room before you hear their footsteps approaching. The startle response is automatic. Fear's job is to give a rapid response so the body can get ready to 'fight, flee or freeze' and keep you safe.

Children can experience fear at any age, and this is a sign of healthy, normal development. In the early years, before the age of three, children are likely to be scared of anything that is unfamiliar, loud or different. This can be the first time they see someone they know wearing sunglasses, meet strangers and hear loud noises they cannot make sense of such as thunder, a dog's bark or the vacuum cleaner. I'll never forget the first time we took our child to a Santa's grotto. It was a gorgeous setting with sweet music and lovely decorations. When Santa waved hello in her direction, our child burst into tears, screaming and crawling all over us. To her, Santa did not appear as a jolly man bringing gifts, he was a scary-looking man wearing bright red.

Around the age of eight, children's fears become more reality-based. Children begin to understand danger, but their imaginations still fuel many of their fears. They may become afraid of fires and the danger they can pose to homes or belongings, of medical appointments, or worry about others' health and fear the possibility of death. But before then, children's vivid imaginations cannot separate reality from fantasy. This makes it possible for them to be scared of things that are not there, such as monsters in the dark. Children cannot make sense of the experience of fear in their bodies without a concrete and literal reason for it. So if they notice fear at bedtime with no one around them, their brain jumps to create something concrete that has made the fear show up. The 'monsters in the dark' many children talk about are a trick of their imagination and the best way a child can articulate how it feels to be alone in the dark with big, scary feelings inside their body that they cannot manage alone.

Without meaning to, many adults fall for the tricks of a child's imagination and end up doing things that are not useful in containing fear and instead can make it worse in the long term. Examples of this are:

- Minimizing the fears by saying, 'It's not a big deal,' or 'Don't be scared.' This can make children suppress emotion or escalate their expressions of fear to help you understand how frightened they are.

- Mocking, for example, calling them a 'scaredy cat'. This brings a child shame and it ruptures your relationship, making it less likely that your child will willingly share their vulnerabilities with you in the future.
- Using logic to convince a child that their fears are unfounded is an intellectual way of dismissing a child's experience.
- Falling into the trap of 'joining their magical world narrative'. For example, if a child is scared of 'monsters under the bed' and you check under the bed, through drawers and cupboards, or get out a 'monster spray', you are reinforcing the idea of the monsters. This tells children that their fantasy is real, and your search for 'monsters' may escalate to more places the next night.
- Forcing a child to 'face their fears' when they are not ready. This intensifies fear because a child has not yet learned appropriate coping strategies to work through it.

Fear calms when it is fully and safely experienced in the body. Children need to receive the message that you believe their experience is real and that you will stand with them against the fear.

Validate their experience. When children know that their feelings are real and they are not alone with them, this means that they can begin to put fear in its place and allows calm to return to their bodies. That may sound like 'I cannot see any monsters but I believe that you are scared right now. You are safe, I am here' or 'I can see you are scared. I am here. I will keep you safe.'

Tell the story of their fear. Wrap your child's fear in the warmth and safety of your emotional regulation to allow them to move through the emotion. Don't try and pull them out of their feeling of fear; instead, add perspective to their experience.

Instead of: 'It's not scary. See – it's fine.'
Say: 'You feel scared at the top of that slide. If you want to go, I can hold your hand. I am right here with you.'

Instead of: 'This isn't scary. Come on. You are a big kid now.'
Say: 'Shadows make you nervous. It looks like they come out of nowhere and move around. Do you want me to show you how we can play with shadows and make hand puppets?'

Break down the fear. If your child is scared of an everyday item (e.g. the vacuum cleaner or the neighbour's dog), create small steps to help shrink the fear at times when they are calm. This may be having them touch or look at a vacuum cleaner while it is turned off, or look at the dog through the window when it goes for a walk and pointing details out. Frame it in a positive way, as simply as you can. This may sound like 'The hoover has a long, wobbly neck. Its body is big and heavy – that's where the loud VOOM sound comes from'; 'Look, it's the doggy again! See how it wags its tail? Wagging is a sign of happiness; it's a dog's way of waving at us.'

Doing this creates meaning, helps children make sense of how they feel and develops their emotional vocabulary.

Calming anxiety

Anxiety is a sign that your child's brain is doing exactly what it should do. It is protecting them from a perceived threat. Anxiety is triggered in a part of the brain called the amygdala, and its only job is to keep us safe. The amygdala switches on when it thinks there *might* be something dangerous – so rather than a child crying and showing fear of an electric hand drier when it goes off loudly, anxiety looks like a child who avoids using a public toilet in case there is an electric hand drier there. A fear of separation, falling sick, something happening to someone they love, feeling excluded, rejected or embarrassed . . . they all count as potential dangers. When a child perceives a danger, anxiety will try and hold them back in an attempt to keep them safe.

Anxiety in young children shows up in strong physical reactions. As they get older, you will also witness their anxiety manifesting in different ways:

- Frequent crying and tearfulness
- Shouting and screaming
- Physical shaking (often hands and wobbly legs)
- Becoming 'jumpy' and on 'high alert'
- Needing to be physically close to you
- Hiding or withdrawing from people, things or places
- Getting angry and more easily irritable
- Having aches and pains around the body (often arms and legs)
- Tummy aches, diarrhoea, nausea or constipation
- Struggling to fall asleep or remain asleep
- Disruptions in their appetite by either eating less or only wanting comfort foods.

Always take your child's aches and pains and physical symptoms seriously. Troubleshoot to make sense of whether they are having symptoms of anxiety or illness, for example check for a temperature, notice whether the pain is relieved with painkillers and/or whether other physical symptoms show up, including rashes, spots and skin-colour changes. If physical symptoms keep occurring for more than three days, go and see a medical professional to check that your child has a clean bill of health. If it makes sense that this is anxiety, focus on bringing back safety to your child's body and understand the core of what they are struggling with.

You are the best antidote to anxiety

We know that when parents understand anxiety and how it can trick children into avoidance, it gives them the knowledge to respond to their child in a way that increases positive behaviours and empowers them to overcome its effects. Lebowitz (2020) carried out a study with ninety-seven children diagnosed with anxiety disorders. Some children received individual cognitive-behavioural treatment; for the others, their parents were offered an intervention that educated them on anxiety and ways to respond to it with their children. The results showed that after ten weeks of treatment anxiety had reduced in all children, but those whose parents had received the intervention had better outcomes in family relationships, lower parental anxiety and more moments of family life without the presence of anxiety. This study has been replicated, and we know from a recent analysis of the most up-to-date evidence on anxiety interventions with children that parent therapy is more powerful than individual child therapy alone (Yin et al., 2021). In simple terms – you are the most powerful antidote to anxiety in your child.

Anxiety isn't contagious, but the behaviours, strategies and adaptations to the environment that you make for or against anxiety can be. I have met many parents who worry that they are responsible for the anxiety their child experiences because they live with anxiety too.

Mercedes reported that she was an anxious child and now felt like an 'anxious' adult. She mentioned she had a fear of flying and was scared of the impact this was having on her son, Raul. She mentioned that they were due to go abroad on holiday and Raul had started to ask lots of question about the flight and whether the plane would crash or not. This had triggered Mercedes' own anxiety about flying, to the point where she considered cancelling the trip.

Rather than worrying that you may be responsible for the anxiety around your child, focus on the power you have to shrink it by focusing on your own self-regulation and by adapting the way you respond when anxiety shows up around you. It can help to use a mantra: 'My child being scared is okay. I am not scared of this feeling. I can stay.'

Don't run away from anxiety

Anxiety is a bit like a wave. It comes and goes. When your child is at the crest of their wave of anxiety it can be distressing, and you may feel tempted to lift your child out to protect them. At first this may soothe them – but in the long term, avoidance shrinks your child's world. It tricks your child into thinking that safety only exists in the absence of anxiety, making new or unfamiliar experiences more difficult.

For example, imagine your child is going to a new activity, such as tennis. Your child begins to cry and says, 'I don't feel well, I don't want to go.' If you lean towards anxiety, you may end up protecting your child from its effects, which may result in them not going to tennis. This can create a cycle of avoidance that makes anxiety grow when a similar event presents itself (e.g. starting a new activity or meeting unfamiliar people).

Mercedes and I explored the reasons she was thinking of cancelling the family holiday, which included Raul's anxiety about flying and her own fears of what could happen. She came to understand that cancelling the holiday would be avoiding anxiety and would in future make it less likely that they could go abroad on holiday. Mercedes was committed to protecting her family life from the tricks of anxiety which stopped her from flying or doing the things she wanted, so she agreed to work on developing coping tools for herself to manage her fears in order to make going abroad as a family a reality.

When the danger is a perceived threat that feels scary but is safe, what your child needs isn't protection, it's for you to be the sturdy ground they can hold on to until it passes. It can help to remember that anxiety is a companion in many of our life experiences and brings richness and fullness to what we experience. Think of a time when you had a first date, or a job interview, or had to do a public presentation. Anxiety is likely to have been part of your experience and, although it may have been uncomfortable, it was also giving you the adrenaline to push you through that moment.

Children who have neurodivergent brains may have to limit certain experiences in order to manage their levels of distress. When experiences have a deeply distressing impact on your child and their brain doesn't have the capacity for regulation, missing out on certain events or activities isn't avoidance. This is adapting their environment to meet their needs.

Meet anxiety with calm curiosity

Mercedes explored her anxiety of flying. What happened to her body when she thought of being up in the air? Where did that take her mind? Mercedes began to recognize that she felt nauseous, 'like on a rollercoaster', and that her mind always took her to catastrophizing the worst possible outcome – that the flight would crash and they would all die. We talked about how normal it is to feel nervous about flying; after all, we are not birds with wings so it can feel unnatural to have a heavy vehicle soaring through the sky with humans on board. And we also talked about the feelings that show up when Mercedes thinks about being on holiday, sunbathing on a beach with a nice cocktail while her boys splash in the water. Mercedes described feelings of pleasure and peace, and also excitement. So we reframed the nausea in her tummy at the idea of flying as 'nervous excitement' about doing something unfamiliar AND going somewhere new to spend quality time as a family. I wondered if this could also be Raul's experience, given that flying was a new experience for him and the idea of being in a warm, sunny place where he could eat ice cream and frolic in the waves was an exciting prospect.

When talking with children, it helps to guide your child's emotional state in your vocal tone, your gestures and your facial expressions. Rather than a very calm 'You are scared', meet your child's energy when you say, 'I wonder if this is nervous excitement about doing a new activity?' Using 'I wonder' introduces possibility and allows for multiple perspectives in that moment.

Soothe anxiety

Mercedes and I worked on developing a toolkit for her to manage the 'nervous excitement' of flying, and to help Raul through this too. Rather than trying to stop the nauseous feeling in her tummy, Mercedes took control of the things she could prepare and plan for. She wrote a list of all the people she knew who had holidayed abroad and made it back home. She made sure to ask Raul a curious question about this so he could find out more too ('Do you know any friends who have taken a flight to go on holiday? Why don't you tell them you have never been on a plane and ask them what it was like?'). On the day of the flight, Mercedes planned to get to the airport extra early and have a nice sit-down meal as a way of starting their holiday. We also practised some breathing techniques and mantras for Mercedes to do before boarding the plane, and she agreed that she would do them at bedtimes with Raul so they could both practise feeling calm together.

You can stop anxiety tricking you into thinking bad things will happen when you are doing something that is safe by grounding yourself in reality and taking control of the things you can predict. I have three simple strategies that are effective in regulating the nervous system. Practise them when anxiety is not around so they become associated with the experience of calm – if the first time you try them is when your child is feeling nervous about flying on a plane or going to a new school, for example, it will doubly confuse them and may lead to an escalation of distress, as doing something new and unfamiliar so often does when anxiety is around. Try to introduce one of these ideas into your everyday life; they only take a few seconds each. They can work well as small rituals during transitions such as bedtime or leaving the house in the morning.

A useful grounding technique that children and adults can do involves focusing attention on the environment. Ask your child to say out loud:

- 5 things they can see [of a chosen colour, e.g. red] . . .
- 4 things they can hear . . .
- 3 things they can feel against their skin (the breeze/the ground/ clothes) . . .
- 2 things they can smell (their hair/the air/something in the room) . . .
- 1 thing they can taste.

The order doesn't matter, but it is usually easier to find things they can see or hear than things they can smell or taste. Give your child more control and let them choose the colour you are looking out for. Practise on the way to school or when you go for a walk in the woods and see what you and your child notice happening.

Anxiety makes our bodies take smaller, shallower breaths. Extending and slowing down our breath brings relaxation to the body. A simple technique that children love to practise with a cup of hot chocolate is what like to call 'hot chocolate breathing':

- Cup your hands like you are holding a mug of hot chocolate (or hold one for real; it's even better).
- Smell the warm, chocolatey smell for three, hold it for one, blow it cool for three, hold it for one.

- Repeat three or four times or as often as necessary for your child to notice a change in their body.

Anxiety can feel flighty, and touch is grounding. One technique brings touch and controlled breathing into a soothing motion that can help dim anxiety:

- Imagine drawing a figure 8 on your skin (arm, leg, back of the hand – wherever feels good) with your index finger.
- As you draw the first half of the figure 8, breathe in for three.
- When you get to the middle, hold your finger still for one.
- For the second half of the figure 8, breathe out for three.
- When you get to the middle, hold for one again.
- Repeat as many times as needed until you notice your breath slowing down and your body feeling more calm.

All these strategies can be something your child can do on their own with your verbal and physical support and, more long-term, quietly and privately, whenever they want to invite calm back into their body.

Protect time for anxiety

Sometimes, when anxiety sticks around for a while, you may notice there are worries that persist and repeat. Your child may keep asking you the same 'what if' questions and you may start to avoid them, telling them, 'You know the answer, stop asking me,' or begin to feel frustrated. Your child is not asking for answers, they are asking you to see that anxiety is keeping them stuck.

Mercedes mentioned that her anxiety would always flare up when Raul asked questions about what would happen if the plane hit turbulence or ran out of fuel or one of the engines flew off . . . By helping Mercedes notice that Raul's questions were not necessarily looking for complete answers but instead were communicating that anxiety was around, she was able to meet him with greater curiosity ('You have asked me about what will happen if the plane shakes while we are on the flight three times today, so I wonder if you really want me to answer that again or you want to talk about what it will be like to be on a flight? What do you think it will be like? Is there something we can research/look up together? How do you want me to help you with this?').

Once you have a better understanding of the worries, what they are and how they are getting in the way, you can begin to problem-solve. It can help to keep a journal or notepad where the worries your child shares with you are recorded. Make sure to have this to hand if worries show up at bedtime, so you can keep a record. Try as best you can to limit 'worry talk' around bedtime as this can interfere with sleep. Instead, tell your child, 'Your worries are important to me. I am going to write them all down so we can talk about them in the morning.' Then, once you have written them down without engaging in conversation, 'Now it's time to sleep. You are safe. I am here. Shall we do some [hot chocolate breaths] together and see if that helps bring in sleepy vibes?'

In the daytime you can check in with your child's worries by going through their list. Don't avoid doing this step, thinking the worries have 'gone', as this may be avoidance on your part or feed into theirs. Instead, focus on problem-solving them using a 'worry tree' (see worked example, p.119) to work out what you can let go of, what needs soothing and where you can take action.

Learning to become comfortable sitting with your child's discomfort is a huge feat, but one that is well worth the work. You cannot fix or take away all your child's worries. Some worries and fears are about the tricky process of growing up, and they are inevitable. The best thing you can do is give your child the message that uncomfortable feelings are not something to fear or avoid; they can be worked through.

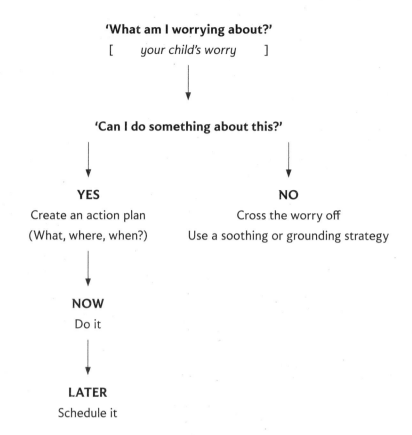

'What am I worrying about?'

[*your child's worry*   ]

'Can I do something about this?'

YES
Create an action plan
(What, where, when?)

NO
Cross the worry off
Use a soothing or grounding strategy

NOW
Do it

LATER
Schedule it

We can learn to get comfortable with uncomfortable emotions when they show up in ourselves and in our children, to bring safety and teach coping strategies that will support them throughout their life.

CHAPTER 7

Shyness

You might not consider 'shyness' a feeling in the same way anger or sadness is. However, unlike introversion, which is a personality trait, shyness is a feeling of discomfort that many children and people experience in new and unfamiliar situations. Most people know what 'shyness' looks like – a bubbly child who suddenly recoils behind their parents' legs, a chatty child who won't respond to 'What's your name?', or the little one who usually squeals in delight at music choosing to sit out of dancing at the birthday party.

It can be easy to get pulled into wanting to encourage your child to join in the fun with others. Shyness can feel confusing and frustrating to witness, particularly when you know that your child will enjoy something. Not all children are social butterflies, and this difference isn't a bad thing. Many of the behaviours children who feel shy display show deep self-awareness, critical thinking and attunement to the emotions they feel in their bodies. A child's temperament may make it more or less likely that they experience shyness in certain situations, and it is how you, their supportive parent, choose to help them navigate these situations that can be the greatest buffer against shyness.

Drop the label

Kieron's parents tell me that he is 'painfully shy'. They describe Kieron as a chatty five-year-old, happy and full of fun, always talking at home and being the centre of every family event. However, when they take him out to parties, Kieron won't budge from his parents' side. His mother reports that they do 'everything' to encourage him to join in, telling him to 'have fun' and looking at how much his friends are enjoying it. They mention that Kieron's friends ask him to play but he refuses, and that's why his parents have decided they won't be taking Kieron to any more parties.

Labelling a child as 'shy' creates narratives about their identity that can be difficult to break away from. Adults often unknowingly reinforce behaviours either by pushing children to join in too soon or protecting them too much. This means that children miss out on opportunities to learn how to become comfortable in unfamiliar situations, and don't learn coping strategies to overcome their experience of shyness. It can help to offer others a more descriptive story of what is happening for your child. This helps others understand the situation and models more appropriate language for your child's behaviour. This may sound like:

'My child takes a little bit of time to warm up.'
'My child prefers to stay with me at the start to get a feel for things. When he is ready, he will join in.'
'Thank you so much for trying to encourage my child to play. She is happy with me for now. I will make sure she knows she can take part when she is ready.'

Empathize with your child's experience

Empathizing with your child's experience is about allowing and welcoming their feelings. In order to do this you have to believe that your child's experience is real and not try and convince them of what you imagine their experience 'could be'.

Kieron's parents have begun to understand that what he needs is a bit of time to settle into a new situation. They help Kieron make sense of what is happening for him just before they get to a party. Kieron's father has started to ask him, 'How are you feeling?', which has helped Kieron name that he feels 'scared' because he doesn't like how loud and busy the parties are. This has allowed his parents to give him a choice to stay with them until he feels ready to join in, and give him time to settle into the new, busy, noisy environment of the party.

Giving your child permission to stay by your side until they are ready offers them the possibility that what they are experiencing in that moment is temporary and other choices are available to them. When you remove pressure, the shy feelings have more space to fizzle out because they are not being forced to stop being there, they can just be what they are until a child has warmed up enough to want to join in.

Get curious about shyness

Some children may need support with overcoming feelings of anxiety and/ or help with skills in areas of social communication and interaction. You will only be able to make sense of the support that may be most useful to your child if you lean into their experiences.

Kieron's parents begin to explore what has happened at the party after the event. Prior to this, they used to get frustrated and ask Kieron, 'Why didn't you join in?' Now that they accept this is part of their child's experience they get more curious about it, for example, 'I noticed you sat with me at the party and didn't want join with the disco. Do you not like dancing with your friends?' Kieron's mother discovers that Kieron is scared of bumping into others when he dances. He has a diagnosis of dyspraxia and his parents had never thought of this being a factor in what they saw as 'shyness'.

After a situation where shyness has shown up, explore it with curiosity without trying to fix it. Listen carefully to the words and labels your child chooses. What feeling do they notice in their body? Are they worried others won't want to play with them? Do they feel unsure of what to say or what to do to join in? Get clear on whether this is a skills deficit or an emotional barrier so you can support your child most effectively.

Prepare and offer choices

Preparation and predictability can help offer your child a toolkit of coping strategies. Before going out to a social situation where you know shyness may show up, talk to your child about what is going to happen. Let them know you understand they may feel uncomfortable. Validate their feelings and problem-solve together.

Kieron's parents took him to the school Halloween disco and, although they thought this would be a 'nightmare', they chose to see it as an opportunity for him to build skills. Before the party they made a plan with Kieron about what would help him have fun on the night. Kieron chose face paints but not a mask and asked to walk in with his best friend. Parents reported that Kieron stood by the side at first, but his friends joined him and, towards the end of the afternoon, Kieron was up at the front, showing his friends how to do the 'floss' dance. More strikingly, Kieron had come up to his parents and said, 'It's okay, you can go. I am fine.'

Build up their toolkit

As a parent, you can offer opportunities for your child to build up social skills and overcome shy feelings. You can:

- Set up playdates with one or two children to help them practise social interactions in an environment that gives them control and helps them feel safe.
- Encourage one or two extracurricular activities that your child enjoys and is good at; this can help them engage with others who have the same interests and boost their confidence.
- Offer social skills coaching. Children who are neurodivergent and those who are worried they don't have the social skills to interact with peers may benefit from learning simple conversational skills through play with you. This can help them have a small toolkit of how to begin an interaction.
  - Giving eye contact and smiling (only if your child feels comfortable doing this)
  - 'Hello'
  - 'My name is . . .'
  - 'What is your name?'
  - 'I like playing with . . .'
  - 'What do you like doing?'

Model what you want to see

Children learn the most through seeing behaviour in context, rather than being told 'to do' things. Being explicit about what you do, and how it feels, can really help your child begin to understand social skills and put them into practice. Talk through moments where you feel uncertain or nervous. Normalize the experience of feeling shy as part of the experience of doing something unfamiliar with people you don't know.

Instead of (when meeting someone else): 'Say hello! Look up, please. Come on, you know how to speak.'
Try (to the other person): 'Hello! How lovely to see you here.'
Afterwards: 'I did not expect to see Lucy in that shop. It was nice to say hello and share some smiles with her. We haven't seen her in such a long time it took me by surprise a little. I think I was a bit flustered. How was it for you?'

Be aware of your expectations

Not all children want to socialize with lots of others, and that is okay as long as it does not impact on their quality of life or interfere in activities they would otherwise enjoy. Be guided by your child. The quality of their friendships is more important than the number of friends they have.

When children feel seen, heard and understood, they feel safe. Safety allows children to explore and try things out. Shyness is a feeling that may show up across a child's life in different contexts and situations. It is also a feeling that often resolves or shows up less frequently as they grow and develop. Notice that your child is already a bright star in their own unique way. Don't be afraid to stay by their side until they are comfortable enough to go and shine by themselves. Trust the process.

CHAPTER 8

Overwhelm

Has your child ever turned around to you and said, 'I can't . . .' when you have asked them to do a task you know they are capable of doing? In the mornings, my child often runs around the house singing at the top of her voice, and when I ask her to put her shoes on she lands in a floppy bundle beside her trainers on the floor and says, 'I can't do it, I'm too tired.' We also get a daily scream from the toilet – 'I can't wipe. I need you here with me!' – even though when we get to her, she wipes her bum completely fine and says, 'I can do it. Don't check.' I roll my eyes at these moments (in my head; not at my child), but I know that she is not being rude, lazy or badly behaved. My child is trying to communicate an emotion that she doesn't know how to communicate yet. That emotion is overwhelm and those are real cries for help.

To give you a flavour of this, try to imagine having a hard day at work and then coming to collect your children, who are wired and full of energy. You look in the fridge and think, 'We don't have much. Great excuse to get pizza tonight. I am shattered.' And that's when your partner comes in, saying, 'I thought we could make a lasagne tonight. Got everything for it.' What if what comes out of your mouth is a disappointed 'Ugh . . . no . . . I can't . . . I don't want to . . .' That is understandable. It doesn't mean you have not got the skills to make a lasagne from scratch. It doesn't mean you don't like eating lasagne or don't want to have a family meal. It means, 'Emotionally, this is too much. I can't. Please make this easier for me.'

What would happen if your partner said, 'What do you mean, you can't? Don't you think we all deserve to eat a nice dinner? Get in the kitchen and start chopping some onions.' Would you feel angry, sad, hurt, misunderstood, alone? How would this then show up with your partner? Perhaps as an escalation that turns into a conflict?

And what do you think would happen if instead, in that moment, your partner said, 'We can split the tasks and get it done in fifteen minutes. I bought the tomato sauce and a cheesy sauce, so it's just a bit of chopping.' Or, even better, 'Wow. You sound really tired. Okay, don't worry, you sit down. I will cook it for us.' How would that land with you in that overwhelmed, exhausted state? Would it help you feel seen and understood? How do you think you would then interact with your partner? Would you perhaps be appreciative of their understanding and like a little extra drop has been added into your capacity to deal with the rest of what's left of your evening?

Children have less capacity than we do as adults to contain all the emotional load they carry throughout the day. As their brains are still under construction, most daily tasks are a lot more effortful to them than they are to us. They might have learned how to put their shoes on, but they still put them on the wrong feet from time to time because it's still not an automatic process; they might know how to wipe their bum, but it still feels unfamiliar in comparison to the many times they have had their bum wiped by you. They might be learning how to draw and write, but it still takes a lot more mental focus and physical precision than it does for you because they are still learning. They haven't really mastered anything yet.

When a child is overwhelmed, they need you to pause, observe and listen to what is happening. They need acknowledgement that something in the here and now feels hard and that they are in a place of 'stuckness'. Sometimes it is a skill they are learning and haven't mastered. Sometimes there is an emotion that is getting in the way. This is always an opportunity for you to understand your child better and become more effective in your approach of validating their experience, empathizing with their struggle and helping them consolidate skills with your support.

'I need nurturing'

Children often whinge or say, 'I can't' because they need emotional and practical support. Although your child may not be communicating their needs with you in the most appropriate way, it matters that you offer validation and empathy to help lift them out of this place of 'stuckness'.

So rather than say, 'Of course you can, come on. Please take your shoes off,' it is better to expand on what you see and lean into their emotion. That may sound like 'Oh, you are so tired you cannot even bend down to take off your shoes [validation]. We did a lot of walking today, I get it [empathy]. Okay, I will help you. I will take off this shoe and you take off the other [skill]. That way we will be done super-fast and you can go and chill for a bit.'

Sitting with your child's emotion doesn't mean you have to do everything for them. With an older child, this may sound like 'Getting dressed is so hard right now [validation]. Can you tell me what is really hard about this today [skill]? I get that you don't really want to go to school and that you feel really sad that the holidays are over. I am going to miss being with you too [empathy].'

Knowing when to ask for help is part of building an 'I can' attitude. Sometimes we need others to carry us through a task so we can carry on with the rest of what is needed from us that day.

'There is too much pressure'

This type of overwhelm often happens after school around homework tasks. Children are often cognitively and emotionally tired from the concentration and focused effort they have expended at school alongside the social and emotional requirements of being with their peers. Homework can be useful to help children consolidate work, but you may need to be mindful of when and how it is done, depending on your child's capacity.

For learning to happen, a task has to be challenging enough without causing too much stress. If the challenge is too great or the stress surrounding the task is too high, then a child may give up trying in order to stop the feelings of discomfort and inadequacy.

Rather than saying, 'Come on, you can do it. You're super-smart,' allow them to pause on an activity they feel overwhelmed by. Taking a pause is not the same as quitting. Sometimes our brains and bodies need a change, to move, to get away from the work that is overwhelming us. This may sound like 'You have been sitting there for a long time [validation]. Want to take a break [skill]? I might not have the answers, but if you want someone to vent to, I am right here [empathy].'

Learn to observe and give permission to stop even if a task has not been completed. Trust that your child is learning how their body feels under pressure, and that learning to take breaks is a skill that allows them to develop self-soothing and self-care skills. You can then support them to return to the task with a fresher outlook and, hopefully, some new ideas of how to approach it.

'Doing this makes me feel bad'

There are activities your child will associate with uncomfortable or difficult feelings. This may be because they had a bad experience in the past, they feel awkward or bad doing it, or they are aware a task is particularly hard for them due to lack of skill or ability.

Rather than end up in a battle of wills, trust your child's experience and that they know themselves best. Meet them with curiosity and an openness to understand. Offer them choices to make sense of whether this is a skill, an emotion, or a little of both, and where your input and support is going to be most useful.

That may sound like:

- 'You never want a shower. I know the soapy water gets in your eyes and it's stingy. How can I help you? Do you prefer having a bath? Shall we use a sponge or the bucket for washing? You choose.'
- 'This is hard for you – you say that every time we pick up a book. I can see you feel sad. Do you think it would be easier with a different story? Maybe a book with more pictures and fewer words? Want to try that?'
- 'I have noticed you don't like drawing. It always ends up with ripped paper. Are the ideas hard to find, or maybe it's your hand that hurts when you draw? If you want to talk about it, I would love to understand what you struggle with.'

Always believe that your child's struggle is real. Sometimes this will be skill-based; at other times it's a real emotion that is creating a barrier to success. Children learn best when they are in a supportive relationship that helps them feel seen, heard and understood. Listening to your child's 'I can't' as a cry for help says to your child, 'I see you, I hear you, I am WITH you.' That can go a long way to supporting them (and you) to find the next best step forward.

Whinging

Whinging is an alarm that you cannot ignore. When you hear your child say, 'Muuuummy!', 'I am huuuuungry!', or even 'It's noooooot woooooorkiiiiing!'

it's a sure way to fire up your 'annoyed' switch. Whinging is possibly one of the most irritating noises a child can make, and it's super-effective. It is a sign of unmet needs that a child is too overwhelmed to communicate appropriately. It is also often a sign that a child is disconnected from you, so when you hear whinging it is also ringing an alarm that says, 'Warning! Meltdown incoming!' Telling a child off or ignoring the whinging means ignoring a child's unmet need, and this can lead to rapid escalation. Whinging signals that you need to take action, and you can teach your child more appropriate communication skills. Here are three steps that will help you shrink whinging, if you do them consistently and in as timely a way as you possibly can.

Respond to their need in the moment
Instead of: 'STOP whinging!'
Try: 'You want a drink? Here you go.'

Offer validation and keep hold of your boundary, as appropriate
Instead of: 'I said we have no juice. Water is all I have got. Stop whinging.'
Try: 'You really want juice. And there is none. It's so disappointing. Water is not good enough, only juice will do. Ugh. How frustrating for you.'

Teach appropriate skills to get their needs met
Instead of: 'I will not respond to you while you talk to me like that. Speak properly.'
Try: 'Next time, you can just say, "Mummy, I want a drink." I will always get you one.'

This isn't giving in to your child, because whinging is not misbehaviour. It's an inarticulate expression of a need when your child is about to hit the end of their emotional capacity. Children's needs are always real, and they are often immediate. Meeting their needs allows you to put a buffer to their emotional dysregulation and prevent the situation escalating into a tantrum or a meltdown.

Emotion check-in

Help your child explore emotions and develop emotion words with this activity. Do this at a time of calm when your child can think and learn. See this as 'structured play', even though you are doing so much more with them.

Materials:
Coloured pens and paper
OR
Different-coloured playdoh (as long as you are okay with colour-mixing)

Use emotion words from an emotion wheel and pick a colour for each one. Allow your child to lead this as much as possible. Let your child get creative with the colours. This may look like:

Red – angry
Yellow – happy
Blue – sad
Green – calm
Purple – anxious

Draw a few circles (as many as your child wants, but starting with two to three is a good idea). These represent activities they do or places they go. Pick one where emotions often escalate and one where you know they find joy.

For example:

- Nursery
- Playing with a sibling
- Bathtime

Talk about each circle and let your child use 'emotion colours' to show what they felt during this experience. This is a really great way of showing children that they can have more than one emotion show up at once and that none is 'good' or' bad'; they all colour their experience and make it richer by being there.

This exercise can help you work out what support they need. It gives you a visual of your child's experience. If you are working on something together (e.g. dimming anxiety or comforting sadness), this can help you to notice changes across days and weeks.

CHAPTER 9

Happiness

Most of us recognize happiness when it shows up. We may see a smile, hear laughter or feel warmth in our heart. Happiness is about finding meaning in our everyday lives. No matter how much you chase happiness for you and your child, it is a temporary emotion and the most important factor in it is the quality of our relationships.

Just like all other emotions, there are triggers for happiness, but we tend to not be very good at recognizing what really makes us happy. There is a fallacy in our society that achievement and status bring happiness. In reality, the grades your child brings back from school, how well they play an instrument or how good they are at sport only bring short-term happiness. Humans tend to overestimate the impact of future events rather than live in the present moment. We also get used to happy feelings much more quickly than we do uncomfortable ones, which means that we stop appreciating our happiness triggers much faster. You can build 'happy habits' into your everyday life through the power of building moments of meaningful connection.

Build happy routines and rituals

What brings children most happiness is grounded in finding pockets of joy, contentment and meaningful connection. We can teach children happy habits that we embed into their everyday life and model the importance of healthy routines and rituals that look after our minds and bodies.

Integrating small happy habits into your everyday life can look like finding moments of joy in the mundane. This can be finding laughter in places you don't necessarily see it, like at mealtimes, by calling foods fun names. This may seem quirky and weird, but stay with me. While on holiday, I asked my daughter if she wanted a 'cheese and ham roll', and she said no, because it looked different to what we usually have at home. After looking at it for a moment, I suggested, 'Hmmm . . . how about a ham and cheese doughnut?' Can you guess her response? YES. She ate all of it! Since then, we have incorporated some fun labels for foods, and although it doesn't always help her eat them, it definitely adds a sprinkling of happiness at mealtimes. Things like Mini Trees (broccoli); Dragon Bites (olives); Monkey Fuel (bananas); Teddy Bear Porridge (lentils); Fluffy Clouds (cauliflower). Feel free to experiment and make up your own labels.

Another happy ritual you can incorporate into your everyday life is to encourage movement and exercise. The impact of physical movement on emotional and mental health is well documented, and in addition to helping regulate their emotions, it also helps children improve their attention and focus. Movement can help children learn more effectively, so fitting this in before and/or after school can help your child learn while also injecting some happiness into their day. Current guidelines recommend that children move for a minimum of sixty minutes a day from the age of five. This can include things such as walking the dog, riding a scooter, using a push bike, jumping, running, skipping, climbing and playing team sports. If while you're reading this you're thinking, 'But we simply don't have the time,' it doesn't have to take time outside of your routine. You can just slot it in, for example by having a morning breakfast disco, or skipping together down the road after school. It doesn't have to take long – five minutes can bring enough of a happy boost of endorphins.

At bedtime you can try and shift the atmosphere from 'battleground' to connection before separating. Think of what would happen if, rather than pushing for the end point of your child falling asleep, you slowed down to be with your child for these last moments of their day? It might make your evening run a little later than you'd hoped, but what will you gain from being more present with your child in these last few minutes, and bringing some joy into your interaction? Physical contact such as cuddling, rocking and massage are linked to increased feelings of security. Activities that offer quiet moments of connection, like reading and singing a bedtime song, offer opportunities for regulation. As your child gets older you can introduce rituals such as inviting your child to put their teddies to bed. This can include:

- Giving the toys a 'role-play' bath and massage
- Reading them a story
- Singing a goodnight song
- Giving them a goodnight cuddle and a kiss
- Placing a little blanket over them
- . . . And switching off the light.

This little ritual can feel soothing, and its playfulness helps children feel more content before bedtime. It also gives them a sense of control when, a few minutes later, you repeat similar steps with them.

Connection is key to happiness

Connection is the best way to boost emotional and sensory regulation. You bond and connect with your child through so many moments of your day, many of which may go unrecognized. Connections don't need a lot of your time or hours of undivided attention. A few conscious moments of being present with your child is enough. It might be, as soon as they wake, starting the day by saying, 'I so look forward to seeing you when I wake up.' Saying, 'Picking you up is the best part of my day' when you collect them from nursery or school and, at bedtime, 'I am so grateful you are in my life.' Simply acknowledging your child intentionally once a day can fill your child's cup with the strength of your love.

One of the best ways to connect and trigger joy and happiness with your child is by being playful. Playfulness with your child can be anything from ball games, board games, role-play with toys, fancy dress, water play, drawing and creating, and getting silly together. Despite what advertising companies might tell you, children don't need fancy toys in order to play, as paper, cardboard boxes and simple everyday items found in your home can lead to creative forms of play that allow a child's imagination to take centre stage. Make sure you protect time for unstructured free play where your child's mind can run free and find joy in the moment. If you are able to join in with them – even better.

Moments of calm

Teaching children to be in the present moment is a skill that can benefit them throughout their lives. Mindful moments don't need to take longer than five or ten minutes, and protecting time for this can strengthen regulation and their ability to find stillness within the busyness of life. This can include going for a walk in nature to look for five minibeasts or spot the colours of the rainbow in plants and animals; watching the sand fall through a glass timer or the shapes in a lava lamp; mindfully smelling things around your home (soap, candles, fresh herbs, flowers, a cinnamon stick) and inviting them to breathe in the smell and to feel what happens in their body as they do so (e.g. 'The cinnamon reminds me of breakfast'). When your child is older, you can also play this as a guessing game with a blindfold, which gives a deeper experience of the smells. As contradictory as it sounds, moments of stillness for our brains and bodies can also be found in movement breaks, or drawing and creating in other ways. If your child is neurodivergent, they are more likely to find activities that include movement or sensory exploration, such as playing a game of throwing soft toys into a box, making a jigsaw or playing with pop-its and fidget toys more soothing.

There is a reason why we all experience emotions – it's because we need them to survive and be fully functional human beings. Emotions and feelings are not enemies we need to shut down, they are important companions in our everyday lives, 'superpowers' that help to inform our choices and the next steps we need to take. Understanding how we and others feel is what helps to build emotional intelligence, which leads to healthy relationships, allows for emotional expression and builds resilience. Developing coping tools for our feelings takes time, which is why it is healthy and important to give children permission to feel, to help them learn how to express feelings in healthy and appropriate ways, and to work on your own emotional regulation and accept that you are a feeling person too.

3

Losing
Control

Understanding different feelings and how you can support your child through them is great – but parenting doesn't always 'work to plan' and this isn't because you are doing something wrong. There are going to be times when your child's feelings get too big and nothing you do or don't do can stop this. Everybody gets emotionally overwhelmed sometimes. This is true for both children and adults. It's a part of the human experience of being alive.

When you witness a child having a tantrum over something you consider to be small, recognize that, to them, it is not small, it is huge. They don't know that a breadstick tastes the same whether it's whole or broken. They only know they were excited to munch on a long stick and it now no longer looks or feels the same. As we have seen, emotional regulation is developmental, so children's brains don't have the prefrontal cortex capacity to buffer emotion – they need external support from a safe and caring adult. Children don't have big feelings on purpose. Their bodies and brains are simply doing what they need to do to bring a safe adult to soothe, comfort and support them. In many ways, tantrums are a golden opportunity to connect with your child and deepen the trust they already have in you. They give adults an opportunity to be with children in the way they need and become a better version of ourselves while supporting our children's needs.

Tantrums and meltdowns are both forms of communicating when emotions flood the body and brain and there is a sensory overload. Although they are often used interchangeably, there is a subtle distinction. Tantrums result from a feeling of powerlessness, often at times when a child has limited tolerance for frustration. In other words, they have a pressing need to eat, to get attention from you, rest or communicate something that to them is important, and when it doesn't happen fast enough their emotions rush through their brain and body like an unstoppable alarm that screams out, 'See my need NOW!' A meltdown is also a form of sensory overwhelm, but it is often due to internal triggers (e.g. the distress from a tantrum has escalated to levels of overwhelm) or external sensory over- or under-stimulation. Although meltdowns are more frequent in children who are neurodivergent because their brains are less capable of buffering sensory stimulation, all bodies can experience the sensory and emotional overload that may result in a meltdown.

CHAPTER 10

Tantrums

Despite what many might have you believe, tantrums are not misbehaviour and they are not a reflection of the quality of your parenting skills. The only thing that reflects on you is how you respond to a tantrum and the words and actions you choose to approach your child with. No one has the power to control another, but we can all choose how we respond.

Tantrums are a sign of powerlessness. When children cry and shout during a tantrum they are regulating their bodies and helping to release the pain of not getting the things they want. This is not a logical and premeditated choice. They are responding from the most developed part of their brain, which is driven by emotion and impulse. Without your calm and safe buffering from the outside, their internal emotional distress will not soothe.

First things first: the goal is not to stop the tantrum. That might be a surprise to you, particularly if you're in public or are already running late, or are overwhelmed yourself. But when you're dealing with a tantrum, the goal is to make sense of a child's emotional distress and meet their need. Once you accept that tantrums are going to happen and your job is not to stop them in their tracks, you won't necessarily feel okay about them, but you may stop dreading them. When the expectation becomes that children do have tantrums from time to time, just like they ask for snacks or want picking up from time to time, you might begin to notice that you approach them differently.

Many tantrums are due to children having a basic unmet need such as hunger, tiredness or connection. You can pre-empt this by making sure you replenish your child's resources by offering them food and snacks, encouraging them to rest and have regular moments of quiet time and, if you have been apart all day, regrounding them in the security of your love with small moments of play, laughter and connection before you get on with the next task of the day.

But it is unrealistic to try and pre-empt all the tantrums. Don't be scared of them; instead, remind yourself this is a healthy part of emotional development. A mistake many adults make is perceiving children to be more reasonable than they can be during a tantrum. Some strategies you may have tried to stop, distract or redirect a tantrum may include:

- Using logic to try and pull them out of the tantrum
- Giving a warning or using a countdown
- Threatening or punishing ('If you don't stop right now, you won't get dessert')
- Giving choices ('If you stop crying, you can have an apple or a banana. Which one do you want?')

These strategies will fail to do what you are hoping for: to stop the crying and shouting, and help your child develop emotional regulation skills. Words are a sensory stimulation and, rather than soothing your child back to regulation, all these strategies place pressure on a child to bottle up their emotion. For some children, these attempts may escalate a tantrum and lead to a longer, louder bout of distress. Other children may bottle up their emotions for fear they will lose the thing they care about the most: your love and connection. A child's brain is simply learning that in order to get their needs met the child has to shout louder, or to suppress their needs to avoid upsetting someone else.

Instead, I want you to sidestep the power struggle. Children often try to show you that they are a real person who deserves to have their wants and wishes acknowledged. As an adult, you don't have to prove to a child that you are 'right' – you may well be right, but pushing the need to 'win' the power struggle will get you nowhere. What your child needs during a tantrum is safety and connection. Emotion needs to be met with empathy, validation and boundaries. When your child feels this, calm will come to them a little more easily, and that's when you can join your child with reasoning and teaching skills.

Regulate yourself first

Tantrums are a stressor on us, the adults around children, and they can flood us with sensory overwhelm and cloud our ability to think. Because they are like resounding alarms, when a child is showing tantrums it fires off your brain into 'fight-flight-freeze' mode, which is an attempt to protect you from the 'alarm' of the tantrum and will give you an urge to fight back (by shouting at them), run away (by ignoring them, which often simply escalates the intensity of the tantrum), or feel helpless and unable to respond to either their distress or your own.

For children to find calm again, they need to borrow your safety. The greatest strategy to support a child in the throes of a tantrum is to learn to work on self-regulation for yourself. A 'good tantrum' is one where you, the adult, are emotionally regulated throughout, no matter how long your child's emotional release takes. I know this is a super-hard ask – it means working on your urges and impulses to scream, shout, punish or reject your child for having emotions they cannot help but express in chaotic and wild ways. In these trigger moments, it's not just your child who is dysregulated. Your adult brain is no longer working from a mature place that can find an appropriate response. When you meet your child's tantrum with shouting or by telling them off, all you are doing is mirroring their tantrum. When this happens, it's as if you have regressed into a 'childlike state', and while you are screaming and shouting you cannot do what is needed of you in that moment. Your sole job when a tantrum erupts is to communicate to your child, 'This is a scary experience for you. I am here to keep you safe.'

So before you jump to react, pause, breathe and tend to your needs. You want to find an effective response that serves you and your child best. A child's tantrum is a cry of distress and needs to be recognized as an invitation to protect, support and guide them through it. Watch your mind during a tantrum, breathe to a count of five and ground yourself:

Instead of: 'My child is manipulating me.'
Think: 'My child is crying out for help.'

Instead of: 'My child is pushing my buttons.'
Think: 'My child is having a hard time.'

Instead of: 'I need to stop this.'
Think: 'I just need to be here.'

If you want to raise a child who can regulate their body and mind to channel emotion in ways that are healthy, you need to embrace the practice of containing emotion yourself first. Once you are more regulated, notice what your child may be trying to communicate through their behaviour. What are their needs in this moment? Are they over- or under-stimulated? What is your role? Is it to support them with communication, a transition, co-regulation?

Tantrums are a cry for connection

Showing empathy isn't a strategy, it is a way of being in the emotion WITH your child. When you empathize with your child's experience, you accept, allow and welcome their feelings, however strong they are and for however long they last. This helps them to know that their experience in that moment is real and that these feelings, as big and dangerous as they feel in their body, will not consume or harm them, because you are there, keeping them safe.

You can embody empathy through the expression of warmth and calm in your whole body, not just the words you say:

- Offer your child 'mutual gaze', looking into their eyes, if they can tolerate it. Do not force eye contact, just stay close and present so you can offer it when they are ready. Children who are neurodivergent may find 'shared gaze' more comfortable. This is the act of looking at something together, for example a train set or a drawing they are doing, without giving each other eye contact.
- Adults tend to mirror a child's tone of voice so, when a child shouts, adults are more likely to shout louder. Work on quietening and slowing down your voice.
- Soften your jaw by keeping your tongue off your palate, as if it is floating in your mouth. This can feel strange at first, but the more you try it, the more tension in your jawline you will release, softening your features.
- Try to hold a warm, open body stance. This may look like making sure your arms are not crossed and that you are closer to their eye level or on the floor. Towering over your child can feel like a threat even if you are remaining calm. When you get closer to their eye level and/or slightly lower it helps a little one feel safe.

Alongside your posture and calm presence, if your child tolerates it, you can validate your child's experience:

'Oh, it is the wrong cup. How frustrating. And the other one is dirty, so that's all you have. It feels wrong to drink from that cup – so, so wrong.'

'Ugh, these shoes don't feel right. I hear you. They're not right. And we have to leave and going barefoot is not an option. This really sucks.'

'Gah! The top isn't right. Nothing feels right on your body today. It all feels wrong. I can tell.'

'Oh, it's broken. It's not right when it breaks. It's not what you wanted.'

Empathy and validation aren't 'mollycoddling' your child. This is a developmentally appropriate step that wires the brain in a healthy way for calm and soothing when big feelings are experienced. In the short term, your child feels seen and understood, and this alone can bring enough safety to stop a tantrum in its tracks. In the long term, this is developing emotional literacy and giving children language to name their feelings; this, alongside emotional regulation, helps a child develop the ability to think while experiencing big feelings.

Of course, none of these steps are 'parent hacks' that will work without fail. Some children may reject your empathy and attempts at validation, and choose to go away to a quiet spot. It is okay to respect your child's choice for space while remaining as close by as they will tolerate. When, during a tantrum, a child says, 'Leave me alone,' this is their way of giving a voice to the shame they feel about you seeing them in this out-of-control state. Say very little, only enough, if it feels appropriate, to let them know: 'I am here.' This helps your child know that you're not afraid of their big feelings. Some call this strategy 'time in' because it is in many ways the opposite of 'time out'. It keeps you connected with your child in their moment of distress, even when they need and want some space.

Children are developing their own sense of how to ride a wave of emotion. Tune in to what your child needs in the moment and don't be surprised this changes depending on the context.

Hold the boundary

It is important to remember that all feelings are okay, but sometimes the behaviour is not. We all feel a huge responsibility to raise children who are 'good' and don't hit or shout while, at the same time, we can understand that children are going to act out in ways adults don't like from time to time because they are still learning. So do you have to give in to your child in an attempt to stop the tantrum? When your child is crying over that broken breadstick, 'should' you just give them another one to stop the crying? Perhaps, sometimes, this will help, and giving in to your child will not do them or you any harm. However, if you disempower your sturdy leadership as a parent on a regular basis because you feel scared of the tantrums, or because you simply cannot tolerate witnessing them in your child, then it can make it more likely that your child will escalate to bigger and louder behaviour the next time they are denied something. As adults, we need to strike a balance between helping children feel seen, heard and valued while teaching them big life skills such as how to cope with disappointment, practise patience, delay gratification and learn the art of accepting that you cannot always have what you want when you want it. These are big lessons that many adults are still learning, which is why it is important to go gently with children and yourself while you navigate the art of setting and holding boundaries.

Holding consistent boundaries offers a child safety; it means they can trust the messages you offer them. It gives them a sense of predictability. For example, when you say, 'It's time to go,' or 'That is the last breadstick for today,' your child knows you mean business, and the more consistently you hold your 'no', the more they can predict the outcome ('Okay ... no more breadsticks for today ... even if I really want another one'). This means that they understand what is expected of them. Over time consistent, predictable boundaries shrink the frequency of tantrums. Clear, consistent boundaries may sound like:

'You watched three episodes of *Bluey* – time to switch off. Bye bye, TV! See you tomorrow.' (And switch off the TV.)

'We have time for one more thing, then we have to go home . . . yay! Such fun. Time to go.'

Use confident momentum

Doing all the steps above may not help your child to move on from their protest. When children keep pushing against a boundary you have set, it doesn't make them bad, disrespectful or problematic. It just makes them children who really want something in that moment. This doesn't mean you have got your boundary wrong or you need to change tack. It means you need to move your child along with confident momentum, because the tantrum may not allow them to do so without your support.

In some cases, this might look like your child running off in the park screaming, 'NO! I don't want to go.' Remember to pause, breathe and regulate. Rather than using your voice to shout, 'Come back here RIGHT NOW,' use your feet to move towards your child and, when you reach them, calmly and confidently stay in your leadership as a parent. That may sound something like 'I know it's hard to say goodbye to the park – it's so much fun. Thank you for letting me know you need some help. I am going to pick you up [while picking them up], it's time to go [while walking with them].'

In other cases, it may look like confidently understanding that your child is going to carry on protesting and that is okay; they are allowed to release all their feelings. You can stay with your child for a while, and you can also let them know you are close by until they are ready. That might sound like

'Three episodes is never enough. I know, it's so hard. I am going to finish making dinner. When you are ready, I have a hug waiting for you.'

Remind your child that they are loved

Children tend to come out of a tantrum physically exhausted, emotionally shaken and needing reassurance. Parents tend to witness the end of a tantrum exhausted, emotionally shaken and needing reassurance that they have done 'well enough' in containing such a huge outburst of emotion. What is the most powerful thing that can help you and your child when the storm of the tantrum has passed? A warm, loving cuddle between you, with some words that reassure and affirm your love, because no matter what has been said or done in the storm of the tantrum, your love remains. 'But wait – if I give my child love and affection after a tantrum, am I not just sending the message that their behaviour was okay?' I understand why so many adults have this fear, and the answer is: NO. Boundaries without warmth and love are not boundaries, they are authoritarian demands ('You do as you are told'). If you only focus on the boundary, without offering warmth, you will come off as harsh and make it more likely that your child fears you and is less able to learn from you. When you connect with your child after a big escalation in behaviour and emotion, you help a child feel safe, which lowers their defences and makes it more likely they can listen to what you have to say. Importantly, children do NOT have tantrums on purpose, and one of the main reasons for their brain to shut down in this way is a lack of connection – with their body, and often with you too. Wrapping your child in the comfort and safety of your love and, indeed, physical body, if they allow it, soothes their nervous system and wires their brain for regulation.

We know that warm, physical touch brings down levels of cortisol and restores our nervous system from a state of 'fight-flight-freeze' into 'rest and digest' mode, where children can begin to think and process an event. Offer calm, soothing touch through hugs and cuddles and words of affection that may include saying things like 'Wowee . . . that was a lot of feelings. It's passed now. I am here. I love you' or 'I am here, I am here. Do you want a cuddle? I love you. It's okay. It's passed now.'

Reasoning can only take place when there is calm

One of the most common mistakes I witness is parents trying to reason with their child while they are in the middle of a tantrum or just about to come out of it but not quite there . . . So often a child will still be crying, or shouting, or beginning to mumble words, and a parent will take this as a cue to explain how they are feeling and/or share a simple story of what has happened. Inevitably what happens is the tantrum escalates again because the child's brain is not quite ready for this additional stimulation, so it spirals back up into overwhelm.

So what do you need to do? Wait . . . and wait a bit longer to be sure. Teaching your child appropriate skills can only happen when you and your child are in a calm state. Learning does not happen when the nervous system is dysregulated and firing off. After a tantrum, when you witness your child seeming a little floppy, tearful, quiet and in need of physical closeness, you may begin to be in a 'safe' place of calm. This can take a few minutes, an hour, or even a day, depending on the context and how intense your child's emotional experience was.

Make sure to set the scene in a way that invites your child's brain and heart to stay in the conversation and share a story about what has happened. That may sound like 'You are not in trouble. I know it's hard that I am the one who makes all the decisions, and you never get enough of the things you want. It's okay to tell me you want to watch more TV. What you want is important to me AND you cannot say mean words to hurt me. That's not okay.' This creates safety to talk about difficult things and helps to build the logical centres of their brain's prefrontal cortex.

Don't forget to teach your child 'how' they can communicate their needs, express a feeling and/or get themselves heard in more appropriate ways. Some examples might be:

'You can say, "I feel so angry." '
'You can say, "I need attention," and I will come to you.'
'You can stomp your feet or roar like a lion.'
'You can ask, "Please, Mummy, can I have two gos on the slide? One is not enough," and I will listen.'

Give your child appropriate alternatives to transform the words and actions they make. When you only say 'don't', you miss out on telling children what they *can* do – and you want them to learn.

Remember that your child is more than their behaviour, and that tantrums are outside their control. Feeling heard and unconditionally cared for during the release of big emotions helps children reconnect with their inner sense of self-worth and builds trust in the relationship they have with you. It communicates that even when their behaviour is out of control you see their inner goodness.

How to help you move your child through a tantrum

In the moment a tantrum explodes it's impossible to keep everything in mind, so here is a 'prompt sheet' for you with the most useful steps when a tantrum shows up:

Pause – surrender to the storm of the tantrum. Don't try and stop it.

Breathe – focus on regulating your emotions. You don't have to join your child's chaos.

Keep talking to a minimum – remember that words are stimulating and can make the tantrum escalate.

Set a boundary if you need to – keeping yourself and your child safe is a priority.

Notice when the madness turns to sadness – you will know when the tantrum has passed when you see your child softening and, often, becoming weepy or sad.

Give them love – a cuddle and a few words that reassure them that you love them despite the tantrum. Remind yourself, too, that you are a good parent. Even if it didn't go smoothly, you did your best.

Reason and teach when calm – wait a while before you teach alternative words and behaviours. Remember that your child is not in control of the tantrum, and teaching moments need calm to be consolidated into learning points.

CHAPTER 11

Meltdowns and Shutdowns

A meltdown is an extreme emotional response to distress or being overwhelmed by something. Meltdowns are often experienced as a shutting down of the senses and often an inability to communicate verbally. The emotional overwhelm temporarily leads a child to lose control of their behaviour. There may be screaming, shouting and crying, and it often involves physical kicking, lashing out and biting. A tantrum can escalate into a meltdown if a child's distress grows too great. Children who have neurodivergent brains are more likely to land in meltdowns than tantrums because of differences in sensory and emotional processing, alongside the extra demands that everyday living places on their resources and capacity to adjust to discomfort and stimulation. Some children may also experience 'shutdowns', often after they have been in situations that demand a lot of thinking, are very emotional, or highly active or physical. In a 'shutdown', a child may become so overwhelmed that they are unable to process what is going on and they may appear mute or completely withdrawn.

Once a meltdown has set in, the best thing to do is to give a child space and help them stay safe. If possible, move the child to a quiet and safe space where sounds and lights are dimmed. Keep talking to a minimum, a reducing the amount of sensory and information overload is key.

Preventative planning

The best way to manage meltdowns is to work on preventative measures that support your child's emotional capacity. To do this, you may need to identify what your child finds overwhelming. Look at your child's environment, the times when meltdowns happen, and the triggers that may lead them to experience complete overwhelm. Keep a diary over a few weeks and see where there may be patterns at particular times of day, in particular places or around certain people.

Once you have a clearer idea of what sets off your child's overwhelm, you can plan things to mitigate against these instances. Some of these things may include:

- Reducing uncertainty by using visual calendars with images and words that help children know what the next steps are
- Creating environments that protect them from overwhelm. For example, allowing children to wear ear defenders or headphones with their preferred music in noisy spaces and dimming the lights when possible
- Protecting soothing spaces, for example setting up a quiet space for a child to get a sensory break after school or following attendance at a party or busy family gathering.

Allow your child to find soothing strategies that work

Witnessing a child soothe themselves can seem odd, confusing or sometimes stressful to adults. Why is a child singing to themselves? Why are they sucking on their sleeve? How come they want to spin objects round and round? Soothing behaviours happen naturally, because our brain and body are primed to help us survive and know what can bring comfort and healing. Often these actions are automatic; children don't register that are they doing them, they simply feel good. This may include licking, sucking, chewing, spinning, jumping, singing, humming, rolling, tapping, jiggling and exploring smells, tastes and textures.

As a parent, you may find that some of these behaviours spark an emotional response in you. So what might happen is that you inadvertently try to shut off your child's natural soothing behaviours. That may sound like 'That's gross, don't suck' or 'Stop it, that's annoying.'

The trouble with this is that when we suppress or restrict actions that are regulating for children without offering them an alternative, it only serves to block emotion inside the body, which, over time, can turn into inner distress (i.e. shame) or outward distress (i.e. meltdowns).

Having a strong reaction to your child's soothing behaviours may be an important signal that, at some point, you learned to shut down some of these soothing strategies yourself. Meet the emotions and urges that come up when you witness these behaviours in your child with curiosity and self-reflection. What is it about this behaviour that brings up big feelings? How would adults have responded if you had done this as a child? Get curious about your child's experience. What does chewing do for your child? Is it stimulating or soothing? Why is it happening now? And use creativity to find other ways your child can soothe if what they are doing is unsafe or no longer working, given their age or stage of development.

When you look beneath the behaviour to understand what your child is trying to communicate with their body, it can help you to find alternative approaches. Every child is different; there is never a 'one size fits all' approach. Here are some possibilities that may be more or less useful to you:

- A child who likes to chew their sleeve may find a chewing bracelet or tag beneficial

- A child who fidgets and jiggles when sitting down may benefit from having a wiggle board to keep them finding balance or a footrest to ground them
- A child who enjoys licking may benefit from a sensory toy they can suck, or food items that allow them this sensory experience (e.g. ice lollies or ice creams and finger foods).

Soothing behaviours allow children to think, respond and engage with the outside world. Children don't need to be shut down; they need support and redirection so your child can find appropriate and safe soothing behaviours as they continue to grow and develop.

Add to their soothing toolkit

Introducing new soothing ideas can be helpful in preventing meltdowns and offering your child pockets of calm when needed. Some simple ideas you may wish to experiment with and consider trying with your child may include using items to look at, touch and smell, for example 'calming stones', beads or a soft toy. Any small object that fits in your child's hand and which they enjoy carrying can be enough. This exercise works best with children around four years of age and older who won't be tempted to put a small item in their mouth and be at risk of choking. Do this as a guided activity to help your child learn the steps and talk it through together.

Look at the item (10–15 seconds) – notice colours, light and dark patches, ridges, scratches and anything else you can see.
Feel it (10–15 seconds) – with your eyes open and then closed, notice what is smooth, rough, lumpy . . .

Smell it (5–10 seconds) – all objects carry a scent, and you can also spray the object with a preferred smell to add an extra soothing element.

Another mindful exercise that can help children find a moment of stillness is watching a sand timer or glitter jar for a few minutes. To make a glitter jar, fill an empty jam jar or water bottle almost to the top with warm water, drop in a few big dollops of glitter glue and some glitter powder. Put the lid on, give the jar a shake and watch the glitter swirl and fall.

Witnessing a tantrum or meltdown can feel overwhelming, make you want to stop it in its tracks, or even leave you feeling that you are getting it 'wrong' as a parent. Try and remember at these times that your child's behaviour is not 'who' they are. Tantrums and meltdowns are not misbehaviour or 'tools for manipulation'. They are physical responses to an experience that has overwhelmed a child. They are part of a child's development, and all the effort you put in to respond with calm to buffer their big feelings will not be wasted, even if you don't see the effects of this until they are much older. Years from now, your child will not remember what you said or did with them during a tantrum, but they will remember how you made them feel when they were distressed, out of control and feeling helpless.

4

Discipline

CHAPTER 12

The Art of Discipline

As adults, we have forgotten what it was like to be a child, to feel misunderstood because you couldn't get the words out to articulate what you wanted or needed, to get frustrated when the adults around you dismissed what you were trying to communicate or pressured you towards saying or doing what 'they thought' you needed, to be so little and dependent and feel emotions intensely while trying to learn how to do things, what to say when, and how to fit into this 'adult world'. And because we have forgotten, as a culture we tend to interpret the things children do that we don't like in negative ways. We think of their behaviours as 'naughty', 'pushing our buttons', testing our limits, as clingy, irrational, oversensitive and impolite. Yes, children can behave in ways that are not appropriate, and they need our adult guidance and support. However, when we forget children are not 'mini adults' and expect them to fit within the norms of adult standards and expectations, is it any wonder children miss the mark and so many parents feel like they are failing? All adults make mistakes, lose their cool and say the wrong thing sometimes, but when we see this in children it becomes a 'punishable offence'. Children act the way children are supposed to – it's not always what adults would like, but it's because children are going through the process of development, and when we understand this with compassion we can begin to see that children are often doing their best every day, and our job is to keep guiding them forward.

Behaviour is the most powerful way a baby or child can communicate. Children tend to act the way their body feels, and they don't have the cognitive ability to understand someone else's perspective. So while as an adult you may interpret a child's behaviour as 'naughty', children are trying to communicate an unmet need in the best way they know how. And because children are simple, there is no need to overcomplicate things. They are often trying to express a basic physical or emotional need:

- To spend time with you and get your full attention
- To tell you they are hungry, tired or need to move around
- To request a moment of quiet and calm when things are too much, or some noise, activity or physical movement to stimulate them when they are bored
- To get a sense of control and feel like an individual person with some power.

Your child's behaviour isn't personal, but it is you who needs to understand. Where you choose to place your perspective can make all the difference. See it as a clue to find out what their needs might be. Leaning into curiosity will help you see your child as a whole person rather than someone who is intentionally trying to wind you up.

Does reading that make you worried that if you meet your children's needs they may become entitled and 'spoilt'? It's a really common fear that has seeped into Western society since the mid-1920s, when the idea of 'parenting' as a skill came to be considered normal practice due to 'behaviourism', the science of predicting how humans and animals behave. Watson (1928), a behavioural psychologist, famously said, 'Never hug or kiss [children], never let them sit on your lap. If you must, kiss them once on the forehead when they say goodnight. Shake hands with them in the morning . . . try it out. In a week's time you will find how easy it is to be perfectly objective with your child. You will be utterly ashamed of the mawkish, sentimental way you have been handling it.' It was not until the 1980s that theories about attachment began to percolate through society; in the 2000s, neuroscience and neurobiology added weight to the science of child development and the impact that warm, loving care has on the brain. Nowadays, thanks to the internet, we have knowledge at our fingertips about the brain, child development and what supports children's wellbeing. We know with scientific certainty that meeting a child's needs does not create neediness. It gives them a message that they are worthy of care and can trust that, when they have a need, this can be met most of the time. It creates security in their relationship with you, which in turn builds confidence in themselves.

So now the question might no longer be 'Why are children so naughty?' but rather 'What impact has lack of knowledge, understanding and empathy for children had over decades on our cultural and societal expectations of what parenting is about?' Could discipline be about how we learn to behave with others, not just for our children, but for ourselves too?

Discipline

Have you ever stopped to ask yourself how we got to a place where adults believe that to make children do better, first we must make them feel worse?

If your child is grumpy at the dinner table and you gently ask, 'Hey, what's up? Are you okay?' and their reaction is to shout, 'Shut up! Leave me alone! I don't want to talk to you!', you might understandably feel the urge to raise your voice and make the point that 'It's not okay to talk to me like that.' And if your child follows this up with further shouting and insults towards you, you might end up shouting, 'That's enough! Go to your room!

We have equated the word 'discipline' with 'punishment'. To be 'disciplined' is a skill, like learning to play music or training for a sport. It's something that you learn and progress at with dedicated and repeated practice. Yet when it comes to child behaviour, we think of discipline in the same breath as punishment. When you think about it – it makes no sense! Punishment does not teach children skills about what to do better; there is no commitment to repeat a helpful behaviour to consolidate its learning – the only repetition is the punishment that keeps happening and often ends up escalating the situation. The act of punishing a child breaks emotional bonds in their relationship with an adult. Children learn more from what you do than from what you say. So whenever you use a harsh punishment such as spanking, raising your voice, or name-calling, it simply tells your child that to use aggression when things don't go their way is acceptable. It's therefore not surprising to know that adults who were punished in harsh ways are more likely to use the same methods on their child – it feels familiar, natural, and even 'right', to do what was done to us. And when you begin using a punishment you are more likely to reach out for it again or escalate it even higher. Punishments give adults a false sense of power; they communicate adult disapproval by passing fear on to children, and for some adults it can be hard to give that up, particularly if witnessing a child's behaviour makes you feel helpless, vulnerable and like you are failing.

Imagine you are out with a friend and you are both having a good time. You reach out for the salt and pour the entire contents of your glass over the table. Imagine if your friend said, 'What is wrong with you? Did you not see the glass right in front of you? Look what you have done. You idiot!' Notice how your body responds to this idea. What are you learning in this moment? About yourself, and about your friend? What if, instead, your friend had said, 'Oh no! Everything is wet. You didn't mean to do that. It's okay, we can fix this.' You might think this example is too simplistic, and yet adults do this to children all the time. Adults hold a false belief that if they frighten, shame or punish a child, the child will learn that their behaviour is unacceptable. The truth is, what children will remember is that you can be scary, mean and inflict pain on them. This is a message of conditional love. Punishments tell children, 'You are bad, and this at times make you intolerable and unlovable.'

Is it time up for time out?

Sending a child to their room when they have done something you consider to be wrong is a form of time out. 'Time out' is an abbreviation of what was originally called 'time out from positive reinforcement'. It sometimes masquerades under different labels, such as 'the thinking chair' or 'reflective time', and it's likely you have heard of it, and/or your child has experienced it.

Time out is a brief period of time when a child is not given attention (i.e. positive reinforcement); this means no talking and no eye contact. It aims to prevent the unwanted behaviour through 'negative reinforcement' (i.e. the hope is that over time children learn that it is better to behave the way adults want than end up being sent away for a 'time out'). This is based on the behaviourist principle that a negative consequence, such as shouting at a child for throwing a toy, is giving attention and this can make it more likely they will do it again (i.e. shouting is a positive reinforcement). It was developed as a last-resort strategy in a fifteen-step parenting framework of positive parenting, to offer parents a non-violent response to conflict with their children. In other words, time out was created to offer parents a less harmful alternative to smacking, spanking or hitting a child. It offers adults a pause to manage their urges and choose an alternative approach.

It was developed for children between three and nine years of age and with clear guidelines never to use it on little ones, as the separation of the parent and the child could impact on the child's physical and emotional needs. Time out is supposed to last from a few seconds to a maximum of five minutes, no matter the age of the child. There is no requirement to place a child on a 'naughty step' or a chair facing a wall, or to send them to another room. 'Time out' was developed so that adults could do it beside a child – if they were self-regulated enough – just by saying, 'I am giving you time out.'

Time out is not given alongside harsh words, shouting, name-calling, shaming or telling a child 'Think about what you have done!', because it does not help children reflect on their behaviour so they can 'do better next time'. Children up to the age of eight act on impulse and are unable to reflect on making 'good choices'. Most child behaviour isn't conscious, it's a reflection of an emotional state.

I have lost count of the number of times people have asked me if time out works. In simple terms, the answer is yes; like most fear-based tactics (a slap, a loud shout, removing a favourite toy), it suppresses behaviour through a startle reaction. But the effect is temporary and, without other supporting strategies, the behaviour will return, and often with a vengeance.

A recent study by Larzelere and colleagues (2018) invited mothers of children who had been diagnosed with defiant or oppositional behavioural problems to use one out of several different parenting strategies, including using age-appropriate reasoning, mutually acceptable compromises, taking away a privilege, offering choices, using warnings and placing a child on a brief time out. The mothers were observed in interaction with their children and measures of behavioural conduct were completed across the week and at a two-month follow up. The results showed that the two most effective strategies overall were 1) giving choices and 2) offering age-appropriate reasoning for expected behaviours. The least effective strategies were those in which parents used power and control, including punishments and time out, with only 12 per cent of children showing an improvement at the two-month follow-up session. More striking was the finding that 35 per cent of children who were given punishments, warnings and time outs displayed *more* unwanted behaviours two months later. For most children, infrequent time outs had no effect on behaviour; it didn't get worse, but it didn't get better either.

The finding that 35 per cent of children's behaviours worsened with the time-out method is concerning, and yet some have taken these findings as evidence that time out is 'not harmful' to children. But that is a long way from saying it is useful. Consider what it would be like if you forgot to pay the gas bill you had promised to take care of and when your partner found out their response was 'Go and sit facing the wall and think about the choice you have made.' Seriously – would that teach you a lesson about your behaviour or would it make you rethink the relationship you have with your partner? And if you think this sounds silly or ridiculous, this is exactly what we do to children when we put them on a time out. The only difference is that they don't get a chance to rethink their relationship with their parent; they have no choice but to continue in it as it is. Why do we think that misusing our power to shame children will bring out better behaviour? None of us learns anything from force or from a place of shame. We learn best when we are self-determined and self-motivated to do better, and that always comes from a place of safety and feeling good about ourselves.

However, I do advocate time out as a strategy for you, the parent. If you struggle with self-regulation and have an impulse to harm a child either physically or through harsh words, time out is for YOU. Set yourself times across the day when you will consciously take a time out – a five-minute break away from your children. If in a moment of overwhelm with your child you feel yourself boiling with rage, say out loud, 'I need a time out,' or, if in a less emotionally dysregulated state, 'I can feel myself getting angry. I am going to go and cool down and then I will be back to help you.' Those five minutes away are a lot less harmful than unleashing your anger on to your child.

Behaviour is always a communication. Listen to what your behaviour is telling you about your needs just as much as you listen to your child's. I want to help you see that your parenting authority doesn't need the use of harsh punishments or to inflict pain to drill in the message; it's firm and confident boundaries that allow you to make the best decisions for your child. You don't have to compromise your relationship to teach your child how to behave well. This is not 'soft', 'gentle' or permissive, it's developmentally aligned and honours the relationship you want to have with your child from now, until for ever. Let me show you how.

Behaviour management without time out

We all want charming children who are kind, polite and well behaved. An inconvenient truth, though, is that children don't behave the way we expect them to, because they are people in their own right, with their own emotions, wants and wishes.

You probably don't expect your partner or friends to always be on board with what you want, but most of us expect our children to follow our lead. If you suggest going out for pizza and your partner says, 'I think I fancy sushi,' your response is unlikely to be 'I will not let you talk back at me like that!' or 'How dare you! I said we are having pizza, and that's that!', or to walk away and ignore them until they have 'made a better choice' (chosen pizza). The false expectation that children 'should' do as we tell them completely ignores the importance of children practising communication skills and developing these in relationship with you, their loving adults. You cannot talk a child into better behaviour – you have to teach them.

I can hear you ask, 'But if we don't give out punishments and consequences, how will a child ever learn the difference between right and wrong?' I get it. It's so hard to think there is a way other than using punishments. There is a fear that if we turned out okay, despite being punished – or worse, physically hit – doing something different might mean we cannot teach our children these same skills. So let's take a moment to pause and think about what you learned growing up. Look back and consider how the adults around you treated you in some of these situations:

- You touched or took something you had been told not to
- You disagreed with what an adult asked of you by saying, 'No,' or 'I don't want to.'
- You lost an item that you loved (would you have told your parents you lost it?)
- You forgot your manners when out in a public situation with family or friends.

Did the adults around you remain calm and listen to you?

Did they try to understand what had happened?

Did they see what had happened as a mistake which they could help you learn not to make, or did they leave you feeling like *you* were a mistake, that you should have known better?

How did this make you feel about the adult responding to your behaviour?

How did this leave you feeling about yourself?

If not giving punishments feels at odds with your experience and brings up some discomfort, this makes sense. After all, a lot of things in our society are based on the principles of reward and punishment . . . but that still doesn't mean that they work. You can do better than using a time out or a punishment to teach your child appropriate behaviours that will stick with them through life.

Connection is prevention

Connection is your most powerful tool. It means 'to be with' your child, fully present in the moment. When a child feels seen, wanted and valued, their behaviour transforms.

Connection does not have to be complicated or time-consuming. It can look like a sprinkling of intentional moments and words across the day, little reminders that you appreciate and love your child for no reason other than to let them hear you say, 'I love you,' 'I am so lucky to have you,' 'You make my day better.'

It can also look like sharing a mutual gaze by joining their view of the world for a few moments and showing interest in what they are doing or enjoying, asking questions about what they are drawing or making, trying to understand the video game they are playing, or simply sitting beside them with the intention of watching them play. If you are having a good day and want to give your child an extra little boost, why not be the one to invite them to play?

This can look like doing something together, such as cooking or helping you with everyday tasks, such as emptying the dishwasher or choosing food at the supermarket, or more personal tasks such as helping you choose what clothes to wear or brushing your hair.

Children don't differentiate between getting positive attention through interaction or from conflict. All they know is 'I am being seen,' and that feels good. When children are acting at their worst, be intentional about the way in which you connect with them. Giving children positive attention can stop unwanted behaviour in its tracks a lot more robustly than any form of consequence or punishment.

Adjust your expectations

Become aware of your child's development and whether what you expect aligns with what they can do. What a two-year-old can manage is different to what a five-year-old can. Ask yourself:

- Is my child able to do what I am expecting them to do?
- Have they successfully managed to do this before?

- If yes, what was different then? What is stopping them from doing it now?
- If no, what do I need to do to support them in learning this new skill?

Being clear about who your child is and where they are at in building skills will help you target behaviour at an acceptable and developmentally appropriate level.

Pause and be curious

Curiosity engages understanding that allows for collaboration. It brings you 'side by side' with your child, rather than 'against them'. When you witness a behaviour from your child that triggers you and there is no urgent threat to safety, slow down! Pause and count to ten before you respond, and use a mantra: 'I can teach my child to do better' or 'I am the parent my child needs.'

See the behaviour as a communication:

What is my child trying to communicate?
Are they overwhelmed/stressed/protesting?
Are they exploring/learning?
Is there anything I need to do to keep my child safe?
Is a boundary needed now?
How can I teach my child a more appropriate behaviour?
What can I model?
What skills do I have to teach?

Dive into your curiosity and hold the most generous assumption about what is going on for your child. They are trying to get your support the only way they know how.

Focus on what you want to see

When we hear the words 'no' or 'don't', it automatically puts us in a position of defence. Without any further information, it is a rejection. For a child, it closes down their voice, their ideas, their possibilities. It can set off emotional overwhelm because hearing 'no' has caused a block for your child, a bit like a rock in the way of their 'flow'.

In contrast, when you focus on the behaviour you *do* want, you are teaching them appropriate behaviour.

Instead of: 'No! Don't jump on the sofa!'
Try: 'You love jumping, it's fun. Jumping happens on the floor.'

Instead of: 'No! Don't pull the cat's tail!'
Try: 'Stroke the cat gently. Look, I'll show you.'

Instead of: 'Stop shouting!' (If you shout this, you're are just reinforcing their behaviours and they may shout louder.)
Try: (in a whisper) 'Hey! Come here. Can you get your voice teeny-tiny like mine? Let's hear it . . .'

Instead of: 'No drawing on the walls!'
Try: 'You can draw on paper, like this . . .'

There will be times where you have to say 'NO' or 'DON'T' loudly and firmly. I suggest you keep this for when your child may be at risk of danger, to halt them in their steps. This might sound like:

- 'Don't touch the candle!'
- 'NO. I will not let you hit.'
- 'STOP! You can't let go of my hand on the street!'

At these moments, see the learning opportunity. What can you do differently next time to ensure your child is safe? How can you adapt the environment/circumstances to make it less likely they will put themselves at risk in this way?

Find your 'yes'!

We know the brain builds connection with 'yes'. Neuroscientists have written entire books on 'the power of yes' (Siegal et al., 2018). 'Yes' is empowering. It helps children listen in to what you are going to say, because 'yes' offers an invitation, it opens possibility:

- YES, I am listening to you
- YES, I can give you attention
- YES, what you are saying is important
- YES, you are allowed to think that, feel that, want that . . . AND I as a parent can hold my boundary.

It says to your child, 'What you have to say has value and I want to hear it.' It allows you to model what respect and acceptance look like, simply by offering them the experience of valuing their voice in that moment.

Instead of: 'Stop annoying your sister!'
Try: 'Yes, it's so lovely that you want to interact with your sister. You know, there is a better way of getting her attention . . . want me to tell you how?'

Instead of: 'No more snacks!'
Try: 'Yes, those biscuits are yummy! You've had two already . . . if you really want one, I can give you another one with dinner. How's that?'

Instead of: 'No, I am not buying you that!'
Try: 'I love that you want to tell me about the things you like. Yes, I want to see the trainers you like. What is special about them? How are they better than the ones you have?'

I know it may seem like a gimmick, but I promise: it works. When you start your sentence with 'yes' it softens the atmosphere and naturally slows you down because it is not the familiar and impulsive 'no' that rolls off the tongue. Anything that will make you pause, reflect, consider the words you are going to speak and the outcome you want to achieve is a good thing. Finding your 'yes' may help you find your curiosity, open up situations to understand your child better and protect you from being drawn into a power battle.

Collaboration breeds cooperation

We all want to feel we have a sense of control over our lives, and it's no different for children. Whenever possible and appropriate, try to offer your child choices, to support your child in following through with their behaviour. You can use 'micro choices' for little ones that sound like:

- 'Do you want to choose a jumper?'
- 'Do you want to go out to play?'
- 'Do you want to take your cup to the table?'

These are small prompts to offer your child a helping hand to get them moving in the right direction.

When your child is a bit older you can offer structured choices, two options at a time so as not to overwhelm or confuse your child. This may sound like:

- 'Do you want to put your clothes on by yourself or do you want me to help you?'
- 'Do you want to wear your sandals or your trainers today?'
- 'Would you like an apple or a banana?'

Offering small choices like this can help children feel a sense of control that keeps their behaviour more settled throughout the day. Whatever choices you offer, stick to them. Your child may try to negotiate, and it's okay to hold the boundary. So, for example, if your child says, 'I want an ice cream!', you can respond by acknowledging your child's wish and sticking to what you want to offer. This may sound like 'Ah, yes, ice creams are yummy. Now is not the time for an ice cream. I have an apple or a banana. Which do you want?' And if this ends in a full-blown protest, you can hold your boundary while prioritizing emotional regulation. Leave the choices off the table for now. You can come back to them later, when calm has returned. So this process may sound like:

Child: 'I want an ice creeeaaaam! WAAAAH!'
Parent: 'Okay. This is a hard choice. Let's give it a minute . . . I am here' (quietly waiting with open stance and relaxed facial gestures).
Child: 'Waaaahhhhhhh!'
Parent: 'You are allowed to feel angry. When you want a cuddle I am here.'
Child: 'Waahhh . . .' And this might go on for a while. But eventually, they will run towards you for a cuddle.
Parent: 'It's passed. I am here. I know not getting what you want is really hard. I love you.'
Child: 'I want an ice cream.'
Parent: 'I know you want an ice cream soooo bad. Today I have an apple or a banana. Do you want either of those?

Child: 'Hmmm . . . okay. Banana' (perhaps your child will make a choice; if not, they may grumble a while longer).

Parent: 'Okay. Here you go. And next time, it's okay to tell me that it's "very unfair" that you are not getting what you want. You don't have to scream. I will hear you if you say, "Mummy, that's not fair. I never get what I want,' and we can talk about it and see what I can do. I can't always give you what you want in the moment. I know that's really hard. I love you, always.'

You are allowed to make choices for your child. Your child is also allowed to speak up and protest. It's their right not to like the choices you offer, and that doesn't mean you have to change your mind. You need to dig deep to remind yourself that you can make the right decisions for them. That is what discipline looks like. It is you taking a leadership role in setting a choice, holding a boundary and supporting your child through it.

Boundaries are your best consequences

In a healthy parent–child relationship, the parent holds the authority and the decision-making. How you communicate your parental authority and leadership can make all the difference. If you show up with the intention of hurting a child in order to 'teach' them a lesson, you will be offering them a punishment. On the other hand, natural consequences are things that happen after a behaviour without adult or child control, for example, throwing a toy car across the room might mean that it breaks. Natural consequences are often upsetting and sometimes uncomfortable and, in many cases, inevitable.

When you choose to communicate your parental authority with warmth and empathy to protect a person, the environment or yourself, we call this having 'boundaries'. A good boundary also takes into account how someone else might feel about it being set. For example, saying to a friend, 'I'm not coming out and I don't have to explain why,' is not a boundary, it's an unkind interaction that may rupture a relationship. However, saying, 'I'm sorry I can't come out. I'm not in a place to want to talk about it yet,' is a boundary of your personal information that acknowledges the impact it may have on the other person. Boundary-setting is not harsh or punitive and it can start with a 'yes' and be playful too.

To hold a boundary more tightly, you need to follow this up with an action that is related to the behaviour, respectful towards your child and reasonably aligns with the stage of a child's development. Actions that follow a boundary should not be punitive, shaming or a misuse of your power – that will turn them into punishments that mask as 'consequences'.

As an adult, you are always in a position of power with your child. Remember that you are responsible for your emotions and it's up to you to regulate them. To find a related consequence, you need to be in a state of regulation. So if your child draws on the table, a boundary would be to say, 'I can't let you draw on the table. Drawing is for paper. Like this . . .' and a related consequence might be to ask them to help you clean it up, or if the child is older, to clean it up themselves with your supervision. Another related consequence might be that you set a higher boundary whereby any time your child wants to draw, this happens under your supervision and guidance, to ensure drawing is on paper and not on any other surface. This will of course limit your child's access to drawing and may mean you need to store away pens and paper until you are available to commit the time to be with your child during this activity.

Stay mindful of the language you use with your child during discipline. If you use shame by saying, 'How many times have I told you not to draw on the table? What is wrong with you? Clean it up. NOW,' you will undermine the success of what you are trying to teach. Breathe – slow down. No matter how bad the furniture looks, this does not need an urgent intervention. Try and suspend your judgement to help your child think about what they have done. That might sound more like 'Oh, what happened here? Looks like you mistook the table for paper . . .' You might be surprised to learn that your child is not trying to vandalize your home, they simply got caught up in their imagination and the playfulness of it all. And this may help you shift your response more easily because you will learn that their intention was never 'naughty' in the first place.

Finally, for a boundary to stick and be effective, it needs to be a good fit for the situation. This means that you can't rely on one boundary for every action or behaviour your child does. So drawing on the table might need redirecting to paper, but if your child is drawing with permanent ink, then the boundary might need to be to ensure all accessible pens are water soluble and all permanent biros are kept high up and out of reach of little hands (until the child is old enough that you know they won't be drawing anywhere but on paper). If you ever look back in hindsight and feel like the boundary was too high, too fast, remember that you can always repair the relationship with your child. Tell your child you got it wrong and work on doing better next time.

After a discipline moment . . .

Discipline doesn't always feel good, even if you are focusing on teaching rather than punishing. It is emotionally exhausting work to focus on the behaviour you want to see, to self-regulate, set boundaries and respond to the emotional whirlwind of your child. It is a lot.

The intensity of your child's emotions is not a reflection of your parenting. The steps you choose to take and how you regulate your emotions are your primary jobs. Your child may continue protesting, and that is okay; it's their job to feel their wants and wishes intensely. This is how they learn about boundaries, and it's a life-long skill that you are teaching them.

Just because it feels bad, it doesn't mean you have got it wrong. Some things that may help you reflect on how well you have carried out your 'jobs' as a parent in these moments of discipline include:

- Did you set a clear boundary?
- Did you teach your child what they can do instead?
- Was your child able to release their emotions, share their protest or offer a different opinion about your boundary?
- Did your child feel acknowledged in what they wanted (even if they didn't get it)?
- Have you repaired your relationship with your child? (Or will you do so in a timely manner when you and they are ready?)

You might not get to feel like you can 'tick off' each off these points every time. You will make mistakes. That's why the biggest tick is the last point – repair. You can learn from the things you get wrong in your relationship with your child and they in turn will also be learning from you.

Teaching accountability without shame

Shame happens quietly and often subtly. It happens in all sorts of families, including loving, attentive, nurturing ones. Shame makes a statement about who the child is rather than what the child has done. It says, 'You are bad.' It happens with words such as 'I am not angry with you, I am disappointed' or 'That's not very nice – do you want to make me sad?' or even 'Why do you make me so angry?'

Rather than focusing on what has happened ('What did I do that was wrong? How can I learn from this?'), shame makes children focus on who they are ('I am a bad child,' 'I am naughty,' 'I am unlovable'). To avoid feeling shame, children become compliant. This is not the same as building an internal sense of morality and accountability. Compliance makes it harder for children to show remorse for actions that hurt others, because shame blocks them from being able to accept the reality ('I did something wrong. I made a mistake. I am human').

If you have ever used 'shame' with your child, even subtly, as a way of trying to tell your child that their behaviour is not acceptable, you are not a terrible parent who has caused irreversible harm. Becoming aware of how you respond to your child can help you tweak things and infuse more love, warmth and compassion into these interactions.

If you want to teach accountability, you need to leave room for your child to accept ownership of their behaviour. I have broken this down into a simple process:

- Focus on the behaviour – keep this as an objective observation, e.g. 'You drew all over the sofa.'
- Focus on your emotions upon witnessing the behaviour – e.g. 'I feel really worried that the ink won't come off and the sofa will be ruined.'
- Invite your child to take responsibility, e.g. 'How are we going to fix this now?' or 'What is your plan?'

Join them in putting things right, and keep talking. This is not a punishment, it is part of making things better and them learning accountability for their behaviour. And for times when your child expresses feeling shame by saying things such as 'I am naughty' or 'I am bad,' you can encourage them to think of behaviour as a choice, and mistakes as learning opportunities. That might sound like 'You made a mistake. That doesn't make you naughty or bad. Making mistakes is how we learn to do things differently next time.' Get curious with them and what they think of others who make similar mistakes; help them find multiple perspectives for their behaviour (e.g. they were absorbed in their creativity and didn't see that the ink was going on the sofa). This isn't about excuses; it's about developing a growth mindset for change and moving towards progress rather than keeping them stuck in shame.

If you find this tricky, I invite you, the next time you make a mistake and you hear yourself go to a place of shame (e.g. 'I am so stupid'), to step back and think, 'What if this was something I could learn from? What would I say to a friend?' You do not deserve to sit in shame, and neither does your child. You can learn to do better next time.

CHAPTER 13

A Toolkit for Behaviours that Challenge

Children are more likely to behave in ways we want when we create environments that are rich in warmth, mutual respect and understanding alongside age-appropriate experiences that allow them to learn and thrive. Prevention is always better than cure, so by better understanding a child you can create environments that are less likely to trigger challenging behaviour and be more prepared to respond in ways that are most effective when need be.

Hitting, spitting, biting, throwing . . . are all developmental

Kitty's parents described how she had turned from a 'sweet, loving two-and-a-half-year-old' into a 'brat' who 'viciously' wanted to hurt them. Kitty's mum explained that she had recently had a baby and Kitty had begun to hit her parents, smiling and laughing as she did so. Her parents felt that Kitty found it funny to hurt them and they were concerned about where their sweet child had gone and what to do about it.

Whenever a baby or child displays these behaviours, it is not a personal attack, even if it feels like it in the moment. Children display these behaviours at moments of vulnerability when big emotions overwhelm them, and these behaviours offer them regulation. They may be practising a skill or following an impulse to explore and make sense of what their body can do. You are not a bad parent if your child does these behaviours, and they are not a bad child. As I did with Kitty and her parents, let's rescript these ideas to find new understandings and strategies that can effectively support children to move through these behaviours with the help of your calm, confident leadership.

Why do they happen?

These behaviours are all developmental milestones. Children are figuring out when and how it is appropriate to hit, throw, spit or bite, and they need your support to guide them. They don't need to see anyone do these behaviours to begin doing them; they are all skills that children move through in different ways.

When little ones figure out how to spit, they tend to do this at mealtimes, when they have saliva, food and liquid in their mouths. It's the perfect set-up! Moving their tongue and mouth into the right position to spit something out takes a lot of skill.

Little ones begin to throw things at the age of around eighteen months. It involves hand–eye coordination and hand agility to hold and release the object. Throwing gives them the opportunity to explore their body within space and context, and it's fun too.

Children explore the world with their mouths because there are more sensory receptors on the tongue than anywhere else. Babies' teeth can also cause aches and discomfort that biting soothes. For a baby or toddler to bite objects and at times people is not malicious in the early years; it is not intended to harm, it communicates a need that must be guided appropriately.

It is typical for children of around eighteen months to start hitting as a sign of frustration, to get something they want or to get someone's attention. Hitting is not a learned behaviour in little ones, it's an impulse and a quick way to get seen, because most adults find hitting hard to ignore.

Kitty's parents started to notice that the hitting was not random. It tended to happen when the new baby was in their arms or they had asked Kitty to 'wait' while they tended to the baby's needs. This told them something about what the hitting might be communicating – a need for attention? An expression of frustration? A desire by Kitty to check that she was still important to her parents and not just an afterthought?

What to avoid

Restricting these behaviours is not the goal; they have a developmental component that is important. Children need to develop these skills in ways that are appropriate, with gentle, focused guidance.

Using punishment and threats for these behaviours can lead to children being locked in distress. Those children who suppress these behaviours will struggle to make appropriate brain–body connections towards emotional regulation. In the long term, they are then more likely to display hitting, spitting and throwing in moments of dysregulation because they have not learned to do anything different.

Kitty's mother said she couldn't help but shout, 'STOP IT!' at Kitty, and that this would make Kitty laugh and the hitting intensify. Kitty's father had hit her back on the arm, not too hard, but enough that it made her cry. He had hoped this would teach her that hitting hurts others, but this had not worked, as she continued to hit back. We talked about what these reactions did – shouting focused on the hitting and reinforced it because Kitty was getting attention, as she wanted, but not as she needed. Retaliating with hitting is an impulse that is never okay. We talked about how, at her stage of development, Kitty would not understand the link between her hitting her father for attention and him hitting her to teach a lesson, so all Kitty was learning in these moments was that her father could become frightening and hurt her.

The more you react to behaviours you don't want to see, the more you increase the likelihood that a child will repeat them. Laughter is often a sign of emotional dysregulation, a nervous laugh that is pre-empting the big reaction you might have. Little ones sometimes find your reactions funny too – your loud voice and change of facial features – but they don't understand that you are hurt because this isn't their intention when they are hitting, spitting, throwing or biting. They are trying to communicate. Rather than placing attention on these behaviours, focus on staying calm so you can set an appropriate boundary.

What works

When children are developing skills of throwing, spitting, hitting or even biting, it is important to give them appropriate spaces and contexts to practise these behaviours safely. The more a child practises a skill in a way that is safe and useful, the less likely they are to do things that are unsafe or dangerous. Promoting safe behaviours teaches your child how to do them in a way that serves a purpose and meets their needs.

For throwing, this might look like throwing bean-bag toys and ball games that incorporate different contexts. For example, throwing bean bags into a box, throwing pebbles into a pond to hear them go 'plop!', playing catch, and throwing a ball for a dog to chase.

For hitting, you may offer toys such as 'whack a mole', swing ball and bat-and-ball games, or tambourines, bongos and drums for tapping and creating sounds with.

For spitting, you may let them practise blowing bubbles in the bathtub or spitting after they brush their teeth.

And for biting, it can help to offer a selection of finger foods to babies, and snacks that crunch for children. Suitable teethers and sensory chew toys as children get older are also good to have at hand. Let a child know that biting is for food and teething toys only.

The message you want to convey with these activities is that throwing, hitting, biting and spitting are behaviours we might do sometimes in appropriate contexts with appropriate items.

Set boundaries

No warning is needed. When you see the behaviour and it is inappropriate, set the boundary firmly.

Kitty's parents worked on setting a firm boundary that communicated, 'I will not let you hit me,' and redirected her to whacking a pillow instead when she was out of control. However, their most impactful strategy was to teach Kitty to ask for her parents' attention with words and actions that did not involve hitting. Kitty started to say, 'I want to play with you,' and her parents started to offer Kitty a 'high-five promise' that they would be with her once they had finished what they were doing. Making regular and predictable times when Kitty was with her parents one-on-one made a noticeable difference to her capacity to wait to be in the presence of her parents. Understanding that Kitty was trying to communicate the pain she felt at losing the full attention of her parents shifted her parents' feeling of anger into one of compassion and care.

Redirecting and moving away from your child is always a better choice than restraining. Never hold their wrists – this can affect their joints. If they are younger than three years old, you may be able to gently hold their arms and redirect them (e.g. 'You can tap on this tambourine like this: tap tap tap'). As much as possible, swap 'hitting' for a less aggressive word when you redirect the behaviour. 'Tapping' or 'whacking' may be more useful terms to move your child away from the focus of 'hitting' and the association of this as an aggressive behaviour.

See the communication beneath the behaviour

Tuning in to what your child is doing and redirecting it accordingly may take some detective work. If you find this tricky – and for many parents it is, particularly when their child cannot yet speak – try following the steps below to make sense of your child's behaviour:

A (Antecedents) – Write down what happened before the behaviour showed up (What was your child doing? Who else was around? What noises, movements and sounds were present?)

B (Behaviour) – Write down the behaviour they carried out and your best guess of what they were trying to communicate.

C (Consequence) – Consider the boundaries you may need to set and how best you will support them to learn appropriate behaviour (e.g. modelling actions alongside teaching them words).

Some prompts to help you:

Is it more common at a particular time of day?
Does it happen around one person more than others?
Is it a sign of hunger or tiredness?
Does it happen when your child feels sensorily overwhelmed by noise, sights and/or movement?
Does it happen when your child feels sensorily deprived (i.e. there is not enough going on to keep them engaged)?

Is your child trying to say something they don't have the words for?

Are they asking others to get out of their personal space?

Do they want to say 'No', 'Stop' or 'Help'?

Are they in a teething phase?

Are any of these behaviours soothing actions they like to do at times of calm or distress?

Are they trying to get your attention?

Is it an invitation to play?

By targeting their need rather than focusing on behaviour, you will support your child more effectively.

When children are defiant

Tanesha's parents told me she had 'no respect' for authority in their home; she was always defying them and refusing to do what was asked of her. At school, Tanesha was a model pupil, and the teachers wished all the children were more like her; at home, she was the complete opposite. Where her older sister was respectful, kind and obedient, Tanesha was rude, wilful and defiant. Her parents resorted to shouting, punishment and, at times, harsh words to get Tanesha to understand that her behaviour was unacceptable. However, they felt that this strategy had not helped Tanesha listen to them better; in fact, it had made their relationship a whole lot worse.

'Not listening' is one of the most common frustrations I hear from parents in my therapy room. So often we think of 'not listening' as defiance, and what we seek from a child is for them to do as they are told – in other words: compliance. The thing is, compliance is not the opposite of defiance. They are sides of the same coin that is founded on power and control. When a child ignores an adult's request it can leave the adult feeling helpless and invisible, and in an attempt to regain control of the situation it is easy to start to shout, or even give a punishment as a way of saying, 'Hey, I am the authority in this house. You WILL listen to me.' The truth is, those reactions only help soothe an adult's feeling of helplessness temporarily, they don't support a child to move through with your request and it doesn't stop them showing defiance. Because the opposite of defiance is actually connection. When a child is not listening to you, it's a sign something is not right in that moment. If you want to regain your position of leadership so your child listens to what you have to say and follows through with your demand, you have to lean into what is happening with curiosity. 'What is going on that my child isn't listening to me right now? Have they got a more pressing need? How can I help them?' When a child feels invisible and disconnected from you, they will tell you by making you feel the way they do.

When a child defies you, it doesn't mean that you have to respond with permissiveness. It means you work *with* your child to move them through what needs to happen. It's not about taking their silence or their 'no' as a fact, it's about acknowledging that they don't want to do something and helping them edge towards it with your help.

Connect before you redirect

Tanesha's father explained how he would have received a slap or a whack on the back of his legs at Tanesha's age if had ignored his father and spoken to him the way Tanesha was speaking to them. He said he often felt shame when his parents came to visit and they saw Tanesha ignoring him. To him, this exposed him as a 'failed father', and yet he did not want to do what had been done to him. He didn't agree with hitting a child, and he didn't want Tanesha to associate his love with force.

When children ignore their parents, it can be a huge trigger from childhood of a time when you were ignored, dismissed or made to feel invisible when you had a need and the adults around you shut you out. As a child, you had no power to make choices about how you were responded to, but now, as an adult, you do. If you want your child to comply, you need to focus on seeing, hearing and connecting with your child in the moment and before you make a request of them.

Tanesha's parents came to notice that she ignored them when they asked her to stop doing something (e.g. winding up her sister) or she was occupied with something, like drawing, homework or play and they needed her to do something. This was usually after school. We talked about how Tanesha was likely to be tired and that her 'role model' student behaviour was likely to have taken a lot of focus and effort, and so her capacity to follow demands at home was limited.

There are many reasons why children 'switch off' from complying to adult demands. They may be immersed in an activity, or they may be tired and overwhelmed by sensory stimulations throughout the day (e.g. from nursery or school), and all of this will affect their emotional capacity to hear your request and follow through. So what can you do? Connect with your child and support them to carry out the behaviour you want to see. No matter how old they are, if you want your child to do something, be prepared to join them in doing it. Don't expect a child to follow your direction when you do so passively by shouting across a room, 'Time to tidy up!' or 'Get your shoes on!' or 'Bathtime, now!' Move your body towards them so you can connect your request with their emotional experience and guide them through it.

Get close

Tanesha's parents had a 'eureka moment' when they realized that Tanesha likes to sit at the front of class and takes any requests the teacher makes seriously because they seem to be directed at her. They began by moving closer to Tanesha and focusing on what she was doing in the moment, offering a comment on her artwork or her play so that Tanesha felt that she was being seen in that moment. They would then invite Tanesha to listen to them by saying, 'Hey, Tanesha, can I ask you something?'

Before you make a request, make sure you are close to your child, ideally at their eye level. Say their name so that they are encouraged to give eye contact (without forcing it) and know that what is coming next is directed at them.

Simplify your request

Tanesha's parents had excused her older sister from participating in house chores because she was revising for exams. They agreed that a few minutes of laying the table would not impact on her revision but would make a big difference to Tanesha, demonstrating that it wasn't just she who had to follow her parents' demands.

Children struggle with demands that have multiple steps, and inaction may be a sign of information overwhelm. It is better to say, 'Put your shoes on,' rather than 'Can you put your shoes on?' Make a statement – don't ask a rhetorical question.

Offer agency

One thing children crave is control. Offer them age-appropriate choices that give them a sense of power in this moment.

Tanesha's parents began to offer her more choices, so, for example, when laying the table, they asked her, 'Do you want to do the plates or the cutlery today?' They also began to offer choices about times when she wanted attention from them (e.g. 'After school, do you want some time to chill or get some one-on-one time with one of us? We are not your sister but we could still do something fun if you want to'). Protecting fifteen minutes of time after school gradually stopped Tanesha from needing to wind up her sister in order to get attention and interaction.

Get playful!

It may help you to get playful with your child to engage their willingness to comply. This might look like putting your shoes on the wrong way round or picking up one of your boots and saying, 'Here you go, put that on,' and when they say, 'That's not mine!', get silly with it. 'Oh, whoops! So I guess these ones on my toes are yours . . . I wondered why only my toes fitted in.' Children are more likely to do things that are fun, and an added benefit of this is that it can make the whole experience feel a lot more connecting.

Pick your battles

Tanesha's parents recognized that school had become more intense for Tanesha and that there were things they could 'let go' of, like they did for her older sister. They started to have a couple of nights a week when the girls were free from chores. On those nights, Tanesha and her sister got to spend a few minutes playing or watching TV together, small moments of connection that had been missing for a while.

When you want your child to cooperate, you are asking them to do something for you. If this comes at the expense of time and/or your relationship with your child (because you end up in a shouting match), give yourself permission to get the task done. This might mean doing part of the task yourself, such as setting the table or grabbing your child's shoes and helping them put them on. This helps children experience you as an accessible, supportive and safe adult when compliance is expected.

When children 'talk back'

If you wish for a child who rarely protests, doesn't take up too much space, appears generous and gives in easily to others' wants or wishes – I get why!

These children – who we often label as 'good kids' – are compliant and appear easy to lead forward.

Now think about what you want to see in your child when they're a teenager. Do you want them to be independent, speak up for themselves and know how to stand up to peer pressure? If you are thinking, 'Yes! I want that too!', there is a mismatch. A child who is compliant does not turn into an adolescent who knows how to protest and say no when things don't feel right to them. If you want to help your child learn that their voice matters, you need to give them the experience of having their voice heard.

Children are allowed to say no!

We need to actively encourage children to say no more often. 'Why on earth would we want that?' I hear you say. Because believing that a child should not 'talk back' to adults is an authoritarian attitude that is linked to greater conduct problems in children and unhealthy outcomes in adulthood. Children who comply easily tend to become adults who find it hard to express their emotions with others out of fear that they will be dismissed. They tend not to make a fuss when something is harming them in relationships for fear of being rejected. They are more likely to avoid new things as they are afraid of failing and instead strive for perfection in the areas they are good at. And they tend to meet others' needs over and beyond their own, needing external validation and approval to make decisions for themselves.

When your child speaks out with 'no', the only thing you need to fight back is your immediate emotional reaction. Every time you are able to regulate yourself, to offer your child a safe space where their opinions can be heard and accepted, even when they lie outside your own, you are teaching them that their voice matters. So when it happens, pause, breathe and remember that your authority is conveyed in your calm confidence, not your loud reaction. This means accepting when your child likes something different to you (e.g. 'You like the potatoes and I like the asparagus.

We can eat the same meal and enjoy different things'). Accept that your child experiences events differently to you (e.g. 'We came to the swimming pool because I thought it would be fun, but you are not enjoying it. You don't have to come in if you don't want. I'm going to swim a couple more laps and then we will go home') and that your child's protests are an opportunity to experience their feelings as valid and separate to yours (e.g. 'You do not want to put your shoes on. It sucks to have to stop having fun. I know, I know . . . I need to buy food, so you have to come. I'm going to help you . . .').

If this feels uncomfortable and sounds like a route towards 'disrespecting adults', I want to invite you to be curious about how much space you were given to question the decisions your parents made. What was it like to disagree with them? What has this taught you about speaking up for your needs as an adult? Lean into your discomfort. Why might you hold a belief that children need to blindly follow adult authority rather than learn to speak up respectfully for what feels right to them? And remember that *the opposite of defiance is connection*, and you can support your child's willingness to cooperate, but only if you engage with them in a way that makes them feel seen first.

Teach your child how to disagree respectfully

Rather than shutting down a child's voice, let's teach them to use it appropriately and respectfully, while holding their right to speak up when needed. Children have limited emotional regulation skills, so when they object to something their emotions often flood them, impacting on their verbal skills.

Rather than focusing on the tone your child uses, listen to the message behind their words. If you only focus on shutting down the 'disrespectful tone', you ignore the need they are trying to communicate and block their opportunity to practise disagreeing with you. In the moment, that might sound like 'I hear that you don't agree with me. That's okay. Can you say that without using a mean word? Try it. I am listening.' Or if your child is younger: 'It's hard to be told what to do. I know you don't want to do this, you don't need to shout – I am listening.'

You can set firm boundaries with respect around their words, but if you don't allow your child to practise disagreeing with you, they will not know how to do it with others.

Help them to build assertiveness

Children should not be afraid to speak up. For some, this is harder than for others. For a child who is quiet, you can encourage this by asking curious questions at times when they have followed a request or given in to another quickly. Things like 'That was kind. Did you really want to give your biscuit away?', 'What would have happened if you had kept it for yourself?', 'If you wanted something that someone else has, how would you ask for it?'

For a child who already speaks up with more ease, your role is to meet them with empathy and guide them in learning how to do this with respect so they build assertiveness, not aggression. Rather than meeting them in a power battle, where you use negotiation and logic to convince your child to do as you say, which may sound like 'You need a bath. Look, you don't have a choice, you cannot say no to me. Stop it!', make sure you meet them where they are, empathize with their experience and offer them a choice, if possible. This may sound like 'It's bathtime and you reeeaaaally do not want to go. Thank you for telling me how you feel about bathtime. Do you want a quick shower instead?' This needs to be followed through with empathetic momentum and leadership so you can bathe your child while making it clear that you understand that they don't want to. That may sound like 'I know, ugh . . . getting wet makes you feel cold, and you don't like it. I am going to warm up the towels and make sure we get your pyjamas on super-fast!'

Two things can be true at once. Your child is allowed to say they don't want something to happen, and you can engage their willingness when this is for their own good. You and your child are allowed to 'agree to disagree'. Empathizing with your child's disagreement matters because you let them know 'Your voice is important. Even when I have to make the difficult choice of helping you do something you don't want to do, you are allowed to tell me how it feels.'

Understand that authority isn't 'always right'

The idea that adults are not always right can be hard for some to accept. Parents are not omnipotent. We all make mistakes. Children need to learn to stand up to things that feel wrong to them, not to be scared of authority but to speak up with respect.

I will never forget the day my child pointed at a painting in our home and declared, 'There is a man dancing.' The painting is of two zebras, so of course my impulse was to respond, 'No, love, they are zebras.' She became more sure of herself and said loudly, 'IT IS A MAN DANCING.' So I paused . . . reflected back her comment and got curious. It sounded a bit like 'Hmmm . . . okay, so I see two zebras and you see a man dancing . . . how interesting that we don't see the same thing. I wonder where this man is on the painting. Can you point him out?' She did. And I saw him! One of the zebra stripes is squiggly, and it does look like a man dancing with his arms wildly in the air. So, to my daughter, I said, 'Wow, I see him now. Thank you so much for showing him to me. He's so funny.' It would have been so simple to say 'Yeah, okay, whatever,' and sit in my parental authority instead of being curious. By doing the latter not only did I model to my daughter how to make sense of someone else's experience when it is different to our own (in a respectful way), but she opened up my eyes to a different perspective.

Don't try and persuade your child that what you know is more valid than their experience. You may learn more from interacting in this way with your child than you think. There may also be times when you forget that how you behave affects how your child responds. If you land in a place where you say, 'Do it because I say so,' remember that you can repair and work on doing better next time.

We do children a huge disservice if we don't guide them in how to say no, how to stand up for themselves and how to speak up when they feel wronged. Our society needs less compliance and more strong voices. With your calm and supportive guidance, the next generation of voices may change the world.

Rude behaviours

We have a false belief that if a child is rude it reflects bad parenting and 'lack of discipline'. Your child's behaviour is never a reflection of your parenting, it's a clue about how they are feeling. What we as adults perceive as 'rudeness' in children is often a sign of immature social skills, a lack of understanding about social norms, an inability to see something through someone else's perspective and emotional dysregulation that has overwhelmed their capacity to use words effectively.

We cannot expect a child to respond with social skills beyond their developmental capacity and social proficiency. If we understood this, perhaps we would judge each other less and offer greater compassion to children, which would help teach social skills a lot more effectively. When you see a child being rude, look out for their unmet needs so you can guide them, not shame them.

Children learn from what you do

Children learn how to treat others by how they are treated themselves. If you hold the belief that children 'need to show respect to adults', begin by approaching children with the respect and politeness you wish to see mirrored back.

I know it can be embarrassing to witness your child being rude to another. It may spark anger towards your child and/or guilt about your own parenting. It is hard not to jump in and make things better, but try and pause. You need to regulate before you can take positive action.

Reframe the rude encounter.

Rather than think: 'My child is so rude! This is awful. What will they think of me/them?'
Remind yourself: 'My child is still learning social skills. I can help them.'

Once you are in a calm position with your child, you can meet rudeness with positive communication that models to your child the language and/or actions you want to hear.

Rather than: 'How dare you speak like that? Say sorry!'
Try: 'I think what you wanted to say was "No, thank you." You are feeling a little overwhelmed right now. That's okay. I am here.'

This is an opportunity to teach acceptable social interactions with others. Saying negative things about your child in front of them can reinforce the behaviour you don't want to see. Remember that modelling is the most powerful teacher. Avoid saying things like 'I am so sorry – they are so rude. It's unacceptable.' Instead, embody your leadership and model to your child what a respectful apology sounds like. For example, 'I am sorry that came out so abruptly. They are learning how to speak kindly when they don't want something from people they don't know well. Thank you for understanding.'

Learn from the experience to prepare your child

Take a moment to reflect on what is going on when your child appears rude to others. Are they in an unfamiliar situation? Do they feel heightened emotions? Are they feeling scared, worried or embarrassed? Knowing the triggers can help you prepare them for what is expected next time and offer them choices that give them safety and control. This may sound like 'Last time we went to Ellis's house his dad was there and I know you found it hard to speak to him kindly. I wonder whether maybe you were feeling nervous because you don't know him . . . Shall we have a think about what you are going to say when he says hello or offers you something to drink? Let's practise it together.'

Being an effective parent doesn't mean you end up with 'perfect' children. Children will do things that appear rude because it's part of the process of learning and growing up. We all have a responsibility to support children in this by meeting them with good communication skills, respect and compassion. Don't for one minute worry that any rudeness you witness in the early years either reflects your child's identity or will get in the way of them building healthy and positive social relationships in the long term. Keep seeing beneath their behaviour and use your social skills to model more of what you want to see.

CHAPTER 14

A Toolkit for Social Behaviours

Children don't just need to learn how to behave appropriately, they also need to be empowered with social tools that allow them to form positive relationships with others. With adult expectations and assumptions, it can be hard to see a child's perspective. Your best tools as an adult are to be collaborative, creative, empathetic and curious. These are the elements that will help you be a role model and teach your child to develop the social skills and behaviours you want to see more of, now and in the future.

Sharing and the rules of play

How often have you told your child to 'play nicely!' with others? It's such a natural hope to get a bit of a break and enjoy some social company or, in some cases, just a little breathing space to yourself. And yet telling children to 'play nicely' doesn't help them understand what 'nice play' looks or feels like, or what to do when playing with someone else no longer feels 'nice' (because the other person has taken a toy they wanted, or they don't want to play the same game, or they just started doing something that feels annoying . . .).

Blake (2009 and 2010) carried out a series of studies with children aged between three and five to understand the concept of 'ownership'. Children were shown a series of videos in which children were either given a gift or had a toy snatched away, and then asked, 'Whose toy is it?' Two- to three-year-olds consistently pointed at the person who had the toy at the end, regardless of whether it was gifted or not and whether the scenario was between an adult and a child or between two children. Only children who were five were able to understand that property can be transferred (e.g. gifting on birthdays) and that it can still be yours even when someone has illegitimately taken it (e.g. another child snatching a toy).

Little ones who refuse to share have become attached to a toy, and their sense of ownership gets in the way of being able to 'loan' a toy to another child. Children don't begin to make steps towards playing together until they are around three and a half years of age, and socializing with others is a skill that takes a lot of practice and a lot of time. Before you can rest in the knowledge that your child can interact 'nicely', they need to develop the following skills:

- To pay attention and be able to concentrate to interact with another long enough to make it meaningful
- To understand verbal and non-verbal communication to make sense of what others want, say and need
- To be able to express in verbal and non-verbal ways what they want, need and have ideas about
- To be self-motivated to interact and play just to have fun
- To have enough emotional regulation to be able to name an emotion, work through it and continue playing with someone else, or say when they want to stop playing when things get too much in a way that is safe to them and the other.

Most of these skills develop around the age of four or five, and mastery takes a lot longer. When you understand this, you can meet your child in a way that aligns with their development and is a whole lot more effective.

Don't force your child to share

Children are not selfish, and we have science to back this up. There is a fair amount of research on the psychology of sharing which shows that children enjoy sharing, but only if sharing is their choice and they haven't been forced into it.

Wu et al. (2017) invited 139 preschool children aged between three and five years to take part in completing a half-finished puzzle and gave stickers as a reward at the end. The children were split into two groups: some were told they had to share their stickers with the child who had helped start the puzzle they had completed, and others were told that another child had helped make the puzzle but the stickers were theirs to keep. All the children were given two envelopes, one for them and one for the other child in the task, and they were left to decide how many stickers to put in each envelope. All the children were asked to rate on a seven-point scale, where 1 was not happy at all and 7 was very happy, how much they had enjoyed the task. Children aged four and older noticeably shared more stickers, which isn't surprising. However, two interesting things happened: children gave away more stickers when they chose to do so freely rather than when they were told to do so, and those who were forced to share scored lowest on the happiness scale, even though they kept more stickers for themselves!

Children find sharing rewarding, but only when it is self-motivated. In reality, when adults force children to share, it's the adults who are sharing, not the children. It is only when a child makes the difficult choice to share and reap the benefit of feeling good about it that they are more likely to share again. When you use force, it doesn't teach generosity, it teaches resentment, because sharing becomes annoying, something a child never wants to do in the first place.

That doesn't mean that when your child is playing with a toy at play-group or nursery they can hold on to it for hours without letting another child touch it. In spaces where toys are shared, children need to learn turn-taking. However, in spaces where children own toys and others want to join in, for example during playdates, there is something more powerful that you can do than forcing a child to share – and it can feel good to do it.

Before a playdate, give your child permission to protect toys they don't want others to touch or play with, and give them the choice of which toys and activities they are happy to share. Allowing your child to put away toys offers them control about possessions that are important to them, and this can help them relax when another child shows up and begins to take up space.

If your child has been invited to another child's home, consider giving them permission to take some toys and/or activities that they can share too. Many children like to take toys that bring them comfort when they leave the home. It's also a gentle way of teaching children reciprocal sharing so that when they are in someone else's home it isn't the responsibility of one child to 'share', there is also an offering back.

Teach children to take turns

Many parents use timers, or smart speakers, as a way of arbitrating on whose turn it is. I don't advise the use of a timer, as children do not have a concept of time until they are six to eight years old. The time you set is an adult expectation of when a child will have had enough of playing, and this may not match the child's reality.

A better option is to help children stay focused on their play until they have had enough and are willing to give it up. Then, the sharing becomes easy and feels good to do, for example, 'Look, I think Anoushka wants to play with the scooter too. When you are finished, can you pass it on to her for a turn?'

For the child waiting their turn, this is a golden opportunity to teach patience. It's a big skill to learn, and many adults also struggle with it. The more practice with patience your child gets, the easier waiting will become. This means sitting with their upset and disappointed feelings, acknowledging that it is hard to wait and helping them move through these feelings: 'I know, you want the scooter. Becky is playing with it now. It is hard to wait your turn. I am here. Let's do something fun while we wait!'

Children who request toys from others are often trying to display control and power. When you force a child to give up a toy to stop another child from crying, you are teaching a child that they can demand what they want and get it if they cry loudly enough. The child being forced to share is learning that to appease someone else's feelings is important. Neither of these messages is healthy, and they don't build up the skill of sharing. Instead, they lead to entitled children who learn that they can get what they want by crying and shouting louder, and resentment from those who are forced to share.

It is important for children to learn that everything they wish for cannot be granted, and that it's okay to wish for things! Wishing for more is healthy; it's where many of us find motivation to move out of our comfort zones. When children have their feelings heard and are gently redirected to another source of enjoyment, they often forget their initial demands and the intensity about having them here and now fades. This is the foundation of patience, and distraction, in this instance, while waiting to get what you want, can be useful.

Teach assertiveness

I know this is going to be hard to hear and will take a moment to sink in: never shame or punish a child who is unable to share. Children are allowed to feel strongly about whatever they have, and it is okay for them not to want to share it. Children are allowed to say no the same way it is okay for you to say no to letting a friend borrow your most expensive piece of tech or your favourite jewellery. Frankly, who gets to touch and use your things is up to you. And the same is true for children.

Rather than expecting children to share, let's help them develop skills to be respectfully assertive. Before the age of three it is acceptable to take a child's 'no' as enough and for you to support them, modelling the language you would like them to use one day. That might sound like 'I heard you say no. You are not ready to give up the swing yet. That's okay. When you are done, we will let that little boy who is waiting his turn have a go.'

As children develop more language and skills, be explicit about what you want them to say. Help them with setting boundaries. That might sound a little like 'I heard you say no. It's okay that you are not finished with the swing. Can you say, "I am still using it. When I am finished you can have it"?'

Similarly, it's important to help children learn how to request things from others in a way that is respectful. Try to model language you want to hear. When they are little, that may sound like 'You really want the swing. Okay, I will help you.' [To the other child] 'May he have a go on the swing after you?' And when they are older, this may sound like 'You really want the swing. Why don't you ask, "May I go after you?"'

Practise turn-taking

Learning to take turns is a skill that needs time to build. Offer opportunities in your everyday life to take turns and practise tolerance of frustration. If your child struggles with turn-taking, keep games to three people maximum, ensuring that one of the people is an adult, rather than expecting a child to take turns while making sense of a game with a peer.

Some ideas of everyday tasks where turn-taking might show up:

- Baking (e.g. using cookie cutters, one of you at a time)
- Breakfast (taking turns using a spoon to take jam out of the jar or scooping out cereal)

- Bathtime (taking turns washing body parts. Also great for building up body-assertive vocabulary and supporting your child to build independence with your support)
- Getting dressed (e.g. 'you do your top and I'll do your leggings').

Games that help with turn-taking:

- Card games such as Snap
- Memory games such as finding pairs
- Snakes and Ladders
- Lotto games
- Bingo
- Four in a row
- Guess who
- I spy with my little eye . . .

Use descriptive praise

At times when your child chooses to share, shower them with praise, but make it meaningful. Phrases like 'You're such a good boy/girl' have no substance. Try building empathy skills by describing what has happened, to give a child an understanding of why 'give and take' is a positive social interaction. For example, 'I saw you give your dolly to Lexie when she asked for it. Did you see the smile on her face? Look! How do you think she feels? I think she really liked that.' Drawing attention to concrete details and linking this with how it makes someone else feel is how you grow empathy and make sharing feel good.

When children are not forced to share, they learn patience, empathy and how good it feels to give and receive. In the long term, this allows children to handle emotionally complex social situations better and they feel a sense of both assertiveness and generosity.

Good manners

There is a strong narrative in our society that 'children must learn to say please and thank you'. Learning manners is a really important skill, much more than the simple act of learning words by rote. 'Thank you', 'Sorry' and 'Please' are phrases that show appreciation of the actions of another person towards us. They strengthen relationships and build bonds of trust and connection.

Has a child ever asked you for a drink or a snack and you have replied straight away, 'What's the magic word?' If you have, as an attempt to remind a child to use their manners, it makes sense. The problem is, this is not teaching a child good manners. It is associating manners with feelings of shame ('I forgot. Now this adult is mad at me'), embarrassment ('Oh no, I feel so bad I forgot'), or even resentment ('I hate being forced to say please'). This can lead to greater resistance with manners because the emotion associated with 'please' is a bad one.

This doesn't mean you have to give up on teaching a child good manners – please do not give up! But there are better ways to do so than using shame, which is a terrible teacher anyway.

Why gratitude matters

Our brains have a tendency to focus on the things that are difficult or problematic because they often stand out more. Gratitude can rewire the brain to focus on the good things you have around you, not because 'thinking positive makes you feel positive' (that is not necessarily true . . .), but because seeing the positives in your day can bring you a more realistic perspective on your experiences.

With curious enquiry, some guidance and empathetic modelling, we can help children attune to their feelings, make sense of another's perspective and show empathy for someone else's actions towards them.

Gratitude is not a 'natural behaviour', it's a state of thankfulness that has to be learned. Studies have shown that many adults have not yet developed gratitude and find it difficult to practise it. And yet we know that gratitude impacts on resilience, strengthening relationships and reducing stress and depression. Emmons and McCullough (2013) examined gratitude and well-being under three experimental conditions. Participants were divided into three groups and asked to keep a daily journal. The first group noted negative events or hassles, the second noted things they were grateful for, and the third group neutral life events. Those asked to focus on gratitude showed significantly higher reports of subjective wellbeing, including better mood and lower anxiety.

Practising gratitude will not shrink the things you find difficult, but it will put them into perspective. So rather than thinking, 'I have had a terrible day!', gratitude can help bring another dimension to this: 'Ugh, it's been such a long day. I am so tired AND we had a lovely moment giggling together on the floor.' There is always space to bring more colour into your day. Gratitude may be an ingredient that you don't give yourself or others enough of, and if you try to sprinkle it into your days, you may notice a positive effect on your wellbeing and that of others.

Model gratitude and appreciation

Have you ever given a child a gift and their reaction was not to beam a smile and a big 'thank you' but to look down, hide or even run away? If you have, perhaps this reaction seemed strange, disrespectful or even rude. In fact, this is really common. Children are not doing this with the intention to offend; they don't even understand what another person might feel. Their behaviour reflects what is happening inside their bodies. When children are given a gift, they often feel overwhelmed with excitement, embarrassment or anxiety at the adults watching their reaction. Their body goes into overdrive because something huge is happening here! When, in the moment, you jump in with 'Say thank you', all you do is shine a light on their emotional overwhelm and the skills gap they are demonstrating.

Teaching manners starts with you. Make sure that 'thank you' and 'please' are regularly being used by you and, whenever possible, connected with a story of what has happened. For example, 'Thank you so much, that is so kind . . . Did you see how that lady let us skip the queue and go in front of her? That was so kind. Now we can get home quicker and make lunch! Such a thoughtful thing for that lady to do for us.'

Embed a culture of gratitude in your home

Create a gratitude jar or a gratitude poster where family members put down one thing they are grateful for a day. At the end of the week, they can be read out loud during a family meal. This is a great way of embedding gratitude in your home. When all family members participate, it can bring you a little closer together, as you become aware that those you live with are appreciating you and are grateful for your contributions.

Actively teach empathy and gratitude

After an event such as a birthday or Christmas, help your child notice what they are grateful for and how they can share their gratitude with another. Use curious questions such as:

'Do you know who gave you this toy?'
'How does playing with it make you feel?'
'How could you share this feeling you have on the inside with the
    person who gave you this gift?'
'What could you do to show how this toy makes you feel?'

This helps children understand the idea of 'giving and receiving'. Stay open to what your child thinks may be appropriate and really notice their intention to show their gratitude to someone else. Often children find much more meaningful actions and words than a simple 'thank you'.

Use role-play to practise saying 'thank you' and 'please'. For example, playing with a tea set and offering milk and cookies. 'Would you like some milk? There you go. You are welcome, panda bear. Ask me for more later if you want a top-up.' Without force, you may begin hearing your child saying thank you as they learn what the sequence of steps is in these social interactions. Trust the process and remember that children don't begin to engage in meaningful reciprocal social interaction until they are around four years old.

Show them gratitude

Children need to experience gratitude in order to understand the impact of the words and actions we want them to use. Show your child genuine appreciation in buckets, every day. This may sound like:

'Thank you for putting your shoes on.'
'Thank you for coming when I called you.'
'Thank you for helping [your sibling] when they couldn't reach their toy.'
'Thank you for giving me such a warm cuddle.'

Watch your child's face, physical posture and overall reaction when you do this. The more your child associates saying thank you with a feeling of deep appreciation, the more likely they are to spontaneously say thank you when they notice this feeling showing up in their bodies. This won't be something they just offer you, it will be words of gratitude they want to share with others when they get this feeling too.

How to respond when others feel offended

We have all been in the awkward situation where our child is given something and the adult expects a 'please' or a 'thank you' that doesn't come. Be prepared to set a boundary if the adult takes offence and insists on it, or utters the dreaded 'What do you say?' I know this can feel cringey in the moment, but if your child isn't able to show gratitude yet, telling them off will not help them learn faster. Instead, ensure you model sincere gratitude to the adult, and rest assured that this is enough.

We cannot make children feel grateful or remorseful for their actions. Only they can truly feel this. Our job as adults is to help them tap into their caring feelings and model this with them and others, so they experience how these interactions are part of the social glue that binds us together.

The value of honesty

We often think of lies as 'bad', things that should be avoided for the more virtuous process of honesty. But to stay honest, first you need to feel safe. If honesty is going to put you at risk emotionally or physically, or potentially break a relationship, then honesty may not be the best thing. Lying is a protective behaviour and it can help to free us from shame or intolerable feelings of badness.

Paolo's mother found out that he had been lying for weeks. Someone had vandalized one of the toilets at school, and Paolo and his friends had all been questioned. He said he had been in the playground and not seen anything. Three weeks later, at bedtime, Paolo starts to cry and tells his mother he knows who did it and that he watched it happen. Paolo's mother's instinct is to tell him off, to emphasize to him the importance of being honest and the disappointment she feels at learning this. She removes his access to screens for the week and tells him he isn't allowed to see his friends at the weekend.

Consider what message you offer a child when you say, 'I want you to be honest with me, always.' Do you mean 'I want to know everything about you so I can feel in control' or 'I always want to know everything so I can be there to support you'? If your intention is the latter, you must meet your child's lies with love and compassion. Does this mean it's okay for a child to lie? No . . . it's more nuanced than that.

I spoke with Paolo's mother about what she hoped to teach Paolo with her response. She wants him to learn that it is not okay to deceive an adult and that telling the truth won't get him punished but that lying always will. I wonder whether the way she has approached this has given Paolo the clear messages she hoped . . . After all, Paolo did tell the truth, it just took him three weeks to have the courage to do so, and he ended up with no access to screens and without playtime with friends. I wonder what Paolo hoped his mother might do when he told her the truth, which he had clearly found painful to hide from her, as shown by his tears when he spoke about it. Paolo's mother acknowledged that he probably hoped she would comfort him and, as he had told the truth, that she would not be angry, but her emotions got the better of her. It also takes courage as an adult to know when we have got it wrong with our child.

Lying can be a way to keep you on their side

Lying in childhood is not done with the intent to deceive. Children who are neurodiverse are less likely to lie because they have a more 'black and white' view of the world and tend to find the subtleties and nuances of social interaction hard to understand. So, instead, you may have to manage honest blunt truths and learn to gloss them over when they happen.

More than anything, children seek adult approval. When they become aware of your reactions, they try to anticipate what you might do. Some of this is a little 'trial and error' – experiments in how far they can push your boundaries, but also how sturdy your love for them is. Children learn rapidly when adults send the message that what they have done is a source of disappointment. Children hate that feeling. We all hate that feeling! To know you have done or said something that has made someone look at you differently can be so painful and invite shame.

Paolo made a choice that turned into a bad outcome. One of his friends thought it would be funny to stuff a toilet with toilet paper. Paolo was in the wrong place at the wrong time and he felt caught between his loyalty to his friend and what he thought was right. Rather than Paolo being punished, he needed someone to be curious about the story of what had happened, without fear that something bad would happen to him or his friends. If someone had done this, they would have heard that Paolo's friend's parents were going through a divorce and Paolo wanted to protect him. If an adult had taken the time to listen and understand, perhaps they would have reached out to his friend, to offer support and a listening ear and, without inflicting punishment or shame, asked him to help clean up the mess in the toilet. And if this had happened, perhaps Paolo would have learned that he can develop skills to stand up to a friend's actions and say, 'I think this is wrong,' and that adults can be a source of safety and support, that boundaries can exist without pain.

If being honest is important to you, don't forget to thank your child when they get something wrong and still make the choice to tell you the truth. No matter what happened or how much time has passed, a child who sees the value of being honest deserves recognition and appreciation.

Lying can be 'wishful thinking'

Have you ever witnessed a child do something like spill a glass of water, and when you ask, 'Did you just spill that?' they reply without flinching, 'No. I didn't'? Or perhaps you asked a five-year-old to go and wash their hands and when they come to the table you know they haven't because they didn't go anywhere near the sink, but when you ask, 'Did you wash your hands?' their response is 'Yup!'

A child lying in this way is not a 'lie' in the way an adult conceives it. Until the age of eight, children are unable to put themselves in another's shoes to make sense of their perspective, and they have not developed the ability to make up an alternative reality or share a convincing story to fool you.

Children blur fantasy and reality, and have a 'magical hope' that something did not happen. This is a form of 'wishful thinking'. Don't bait them with a question in order to catch them out ('Did you spill that water?'). This is unkind and manipulative. Instead, name their wish and take positive action: 'Ah, you wish you had not spilt that water. It's okay. It happens to everyone. Come on, let's wipe it up.'

Beneath every lie, there is always a wish, a desire to please or to protect. When you see your child's wishes beneath the lie, it can make it easier to approach them. You can then model honesty in a way that teaches them that when they mess up, you won't attack them.

Lying can keep you connected

Children who are punished repeatedly for faults, mistakes and 'hiding the truth' tend to become master liars and may hide the smallest of things for fear of rejection. If your child lies about something and later you find out the truth is different, rather than being guided by your feeling of deceit or disappointment, which may lead you to say, 'You lied to me,' you can choose to regulate your emotions and meet your child's 'new-found' honesty with curious appreciation. With Paolo's mother, that might have sounded like 'Thank you for telling me the truth. It must have been hard to keep that hidden for so long . . . Why did you tell me now? What stopped you telling me last week? I am listening. I am here.'

What you teach here is far more important than honesty. You teach that you are an adult who can be trusted to see the best in a child, even when they mess up, make the wrong choice or get it wrong. You see their goodness. When children learn there is a safe sanctuary in your presence that won't judge or punish but will instead listen, understand and support, they are more likely to stay honest.

Be the role model of honesty you want to see

When children witness adults around them tell lies to either get what they want, manipulate situations in the direction they wish or evade a consequence, they learn this is normal social communication. And, of course, we all lie sometimes. What matters is that we are aware of when we lie and whether it is necessary or not.

Rather than manipulating your child with a story to convince them to comply, for example, 'No, darling, Thomas the Tank Engine has gone to bed, so we cannot watch him any more,' model speaking the truth: 'It's time to say goodbye to Thomas the Tank Engine. Screen time is up. You can watch some more tomorrow.'

Or when you really do not want to take your child to the park, avoid saying, 'When it's wet, they close it.' Instead, be honest: 'I am sorry, I don't want to go to the park today. It's raining and cold. We can do something else together. What would you like to do?'

You cannot ask something of your child that you are not willing to embody yourself. Try to notice when honesty does and doesn't feel safe to you. Are there people or situations that make it more likely that you will drop a lie to protect yourself from feeling embarrassment or shame, or stop the other person from seeing a side of you that you would rather they didn't know about? Realizing that you use lies to make your life easier with others, including your child, may help you meet lying with compassion when it happens. Honesty flourishes where messiness and lies are understood and given empathy.

When children reject you

There is going to be a time when your child will say mean words to you. I am not talking about swearing or being rude, I am talking about saying hurtful words that may sound like:

'I hate you!'
'You are the worst mummy/daddy ever!'

'You are so mean!'
'GO AWAY!'

When this happens, it will break your heart. But take comfort in the knowledge that what your child is trying to communicate is not hate towards you, even if that is how it feels in the moment – they are trying to say, 'I need you.' Because what lies beneath these words is often painful feelings of sadness, hurt, anger, or feeling unloved, unheard or misunderstood. Often this comes alongside a child's pull for independence and at times when you are setting a firm boundary. They want to get away from you while knowing that they still need you. This is deeply frustrating to children who want to 'grow up' and have control over their choices and their lives. The feelings that lie beneath the hurtful words are what you need to see and tend to.

It makes sense that when we feel hurt we try and shield ourselves and perhaps protect our vulnerability by retaliating with words such as 'I hate you too!' or 'Ugh! If only you knew how hard it is to have a child like you . . .' Of course, this won't get you far in bringing soothing to your child and supporting their needs, or making you feel more lovable either! Sometimes we can bring more compassion just by remembering that, as adults – even with mature brains and years of experience – we still mess up too.

Before you take steps to support your child, make sure you tend to your own heartache. Say a mantra: 'This anger I see is not about me.' Do some 'up breathing' (i.e. breathe in for a count of three then breathe out slowly for a count of eight). Remember that your calm is just as contagious as their anger. When you regulate your emotions, it sets up a starting point where change can happen.

Connect with your child's pain

Name their feeling: 'Wow, you must be feeling really hurt to say those words to me.' When you see your child's pain, it's much easier to let the words fly straight past you, like a ball you are intentionally trying not to catch.

Hold a boundary

Teach your child that all feelings are allowed, but hurting others is not. This may sound like:

> 'Those words you have said to me are not okay. I know you are in pain. I will be here for you to talk later.'
> 'You want me to feel as sad as you do. I won't allow you to hurt me. I am going to let you cool off for a bit and then we can talk.'
> 'You are allowed to feel bad, and you can let me see this without being unkind. We can figure this out later.'

Set a clear boundary that gives your child an unambiguous message about how much pain you are willing to hold in the moment. This tells your child: 'I can tolerate your pain AND I won't allow you to hurt me on purpose.'

Whether you stay with your child in this moment or leave them in a safe place and take a break so you can regulate your emotions may depend on the context and what your needs are in that moment. Both can be good ways of breaking up the tension so you can come back together in a different frame of mind.

Some last reflections . . .

Parenting is exhausting, and you don't really get an immediate pay-off that gives you reassurance that what you are doing is 'right'. It can feel like these strategies are 'not working' when a child continues to do the same behaviour over and over again. This might make you want to find a strategy that gives you more control over your child's behaviour, and often that will be a punishment. Before you do, please take a moment to revisit your expectations of your child. Consider whether they are capable of doing what you are asking them to do. Ask yourself, 'Does my child have these skills? Have they demonstrated having a good grasp of this before? Or is this new and so will take time and practice to learn and get right?' And if your child does have the skills needed to follow good behaviour, be curious about why right now they cannot do so and, most importantly, focus on how you can help them.

Remember that parenting a child is a tiny chapter in your parenting story. You are shaping a person's sense of themselves in relationship with you. This is a huge task that doesn't happen overnight. Notice and hold on to your wins. I know it's easy to let go of them at times when things don't work out. Remember that you can repair when needed, to use your words more than their actions, show manners spontaneously, meet others with generosity, speak up for yourself and value honesty. These are lifelong skills and it might come as a surprise that you will be learning too while you teach all of this to your child. I know it's hard work, but I promise it is absolutely worth it.

5

Skills for Living

Watching your child learn to navigate the world is one of the most beautiful parts of parenting. Seeing them zip up their coat on their own, watching them use a knife for the first time or do up their laces without your help feel like momentous occasions – little firsts that build up to big independence. When we incorporate the teaching of life skills early on, the more easily children learn. There are many skills children need, but I am going to focus on the three most common ones: eating, learning how to use the toilet, sleeping – and I have added a fourth skill: play.

Play is not just fun. It's a skill that helps children grow resilience, a space where they can express their emotions, replay scenes, voice fears or show their understanding about everyday situations. It is through play that children first learn to make decisions, solve problems, exert self-control and follow rules. And it is also through play that children connect best with you – their loving adults. Play is also important for you, to focus on enjoyment without the mental demands of work or house chores. It gives our mind and body the possibility to relax and find a positive mood boost. And who doesn't need that once in a while?

Although you probably feel quite skilled in all of these areas, some of what I share may offer you a small reminder that there are areas you can work on for yourself. Because, like everything we have talked about in earlier chapters, children learn best from what we do, not from what we tell them.

CHAPTER 15

Good Eating Habits

How many of these messages did you hear, growing up?

- 'Finish everything on your plate.'
- 'Sweets are treats.'
- 'If you finish your vegetables, then you can have pudding.'
- 'Naughty children don't get dessert.'
- 'Be good at your friend's house, and eat what they give you.'

These stories don't just shape how you relate to the food you eat and the choices you make, they also influence how you respond to your child's likes, dislikes and responses to food. To support your child in building a healthy relationship with food you can set clear boundaries around the job you as a parent have at mealtimes and what your child's role is.

The 'Division of Responsibility' is an authoritative feeding model that has been shown to support children in developing healthy relationships with food and preventing eating difficulties and fussy eating behaviour (Satter, 1990; Haines et al., 2019). It encourages parents to set boundaries at mealtimes AND offers children a chance to trust their own hunger and fullness cues:

- Parents focus on: the WHAT, WHEN and WHERE of feeding
- A child focuses on: deciding WHICH foods on offer they want to eat and HOW MUCH (i.e. portion size based on what is served).

Focus on what, when and where

You are the adult – you have the authority to choose 'what' foods you serve at mealtimes and as snacks, and where you wish your child to eat them. I want you to really own this leadership role you have with food. This doesn't mean you should completely ignore your child's preferences. Offering a child one or two foods in every meal that you know they 'typically' enjoy is good enough. But you don't need to offer your child an alternative food or meal when they say they are not hungry or refuse to eat what has been served.

Billy's father was the main cook at home. He planned three meals at a time, and if he made pasta and Billy said, 'Yuck, I don't want it,' he would quickly dish up something else, like beans on toast, and if that didn't appeal to Billy, he would make an omelette or a sandwich. Despite his best efforts, Billy's father didn't always succeed in getting Billy to eat more than one bite of his meal (whichever one Billy chose to try).

When you choose a meal for your child you will typically consider its nutritional needs, the balance of foods, the time it will take to prepare and the cost of the ingredients. I want you to know that doing all these things is good enough. Your child choosing to eat what you serve is about them, not the meal you have put in front of them.

Billy's father began to recognize that he offered alternatives because he had been brought up to associate food with love. He talked about how he would always finish whatever his parents served and even now when he went home his mother would be offended if he didn't take a second portion, asking, 'Did you not like it?' even if he had wiped his plate clean.

Understanding this helped him think about his relationship with food and what he was bringing to mealtimes with Billy – a need to please him and feel appreciated for his cooking.

Let your child choose 'which' foods to eat and 'how much'

You might have an idea of 'how much' food is right for a child based on your food experiences, how much you enjoy eating and what portion sizes look right to you on a plate. However, a child's stomach is not the same size as an adult's, and only a child can truly know what the right amount of food is. A child's hunger varies from day to day and meal to meal. Stress, anxiety and worry suppress appetite, because when a body is in a state of 'hyper-vigilance' it is getting ready to 'fight' and eating is not the immediate priority. A change in routine, feeling sick, big emotions (e.g. the excitement of being at a party), running around more than usual or being more sedentary (e.g. after a long car journey) will all impact on appetite and how much a child is willing to eat.

Billy often said, 'I am full' after two mouthfuls but half an hour later would ask for a snack. Billy's father was quick to offer something he knew Billy would eat, such as yoghurt, fruit, or jam on toast. After a few sessions of working together, Billy's father started to own his authority around food and set firmer boundaries. So when Billy said that he was finished, Billy's father would set a limit: 'Listen to your body. If your tummy is saying it's full, that's okay, you can leave the table. If you change your mind, you plate will stay here until we finish our meal. There will be no food after that until snack time.'

When a child says, 'I am full,' or 'I am not hungry,' or requests a snack after eating a good-sized meal, your job is not to figure out 'if' they are telling the truth or not. The only responsibility you have is to trust that your child can listen to what their body needs. Your job is to trust yourself to do your job well, by serving foods that you think are good for them and setting boundaries as necessary.

We set up a plan to cull the 'after-meal snacks' by setting a more structured meal and snack routine, and offering Billy a piece of fruit, some yoghurt or half a slice of toast with jam alongside his main meal. So whenever Billy asked for a snack after the meal his father felt much more confident in saying, 'Mealtime is over. You can have a snack in a few hours, but not now.' At first Billy protested against this new routine, but over the course of a few weeks, as it started to feel predictable, he stopped asking for a snack and, to the wonder of his father, started to eat a little more at mealtimes.

Things to avoid around food

There are a few strategies that will always backfire with food: bribes, punishments, coercion and restriction. Don't be fooled into thinking these tactics works – they only set up unhelpful dynamics around food and mealtimes.

Bribes, punishments and coercion

You can inadvertently heighten the value of foods by explicitly and implicitly associating them with emotion. Any time you use any of the below, what you are doing is building the idea that certain foods are 'special' and others are 'bad':

- 'If you have one more bite of your meal, I'll give you a yoghurt.'
  (Bribe – yoghurt is layered with special status.)
- 'If you don't finish your peas, then there won't be any dessert.'
  (Punishment – dessert is a reward.)

- 'I will give you ice cream if you finish your chicken. Deal?'
  (Coercion – ice cream is the desired food.)

You might be tempted to use some of these strategies to get your child to eat something – anything. This fear tends to be more common if you were brought up being told to 'finish what is on your plate' or had strict orders around how much and what to eat. Pause for a moment and take a breath. A healthy relationship with food is not built on force. It is built on listening to your body's needs, knowing when you have had enough and when your body needs more.

In the short term, these strategies might trick you into thinking they work because children tend to comply to get the 'reward food'. However, if you watch carefully, children's emotional experience around food is heightened, and not in the way you intend.

Kimmy had fish and chips on her plate, but she just wanted chips. Her father took her chips away and told her, 'You can have two chips for every bite of fish you eat.' Kimmy started to cry. She came off her chair and sat under the table. Her father put a few chips on her plate to get her back on to her seat. He tried to emphasize why eating fish was healthy and that two chips for a small portion of fish was a 'really good deal'. Kimmy smelled the fish and grimaced. 'Come on, it's yummy' came the encouragement from the adults around the table. Kimmy licked some fish. She took a minuscule bite with her front teeth and exclaimed, 'There! Now can I have chips?'

When you use bribes, coercion or punishment you are not teaching a healthy relationship with food, you are forming a punishment-based cycle with food that makes it less likely that a child will eat the foods you want them to. You have to dig deep into your leadership and authority. Serve your child meals you think are appropriate and let them choose what and how much they eat. If, as in Kimmy's example, you know your child will just want to eat chips, offer a smaller portion alongside other foods on offer and then let them get on with it.

Kimmy had a small frame and her father was anxious that she didn't eat enough. After being reviewed at the doctor's he was reassured that Kimmy was tracking well on her growth chart, despite being on a lower percentile than most children her age. This allowed Kimmy's father to begin to reframe what was happening at mealtimes from 'I have to make her eat something' into 'I am the one who feels anxious. She is petite and I can trust her when she says she is not hungry.'

If your child's weight and/or growth is a concern, do get them checked with a medical professional who can let you know whether they are tracking in line with their size and age. When your child's physical health has been given the green light it can allow you to reposition anxiety as something for you to work on, rather than pressurizing your child to make anxiety shrink.

Restriction

When I talk about 'restriction' I am not talking about foods you have to avoid for a child's wellbeing or safety, such as those that cause allergies or are choking hazards. When I talk about restriction I refer to foods you ban because you deem them to be unhealthy or 'bad' in some way. Often these are sweet foods, 'junk foods' or pre-packaged snacks.

Yes, setting limits around sugar and 'junk foods' is a good thing. Guidelines suggest that children below the age of three should have sugar restricted to prevent dental issues, keep them safe from choking hazards and promote overall health. But setting limits is not the same as demonizing foods such as sugar. When you call foods 'bad' or 'good', children make the connection that they are 'bad' or 'good' when they eat or don't eat certain foods. We place an emotional and moral burden on children, and we miss a golden opportunity to teach balance and self-regulation around food.

Rollins et al. (2015) carried out an experiment with forty-two children aged between three and five years old. They were invited over a period of three weeks to participate in an activity, with a fifteen-minute break with snacks. Some snacks were freely available while others were taken away after five minutes. All children attended a 'post-test' session where they had unlimited access to generous portions of restricted and unrestricted foods. Although this is a small study with a tiny sample, it was a replication of a larger study (Fischer & Birch, 1999) and the findings were clear: children ate restricted foods in larger quantities and they showed stronger emotions around them (e.g. 'I want it'). Children whose parents used restriction as a strategy ate more of these snacks than those who were sometimes allowed to eat similar snacks.

These findings make sense. Restricting foods gives them a 'special' status that increases their appeal, so when children get their hands on them they eat as much as they can because they don't know when they will next get to eat them. To avoid this you have to move away from 'food restriction' and focus on 'food education'.

Think about what you want to teach your child about healthy and balanced eating:

- What values around food do you want to communicate to your child?
- Are there certain foods you limit in your child's diet? If so, why and how much?
- How do you set a limit around these foods?
- What will you do when your child resists your limits (or sneakily eats the restricted food)?
- How will you talk about these foods at times when they are readily available and outside your control?

We restrict certain foods in our home due to food allergies, but there are firm limits on sweets, chocolate, cake and 'treat' foods. When we go to a party or someone else's home where I have no control over what is served, my child knows it is okay to want to eat something and she needs to check with me first for safety purposes *and* because sweet foods can make our tummies hurt and our bodies feel sick. When my child is at a party where there is a big 'free-for-all buffet' or she is on a playdate I loosen the boundary and I let her decide how much and what she wants to eat of what she can have. These are special occasions where I want her to enjoy herself and make memories, not focus on food and what is or isn't restricted. I try to go with the flow while encouraging her to listen to her body when she has had enough. At home we serve cake, chocolate and, on extremely rare occasions (like Halloween), sweets alongside a meal so she sees them for what they are – another food group that we don't have in big quantities or every day but can enjoy together sometimes.

If while reading this you are thinking, 'If I offer my child cake with their meal they will fill up on it and won't eat anything else,' remember that you are the authority when it comes to serving food. The portion of cake you serve is up to you. You can make this as small or as big as you like. Your child's job is to choose how much they eat of *what is served*. You can state a clear boundary about your choices with warmth and empathy: 'Yum, you gobbled that up. I know you love cake – there is no more for today, but I promise to offer it again.'

Reframing 'fussy eating'

James was seven when his parents sought professional support. He had a choking episode at the age of three, an experience described as 'traumatic' and which left family wounds around food and mealtimes. James described himself as 'fussy' with food, preferring soft, beige foods over anything else. His favourite meal was pesto pasta or chicken and roast potatoes. He refused to eat crisps or fries because they were 'too crunchy', and the only fruit he would eat were strawberries and raspberries. James had a 'sweet tooth', enjoying ice cream, cake and pastries. James's parents wanted to bring back variety and enjoyment at mealtimes to help James eat more balanced meals.

We all have eating preferences, foods we enjoy more than others. Eating is a learned skill. To become familiar with foods, we need lots of opportunities to explore textures, colours and smells. During the first year of life, children only need to see foods once to give them a taste and accept them as good enough to eat. This is because they are in 'exploration mode'; they have limited awareness so everything is new and exciting to them. However, around the age of two children begin to go through a developmental phase that is known as 'neophobia'. This is the refusal to try new or unfamiliar foods, and they often avoid bitter tastes, strong flavours or bright colours . . . in other words, most vegetables and meals that have flavours mixed in. This phase is a healthy part of development; it's a time when children are becoming more aware and beginning to take up more space in the world. Making choices around food is part of how a child develops their identity. Neophobia is a transitory stage and it tends to pass naturally. However, if your child has a neurodivergent brain, food preferences may stick, and we think of them as 'sensory preferences'. All children can be supported to accept new and different foods, but the portion size and frequency with which you serve them will be unique to your child. If they have a sensory preference, a fingernail-sized portion of a new food on the side of their plate can be enough.

'I don't like it' is always temporary if you don't give it the power to stay

James often said, 'I don't like it,' about foods he had never tasted. His parents said he would sometimes ask questions like 'What is in that sandwich?' and when they told him he would reply, 'Yuck. I don't like it.' I wondered what would happen if his parents asked James to help them make sandwiches with those ingredients he thought were 'yucky' but made it clear that he didn't have to eat them, he was just helping with the food preparation. His parents were baffled by the idea of having anything on the table that James didn't like – they were scared he would refuse to sit at the table.

Sometimes your efforts in the kitchen will feel futile, and this will feel hard. I know how disheartening and frustrating it can be when your child rejects food you have lovingly prepared. It is even harder when this food is something you know they enjoyed last week but today they declare, 'I don't like it.' After this happens a few times it is unsurprising that you might choose to stop serving these foods, to avoid the next rejection. But your child rejecting your home-cooked meal doesn't mean you have got it wrong; they are just doing what they're supposed to do.

When your child says 'I don't like it' it is 'child speak' for:

- I don't fancy it *today*.
- I don't like the way it looks *today*.
- I don't like the texture of it *today*.
- I don't like the way it's cut *today*.

Adults need to understand that 'I don't like it' is not a for-ever statement. *Today* isn't every day, and it doesn't mean your child won't learn to like it 'one day'. When adults take this communication at face value and avoid certain meals and foods, children miss out on food experiences, including seeing others enjoy these foods. There is no possibility of 'food exploration' if you hide foods away. Unless your child has a sensory preference that will mean they will be highly distressed, or an allergy that could put them in danger, don't avoid foods just because your child says one day, 'I don't like it.' Give your child a chance to experience all foods, even if initially it's just through you eating the food in front of them.

They're not 'fussy', they're exploring

When children begin to choose foods based on texture, smell or taste, adults often stamp on a label of 'fussy' or 'difficult eaters'. These labels are unhelpful because they keep adults and children stuck in negative cycles around food. Adults tend to limit the foods that are served and children's preferences become formed around the narrow choices that are on offer.

James's parents had adapted their meals to suit James's preferences and went the extra mile. Whenever they were invited to eat out with family or friends, they checked there was something on the menu that James would eat and often would take a packed lunch 'just in case'. They explained how this was the only way they could encourage James to join in social events that included food, because his anxiety was so great he would panic and refuse to sit at the table or touch anything that was offered. James talked about himself as 'not a good eater'. He feared being judged by others at mealtimes, that someone might force him to taste things he didn't want to try, or judge him for not eating. The pressure at mealtimes was so big for James that it filled his stomach up with anxiety, leaving no room to explore foods or eat.

I want you to become more aware of the language you use around food. Rather than 'fussy eaters', think of children as what they are – 'food explorers'. They are at the beginning of their journey with food; exploring what they like and dislike is part of the process of developing tastes, and this changes moment by moment if we allow it to, by allowing children to see, touch, lick, taste and even refuse foods. Learning to eat is a non-linear process that takes time. You can respect a child's right to not want to eat something AND continue to offer the food in different ways, to keep exposing them to it.

Sensory exploration is just as good as eating

We used a very gradual approach to food exploration with James, one where he could see and touch foods with no pressure to eat them. The parents asked James to watch them prepare foods, for example slicing, dicing and mashing vegetables, and help put them in the pot or roasting dish. They also asked James to select foods at the shops and got him touching different textures of the same food (e.g. frozen peas versus mushy peas). James was told that taking part in these activities was enough, that the goal was not to eat or try these foods but to get more comfortable around them to be able to shrink anxiety at mealtimes.

Research shows that increasing familiarity with foods is more important than whether children taste them or not. Positive activities that promote multisensory exposure have been shown to positively impact on children's curiosity to taste foods. Yes, you read that right. The more they play with foods, the more likely they are to give them a taste. Below are some fun and positive ways of making foods less scary and therefore more acceptable:

- Painting with food (e.g. broccoli heads and carrot tops as paintbrushes, potatoes and peas for stamping)
- Growing food from seed that you can pick and eat, such as cherry tomatoes, strawberries, peppers and courgettes
- Inviting your child to join you in preparing and cooking a meal.

Take the pressure off food and make it FUN

Talking about and exploring foods can help children become curious and so, in their own time, they may be willing to taste them. Consider all the senses and pick one that feels easy for you (some prompts are easier with different foods). Invite your child into the exploration, but don't push them to 'try', as this may mirror their experience of eating and make it less likely that they will join you.

Prompt: What colour is it?
Your child may hear you say: 'This tomato is red and orange. How different is that?'

Prompt: What shape is it?
Your child may hear you say: 'Aw, look, this broccoli stem looks like a tiny little tree.'

Prompt: What does it smell like?
Your child may hear you say: 'Hmmm, these strawberries smell sweet.'

Prompt: What does it feel like?
Your child may hear you say: 'This cauliflower is all bumpy. Hmmm . . . I wonder if it feels the same after we cook it . . .'

Prompt: How does it sound?
Your child may hear you say: 'Oh, these lentils sound a bit like rice when I put them in the pot. I wonder, if you just listened, could you tell the difference?'

Children learn by example.

James's father came to realize that James had strong preferences with food and unintentionally was sending the message that some foods were 'disgusting'. We worked on changing his expression from 'Gross. That has peanuts in it' to a more neutral communication of 'I am still learning to like peanuts. They're not my favourite.'

Focus on positive language around food and the possibility of change, rather than strong expressions of disgust. Food should be something we enjoy, and of course you are allowed not to like everything. But using neutral language around food can help to increase acceptability for your child and, to the adults around you who may enjoy the foods you don't like, this is also a lot more respectful.

How children feel at mealtimes is more important than what they eat

Mealtimes feel unpredictable to children. What food will be served? How will it smell, taste, feel? What will adults say and do? Will they get angry, upset or annoyed? As adults, you may also feel pressure or anxiety because your child gags at certain foods or you are unhappy about the nutritional content of what they are eating.

A big chunk of James's anxiety came from pressure at mealtimes. So we worked on associating meals with fun rather than food. We agreed that no matter how much James ate, once he said he was finished, he would put the plate to one side and remain at the table. They loved the game Articulate and turned it into a dinnertime activity. This led to longer mealtimes, with James often laughing and, every now and again, having a few extra mouthfuls of his meal.

Approach family mealtimes the same way you would approach a social meal with a friend. Spend more time talking and enjoying each other's company than counting how many bites your child eats. Notice how your body posture, actions and words around food and mealtimes offer a sense of freedom or pressure and control. Remember that emotions are contagious, so how you show up at mealtimes will impact on how your child feels about them.

Mealtime rituals

Rituals are quirky little habits that offer predictability about what is to come. From the steps we take to get dressed (are you a bottom-up or a top-down person?) and how we shower (face, then body, then hair . . . what do you do?), rituals bring comfort to our daily actions. This can calm anxiety, allowing the nervous system to find a point of rest.

Rituals may include:

- **Making dinner together.** Giving children age-appropriate roles can open up curiosity to explore foods. This might include getting foods out of the fridge, stirring or mixing, washing, peeling, cutting or putting chopped foods into a pot.
- **Giving your child a role.** Have your child lay the table or have certain items that are their responsibility (e.g. our daughter sets out the breakfast bowls and cutlery). This gives children control, which helps to shrink anxiety.
- **Having a mealtime signal.** Give a five-minute warning of when food will be served. An alarm followed by your verbal message can work well.
- **Connecting.** Maybe wash your hands together and get playful with the soap. Where there is laughter and playfulness, anxiety cannot take hold.

Food is food: you don't need to praise your child for eating

James's parents initially celebrated every time he touched a new food with big exclamations such as 'Yay! You smelled it! I am so proud of you!' I explained that praise is a form of pressure and when we praise touching, tasting or eating food it tells a child, 'This is a BIG deal.' This centres an adult's point of view and takes away from the experience a child has in the moment about how a food smells, looks or feels. James's parents started playing it cool when James touched a new food and just kept eating their meal or minding their own business in the kitchen. Little by little, they noticed that James grabbed a piece of chopped carrot from the counter, licked the potato masher and ate mushrooms out of the punnet. And when they served him a meal, they swapped 'I know you don't like fish, but please try it' for 'Here is your dinner. You don't have to eat it.'

It may sound counterintuitive, but using praise or rewards makes foods less appealing. Playing it cool can release pressure and make children curious to try. Remember: food is food. If you don't cheer when your child takes a bite out of their buttered toast, don't cheer when it's something they have never tried before. And if your child is like mine and tries to grab your attention by saying something like 'Look, I'm eating broccoli,' respond with a neutral comment such as 'It's yummy, isn't it?' rather than 'Well done.'

Food preferences can be stressful, and a small bite is a big win. Do celebrate with a partner, a friend or just yourself when you're out of your child's sight. Just remember that your child doesn't need to know it's a big deal for you. It's best that children don't know what foods they are 'fussy' about. A child's relationship with food is their own individual relationship, and it doesn't end in childhood. It is a lifelong journey, and you are their first guide. Approach all foods as opportunities to explore, have fun and get familiar with them. Trust the process.

Some final thoughts . . .

We know that children who get early support around issues with food tend to do better long term. This might be a few sessions to work on anxiety around mealtimes (for you and your child) and some individualized strategies to guide you, or a bit more, depending on your situation. Seek support if this is an area of struggle in your home.

CHAPTER 16

Learning to Use the Toilet

From eating into toileting ... Sounds like a smooth transition; however, supporting your child to toilet-train can feel like the biggest hurdle, one where your worth as a parent seems to depend on it.

Most 'potty training' ideas follow classical conditioning rules of behaviourism, rewarding behaviour you want to see (eg. give them a chocolate when they wee on the toilet) and punishing anything you don't (e.g. don't give eye contact when they have an accident). It follows a structure with simple, logical, actionable steps towards an outcome. If, after a few days, it isn't working, this approach might make you question, 'Are you really doing it right?' The answer is: you and your child are not the problem. The method you are using might be.

If you used this type of behavioural schedule and it worked for you, that is great, and you may wish to skip this chapter. If, however, this method worked initially but six months or more later your child continues to have accidents, they don't make it to the toilet unless you prompt them, or they struggle with some aspect of toileting (e.g. refusing to do a poo), then this chapter offers some new perspectives that you might find useful.

Toileting is about developing independence and body autonomy

There is limited research on what the 'right' way to toilet train a child is. However, we know that using the toilet is a developmental milestone, a process children go through that adults can support and guide. Unless there is a physiological issue, your child's body has known how to poo and pee since the day they were born. Learning to use a toilet or potty are steps we can teach them with the right opportunities, while staying sensitive to their motivation. Doing this follows 'the child-oriented method' developed by Brazelton (1962), a gradual approach that has been found to be effective.

Every child is unique, and moving through this process will look different depending on multiple factors. If you have more than one child, you are likely to witness different responses and need to support different skill sets. If your child has a neurodivergent brain, they might take a bit longer to link their body sensations to weeing and pooing, and including a bit more structure such as using a small alarm or visual chart may be useful to support them. You can do this and anything else you think will support your child alongside any of the steps below.

Unless there are physical or cognitive weaknesses that need extra support, no child remains in nappies into adulthood. Most children use the toilet by the age of four and it's not because parents have finally 'got it right', it's because all children become developmentally able to use the toilet eventually. Let go of the pressure of society and other parents around you. Focus on your child's individual process and let them guide you as you coach them forward.

Readiness has nothing to do with age

Age is not the key to success. Starting too soon can make it difficult in the long term as younger children struggle to consolidate toileting skills, leading to more accidents, instances of refusal and a greater need for you to prompt and support.

Your cue to start is not when other parents with similar-aged children begin, when professionals from childcare or nursery suggest it, or at the same time you did with your eldest. Start when it is right for your child and when it works for you. If you are in the middle of big family life-changes such as moving home, changing jobs or soon to have a baby, it may not be the best time to begin this process. Wait. There is no rush. Your readiness matters too. Think about how you feel about going through this process with your child. Does it feel exciting or bring up feelings of disgust? Do you look forward to building up your child's independence from you or does it bring up anxiety?

Your emotional responses to these questions matter. If what you notice in your body feels like discomfort, this is a good thing. Having a 'preview' that you might find this hard to navigate gives you the opportunity to practise self-regulation skills and set up a plan. Do you want to adapt your home in order to feel more comfortable about the mess? Do you need to protect time for yourself? Who can support you through this? Having your needs met will help you better support your child's.

When it comes to your child's signs of readiness, they often begin around two to two and a half years of age and can give you a clue that your child might be a willing participant to learn how to use the toilet soon:

- Can they follow simple steps?
- Are they dry for one and a half hours during the daytime? (Any less will make it hard work.)
- Are they showing discomfort in nappies?
- Can they communicate their wants and needs (verbally and or non-verbally)?
- Are they becoming independent with personal care (e.g. getting dressed, putting shoes on, drying themselves after the bath, putting on moisturizer, etc.)?

Many children will meet some of these signs of readiness but not others. Use this as a guide to understand how much readiness your child has, rather than a blanket 'Are they ready or not?' When you see this as a process you might feel more confident in incorporating some of the steps below before your child is ready to use the toilet.

Focus on the process more than the outcome

The outcome you want is obvious – to lose the nappy and for your child to do wees and poos in a toilet. If you focus only on this, following a schedule of 'drinking and placing your child on the toilet' might mean you reach your goal within the first one or two days, but that doesn't mean your child has learned 'how' to use the toilet. They have only learned to follow your prompts.

To use the toilet children need to learn:

- That a toilet/potty is where wee and poo goes
- To understand and differentiate their body's signals for peeing and pooing
- To make it to the toilet/potty on time
- How to undress and sit down on the toilet/potty
- How to wipe, get dressed and wash their hands.

I hope this shows that you can begin to teach some of these steps before your child is fully ready to toilet train, away from the pressure of using a toilet. The following are ideas to move through this process. When you do what will depend on your child.

Associate wee and poo with the right location
This is going to sound obvious, but children need to learn that wee and poo go in the toilet. For much of a baby's life they have been laid down for a

nappy change in bedrooms, lounges and other spaces that are not the bathroom and have nothing to do with toiletting. You can begin to build an association with the toilet simply by carrying out nappy changes in the bathroom. If you are still laying your child down, get a soft mat and put it on the floor. If your child can stand up, consider using pull-up nappies and change them standing up by the toilet.

Whenever they do a poo, flush it down. It's a good opportunity to share a 'poo story', which can put fear about poo in its place. If you want to take this a step further, invite your child to sit on the toilet or potty so you can wipe them more easily. This offers them low-pressure exposure of sitting with a bare bottom on a toilet seat.

A toileting story

Many children find letting go of poo difficult. For some, pooing feels like losing a part of themselves. Little ones do not understand the idea that we have organs inside our body. They only believe what they can see. Poo can feel like it's a part of their body falling out. Fear of pooing can also mirror their experience of 'losing' the nappies, which inevitably means losing times of care with you, their parent. For other children the sensory experience of a bare bottom and hearing poo fall into a toilet is unfamiliar and frightening. Others may suffer from constipation and associate pain with pooing, which makes withholding more likely.

Having a story about poo and pee can help. Keep it simple and honest while remembering that children won't understand words such as 'bladder' and 'digestive system'. Some children worry that the 'wee' or the 'poo' will get hurt or be lonely in the toilet, so try making the experience playful. I know this may seem ridiculous to you as an adult, but this is one of the outcomes of children blurring fantasy with reality. Play along if it helps your child feel more comfortable around the toilet.

The story I shared with my child is below. Adapt these words as you see fit so they feel genuine when you say them:

When we drink water, it goes into our tummies and into our bodies. Our bodies are very clever, and any extra water our body does not need comes out as wee. This makes space in our tummies for our next drink of water.

When we eat food, it goes into our tummy. Any food your body does not need becomes poo. Poo is not a part of your body, it's extra food your body doesn't need any more. When your tummy is ready, it gives you a signal to let go of the poo to make more space for yummy food and snacks.

Poo and wee want to go inside the toilet – it's where all their friends go swimming too. When the flush goes 'whoosh' it's like a big slide that takes poo on its way. We can wave 'goodbye' to poos when we flush. They're on their way to meet their friends.

If it feels comfortable, say, 'Bye bye, poo!' whenever you flush, and make it positive. This can help your child feel less fearful of letting go. When they feel the experience of using the toilet can be fun and something they can still share with you, they associate the toilet with calm. And feeling relaxed is key to stopping withholding and allowing our bodies to poo.

Use neutral language around wee and poo

When you think about wee and poo, what does it bring up for you? Does it make you snigger and giggle, or perhaps bring up feelings of disgust? Or do you think, 'It's something all humans and animals do.' It's important for you to know what messages you are giving your child.

I will tell you a universal truth: children never want to be a source of disgust to their parents. The way you respond to your child's bodily fluids matters, even while you are changing their nappy. If you hold your nose, turn away from your child or use words such as 'yuck', 'gross', 'it stinks', be mindful that although all these statements may be true, your child does not know poo and wee come out of them, so these comments get easily absorbed as statements about themselves (i.e. 'I am yucky,' 'I am smelly,' 'I am dirty').

Using neutral language and focusing on the positives is protective. You want your child to feel good about toileting. You want to build their confidence about their body doing the right thing: 'Oh! Your tummy has done a big poo. That's so great, your body knows what to do so well' or 'What a lot of wee. That tells me you have been drinking lots – that's great.'

Help your child learn about their body

Poo and wee in a nappy are silent and invisible. A child has never heard 'psss' or 'plop'. Seeing their body release wee and poo for the first time can make some children curious to touch, explore and understand what it is; for others, it can be frightening and scary.

It can help children to see you do a poo and/or a wee in the toilet. To some adults this can feel uncomfortable; we think of using the toilet as something private that we don't let someone else watch. And yet this can normalize the experience of toileting, to know the sound of wee and poo in the toilet, and make it fun if you feel able to (e.g. 'Did you hear that? What sound did it make? Plop. Yes! It's a poo! What a funny sound'). You can also show them before you flush and talk about the colour or the shape (e.g. 'Look! My wee is yellow'). This increases familiarity, which shrinks fear.

If your child wants to touch inside the toilet, set a boundary and use it as an opportunity to teach about hygiene, keeping your language neutral. That may sound like 'Wee and poo go in the toilet. We try not to touch them, but if we do that's okay. That's why we always wash our hands after we use the toilet.'

Use modelling to teach children to recognize their body signals

Children model themselves on us. That's why they want to play with your phone and try on your shoes and grab hold of the scissors and knives they see you use. They want to do whatever you do. You can use this to your advantage by modelling the steps of how you use the toilet explicitly. Help your child connect the idea that there is a link between how their body feels and the process of toileting. Next time you need to use the toilet, say out loud with gestures, 'I think I have that funny feeling in my tummy . . . [while rubbing your tummy] Hmmm . . . yes, I think I need to sit on the toilet. I think there is a wee that wants to come out.'

When you talk about it, model it and name times when you may be unsure about using the toilet – this reassures children that it's not just them who find the toilet strange. Think about a time when you needed to use a public toilet and it wasn't the most pleasant experience. Perhaps it was at a music festival or in a service station. Can you remember how it felt to physically need to go but emotionally want to pull away? That's how your child may feel about doing this. The toilet is scary and unfamiliar; their body might want to but, emotionally, they pull back. Your words and actions can wrap your child in the emotional reassurance they need to give it a try.

Model uncertainty: 'Oh, I don't know if I want to sit on the toilet, it's cold . . . My tummy says I really need to go. Okay. [Big breath] I can do this. It's only a moment. [After sitting] Ow, yes, it's cold, but ahhhh . . . that feels better. I think this seat feels warmer now. I am okay.'

Model times when you don't want to stop what you are doing: 'I think my tummy is giving me that funny feeling that I need a poo, but I don't want go now . . . [A few seconds later] Okay . . . I have to go. Can we pause the game? Everyone – pause. My body says I have to go.'

Model near misses: 'Oh, nothing is coming . . . maybe I need to wait a little longer . . . Hmmm . . . okay. I will get up and come back to the toilet later when my tummy gives me a stronger signal.' (Go back a little later.)

Near misses don't mean you have to wet or soil yourself, but if you have a big sneeze or a cough and a little drop of wee comes out, use this to your advantage. Show your child you had a little accident too. It's not embarrassing or silly; it's important to normalize that accidents are part of the process.

Use play to problem-solve and consolidate skills

There are lots of toys on the market, for example small potties and toilets. Dolls that drink water and 'do a wee' in a potty can help children understand that our body flushes excess water out, and you can place favourite toys or teddies on a potty or toilet to create stories around toileting. Use real-life scenarios that mirror your child's experience to help you make sense of their feelings and find where you can problem-solve. For example, one of the teddies could have a toileting accident and you could ask them questions like 'How did that feel?' and 'Are you disappointed you didn't make it to the toilet?' alongside reassuring language such as 'You just didn't get to the potty on time. You are one step closer to the potty. I think next time you might make it. Now let's clean that up.'

You can also play out situations that your child experiences. This may sound like 'Oh, you don't want to sit on the toilet. Okay . . . what is wrong?

What don't you like? I don't like sitting on the cold toilet sometimes, it's a bit tricky . . .'

This type of play offers your child an outlet for their feelings that makes it less likely for them to act out in their behaviour (e.g. having lots of accidents or refusing to go into the bathroom). If your child responds well to this kind of play, you can also invite their preferred toy to come with them to the potty or toilet when they begin to use it so they can be their 'role model', sitting beside them. In this way toys become 'transitional objects', items that bring your child safety, the same way they feel safe with you, and can support them to use the toilet more independently.

Play was one of the most powerful things we did with our child in this area. She loved her toy refusing to use the toilet and she reassured it about what was happening with words we were saying to her. All the while she was giving herself reassurance, building up her confidence in each step, and feeling a lot less alone in the process.

Accidents are part of learning

Accidents might dishearten you, but they are key to learning to use the toilet. Wetting or soiling themselves helps children learn how the signals inside their bodies match something they can see on the outside. It differentiates between the 'wee signal' and the 'poo signal'. Accidents help children experience these sensations and learn from them.

Whenever an accident happens, stay calm and avoid placing shame (e.g. 'Oh, not again' or 'Okay, so you are still a baby, you're not a big girl/boy yet'), blame ('The toilet is right there' or 'You are too focused on playing') or expressing how it makes you feel ('What is wrong with you? Why don't you get this?'). If you notice this happening, slow down and ground yourself: 'My child is learning. This is part of the process. I have the skills to help them.' Poo and wee are wipeable, and anything that has got wet is fixable. Reassure your child that what has happened is okay; in fact, it's useful. Keep it positive and reassuring:

'You are learning something new, and it takes time. Now you know what
that funny feeling in your tummy is, you might catch it next time.'

'Oh, your leggings are wet. Let's get changed.'

'I am here for you. Next time that funny feeling in your tummy shows
up, you can say, "I have that funny feeling" and I will help you.'

Let your child's 'wow' moment come first

This might be the hardest thing for you to do – and it can be the most powerful too. Yes, when your child makes it to the toilet, you will want to celebrate.
And so you should – it's a massive win! And I want you to count to ten and
take a pause before you give your child your 'wow'. If you are thinking, 'But
why? Praise feels good and my child deserves to be celebrated,' yes, but this
is their process and their achievement. The 'wow' needs to be theirs.

Adult excitement and praise are a pressure to children. When learning a
new skill, such as toileting, there are going to be times when children mess
up. When adults praise the outcome, it makes children feel shame when
they don't get it right, because the praise and celebration won't follow and,
to a child, that feels like they are disappointing you.

If you are a 'praise junkie', like I used to be, here are some words that can
help you offer appreciation of your child's process while not adding pressure:

- 'You did it!'
- 'You listened to your body!'
- 'You noticed that feeling in your tummy and you made it to the
  potty!'
- 'Yes, I heard a plop. You did a poo!'

Counterintuitively, the biggest boost to a child is when someone wit-
nesses their success. In our home, when our child first sat on the toilet, she
said, 'It's a wee!' She said it in a high-pitched voice. Was it a celebration or
fear? I don't know, but I paused for longer than I should have because I

definitely felt nervous excitement about what was going on. When she looked at me, what I finally said, in as calm a voice as I could offer, was 'Yes. It's a wee. You did it.' She didn't smile, she didn't celebrate it, but she has continued to use the toilet ever since.

If your child is boosted by praise and their response is 'Look! It's a wee. Woohoo!', join them. High-five, do a little dance – whatever works. All children are different. Praise your child, but do it for them; it is not a celebration for you.

Night-time dryness happens in its own time

For most children, becoming dry at night happens naturally as their bladders grow, their sphincter muscles become stronger, and hormonal and growth development happens. Often this is around the age of five or six, but it can happen sooner.

Most night-time wetness happens during deep sleep, so waking your child in the middle of the night to have a wee doesn't teach their body to stay dry at night, it teaches their body to wake up for a wee.

My professional recommendation is to keep your child in pull-ups at naps and bedtime until they are consistently dry for two or more weeks. When you think it's time, you can invite your child to wear underwear. Just remember that even if your child is dry at night, they might wet the bed sometimes as their bladder grows and perhaps when they are ill or some change is going on in their routine or life. This usually resolves once things settle and without you having to do anything.

If there is one big takeaway I hope you get from this chapter, it's that your child does not need to be trained to use the toilet. The same way you did not give them a chocolate every time they said 'Mama' to teach them to speak – you just kept talking and expanding your vocabulary around them – you can teach toileting through explicit modelling, helping them focus on their bodily signals and using play with concrete language to help them move through this process.

CHAPTER 17

Sleep

Tell me how often you talk about sleep and I will tell you whether you are a parent or not. From the day my child was born I was asked questions like 'How does she sleep? Is she a good baby?' and was offered advice such as 'Don't touch her at bedtime or she will never learn to self-soothe' or 'Let her cry. That's how they learn to sleep.' These comments came from family, close friends and mothers with babies of a similar age. As a clinical psychologist, with a clear understanding about infant and child sleep, and clinical experience in this area, it was still confusing and stressful. When you are in early parenthood and you are sleep-deprived, exhausted and uncertain about life with a new baby, is it any wonder parents look to Google for support on topics such as 'How to teach my baby to sleep alone/through the night/without being held'?

Like many things in parenting, there is no straightforward 'one size fits all' solution. Responding to sleep is bidirectional. Your child's unique needs and temperament influence how you respond, and the responses you choose depend on your individual preferences, personality and sleep needs too. Some children are comfortable lying in a cot from the get-go, while others can't sleep without being held; some appear to sleep through the night early on, while others need active support to settle. They're all different, and that's why the topic of sleep is such a minefield.

Talking about infant and child sleep is confronting because being chronically sleep-deprived has real consequences on mental health, physical health, energy levels and daily functioning. I want to steer away from judgement and offer you actionable, evidence-based strategies that support sleep, reframing the idea of sleep from our adult perspective to a child's point of view. And I want to dispel some common myths, to help you make an informed decision about the choices you have.

'Sleeping through the night' is a myth, no matter how old you are

No one sleeps through the night, whether they have a child or not. Everyone wakes at the end of a sleep cycle, although for adults this may only be for seconds (Colten & Altevogt, 2006). It's normal to roll over, adjust the covers or even respond to noises briefly in the night and then go back to sleep. When babies wake up it's normal that what they do is cry and reach out for us.

Sleeping through the night is biologically unsafe for babies. They are primed to wake frequently to get protection, food and warmth. A baby's brain doubles in size in the first year of life and with physical growth comes pain and discomfort. Babies cannot tell us that they are in pain, but they can cry to communicate discomfort. At times when you cannot see what is wrong with your little one, it is likely that there is a sensation causing them distress. Babies cannot self-soothe and for sensory stimuli such as wetting, soiling, rubbing, touching or even eating (e.g. reflux) they need a warm caregiver to bring calm back into their bodies. For the first eighteen months babies also teethe. Pain is more intrusive at night-time because there are no distractions or ways to soothe pain without you by their side. Holding, rocking, singing and just being with your baby to help them find sleep will never create a rod for your own back. They are all necessary steps to help babies find sleep.

Somewhere around twelve to eighteen months, children begin to sleep for longer stretches, but waking between one and four times a night is still developmentally normal. This is a time when you may witness nightmares, night terrors and/or fears of the dark. Inevitably, children also fall sick, and this may interfere with their sleep, and of course yours too.

When children reach adolescence you may see a shift in their sleep. Suddenly, they won't want to wake up. This has nothing to do with being 'lazy' and everything to do with brain development. The adolescent years are the biggest developmental transition since birth. Sleeping allows adolescent brains to consolidate learning during the day and rest so they can keep learning tomorrow.

And then, at some point, we are adults. On a scale from one to ten, how good is your sleep? Things like your age, illnesses, hormone changes, work stress, what you ate, whether you drink alcohol or take drugs, how much you moved during the day, how much natural light you are exposed to, whether you have jet lag, are experiencing grief, have changed your lifestyle and, of course, whether you are a parent, all impact on sleep quality.

The message I want to get across here is that there are many factors involved in sleep and the wish for 'sleeping through the night' can be developmentally unrealistic and bring you disappointment and frustration.

Nightmares and night terrors – what is the difference?

These terms are used interchangeably, but 'nightmares' and 'night terrors' are qualitatively different and understanding this can help you to approach them more effectively.

Nightmares

Children typically wake up when they have had a nightmare and call out for your support. These generally happen in the early hours of the morning, when children's sleep is lighter. Most children will explain their dream to you, cry and seek verbal and physical reassurance. Offer comfort in hushed tones and remind your child they are safe. Promise to talk about the nightmare in the morning, which children often will remember to do. If the nightmare sticks around and brings up fears at bedtime, invite them to draw out what they remember (if they're old enough), or role-play and talk about it. Children and adults always wake up at the scariest part of a dream, so you never get to experience the ending. Get your child to visualize a 'good ending', something that makes them laugh can bring back safety to sleeping and dreaming the next night.

Night terrors

Children are in deep sleep when they have a night terror. They typically happen in the early part of the night, usually before midnight, when their brain is in a deeper state of sleep. Night terrors are similar to 'sleepwalking' and some children may open their eyes and even jump out of bed, screaming, shouting and crying, but their brain is asleep. You will know if it is a night terror because your child generally won't say anything coherent and, in the morning, they won't remember it happened.

Don't try and wake your child or have a conversation with them. Instead, soothe them with comforting touch (if they allow it) and a hushed tone of voice. If need be, redirect your child to bed with minimal talking. Remember, they are still asleep, and if you wake them it is likely to take a lot longer to settle them back down.

Night terrors are common around three to five years of age

and tend to pass on their own. They can be triggered by sickness with a high temperature, overtiredness, or life changes that bring a child stress.

If your child has persistent nightmares or night terrors that happen most nights and you are concerned, always seek reassurance from a healthcare professional.

To sleep train or not to sleep train . . . what's the evidence?

Did you 'sleep train' your baby? Are you in the camp that says, 'It works,' or the one that says, 'It harms'? I know how polarizing conversations about 'sleep training' are – so much so that I was hugely conflicted about writing this section. And yet avoiding talking about something does not make it go away, so I am delving into my courage to put this on paper, and if what I share helps one person make a better-informed decision, that is good enough.

Sleep is a societal problem

I cannot talk about sleep without naming the elephant in the room: our society's lack of support for parenthood. Many families rely on having two incomes, and it's often the mother who has access to parenting leave and is therefore most likely to suffer the consequences of frequent night waking. The pressure of needing a solid night's sleep before a child is developmentally ready to do longer stretches is something we need to bring greater awareness to. Wolke at al. (1995) carried out what's called a prospective study that looked at how 4,000 babies' sleep changed in the first five years. No matter what strategies parents used, 71 per cent of children stopped night waking before their second birthday, and 89 per cent did so by the time they turned four. Compare this to the amount of time our society deems is appropriate for maternity leave (fifty-two weeks in the UK with only thirty-nine of these weeks eligible for statutory pay; no obligation to offer maternity leave or pay in the USA, as it is seen as a 'benefit'; and sixteen weeks in France) and paternity leave (ranging from two weeks of statutory pay in the UK, sixteen days of paid leave in Spain – only if the mother chooses not to go on maternity leave – and twelve weeks in Japan), and therein lies a big part of the problem.

Without societal and community support, parents have little choice other than to resort to strategies that help them survive the early years. If the concept of 'sleep training' makes you wince or you find it upsetting, I can understand where this feeling comes from. And at the same time I am aware that circumstances differ and some parents, myself included, are more fortunate in terms of personal, financial and social privilege. Sharing evidence-based information to support parents to make the right choice for them, void of judgement and polarization, is crucial, and disappointingly hard to find.

What is 'sleep training', and does it work?

It's hard to talk about 'sleep training' because no one has managed to agree on a definition of what 'sleep training' is. It refers to any strategy that encourages a baby to fall asleep. It typically means letting your child 'cry it out' but can include staying beside your baby at night, rocking, singing or simply putting a comforting hand on them. It can also mean reading your baby's sleep cues and knowing when they are going to get tired, and supporting them in associating this with naps and following a regular bedtime routine.

Most studies in this area are impossible to critically evaluate in terms of evidence because they use non-randomized samples where parents make a choice about the 'method' of sleep training they want to try. They are typically 'single case studies' with sleep diaries or 'self-report' question-naires, which leave results skewed to individual bias. Furthermore, they have a significant 'drop-off rate' of 50 per cent or more, with no data for those who found 'sleep training' distressing or difficult. In other words, positive results tend to be biased towards those who respond best to 'sleep training'.

A recent meta-analysis looked at 476 peer-reviewed papers (Reuter et al., 2020). Unsurprisingly, only twelve studies were 'good enough' to meet standards of inclusion for the review. The conclusions were that current 'sleep training' studies are of poor quality, with too many knowledge gaps to offer a clear overview of the consequences and impact of these inter-ventions. Any short-term effects of 'sleep training' may therefore be due to individual child-development factors rather than demonstrating the 'effi-cacy' of any one method.

It is for this reason that, as a professional, I am always cautiously scep-tical of anyone who sells parents the idea that there is a model of 'sleep training' that works. What most people don't talk about is that under-standing your child's sleep needs, what helps them feel safe and secure, and the methods you feel comfortable using are unique to you and your child, and key to supporting sleep. Just like learning vocabulary at a different pace, some children need more sleep than others and their sustained sleep increases sooner than others'. It's a matter of 'when' not 'if', and this isn't dependent on what you do or don't do, it depends on a child's unique needs, their temperament and their sleep environment.

To 'cry it out' or not to 'cry it out'? It's a controversial question

How do you feel about a baby going through 'crying it out' to sleep at night? Your answer is likely to depend on your age, your experiences with sleep and how much you know about this method. I was interested to learn that it was the Industrial Revolution, when parents needed to work longer days, that prompted Western society to tell parents that babies should sleep 'independently'. Paediatrician Emmett Holt became famous for saying, 'Crying alone is good for children . . . they should be allowed to "cry it out" for an hour and in extreme cases two or three until they no longer request parental attention' (Rosier et al., 2021). However, it's the 1980s that made 'crying it out' infamous. The Ferber Method is well known as *the* method of 'controlled crying'; it involves leaving a baby to cry for longer and longer periods of time without parental support until they eventually find sleep. Despite Ferber writing a book (2006) that reads as an extensive apology to anyone who has used 'controlled crying' and states that 'co-sleeping works' and 'babies should not be left to cry for long periods of time without parental support'(!), a big portion of 1980s parents and beyond have held on to the belief that 'crying it out' is a rite of passage that teaches children to sleep, and that holding or soothing a baby creates unhelpful associations.

A review of modern parenting books that talk about sleep found that 61 per cent endorse 'crying it out', and many suggest using it with newborns (Ramos et al., 2006). This data is concerning, given that the last twenty years of research in this area clearly shows that 'crying it out' or any form of 'sleep training' that involves a parent withholding care in the first six months of life poses serious risks of sudden infant death syndrome (SIDS), heightens the risk of maternal anxiety and depression, and increases the risk of behavioural problems in childhood (Douglas et al., 2013). Babies don't cry for attention; they cry to communicate their needs. Risks are heightened for children who have experienced trauma and/or have sensitive temperaments. Unfortunately, it is the parents of children most at risk to the impact of 'crying it out' who often choose this method, because these children tend to cry louder and have frequent night wakings. Their needs are greater and therefore the impact on parental sleep is significantly heightened.

One of the few randomized controlled trials (RCTs) looked at 'controlled crying' with 235 babies aged between six and eight months brought up in a two-parent household (Hall, 2015). Parents received education on normal infant sleep, including information on development which broke down unrealistic expectations (e.g. helping parents understand that less napping and late bedtimes don't promote night-time sleep, while regular napping and bedtime routines do), and training in a sleep method: either 'controlled comforting', which encouraged soothing babies at night-time, or 'controlled crying'.

Parents in the control group were given only sleep education, with no formal guidance of how to support their child at night. Alongside sleep diaries, this RCT used actigraphy, a wearable device that registers a baby's sleep–wake patterns. The sleep diaries showed that parents who used 'controlled crying' recorded longer periods of sleep than those in either 'controlled comforting' or the control group. However, actigraphy readings showed a different picture: children who received 'controlled crying' woke up just as often as the children in the control group, and at the six-week follow-up their night-time waking did not improve. In other words, parents who used 'controlled crying' slept for longer because their babies stopped calling out for them, not because 'crying it out' taught them to sleep better.

Pause for a second and notice what reading this brings up for you. To the researchers who led this study, these findings were deemed 'a success'. Parents sleeping for longer and children not crying was interpreted as a sign of 'self-soothing', despite the babies remaining awake.

My professional view on this? I think parents sleeping better is a win, but sugar-coating what this does to an infant sits uncomfortably with me. What I read in this research is that 'crying it out' does not support a baby to self-soothe to sleep. It trains their brain that crying for help is futile because no one is coming. In psychological jargon, it teaches them to dissociate from sensations of discomfort in their bodies. For a baby's brain to shut down distress early on in development is a red flag for me. There is a large body of research that shows the impact of dissociation and emotional suppression on mental, physical and psychological wellbeing. In my professional capacity, 'crying it out' is not a method I can safely advocate. Do I support parents getting a better night's sleep? YES – through education on normal sleep and strategies that maintain parent–child bonds and have a positive long-term impact on sleep. Do these methods help parents sleep for as long stretches of time as 'crying it out' promises to? In all honesty, probably not. They work on developing long-term sleep habits that benefit children over time, so they are not a short-term fix, but they safeguard your child's wellbeing and the most important thing they have: their relationship with you.

What works for you and your family is not something I can decide for you. All I can offer is to weigh up the pros and cons of the science we have on sleep, and let you take the reins of whether 'sleep training' is worth it.

Focusing on good sleep habits will help your child learn the cues of how to sleep

Whether you choose to 'sleep train' or not, it can help to embed healthy sleep habits into your everyday life, the same way you do for eating or personal hygiene. There is good evidence of practices that support a good night's sleep for children and adults. You can begin to put these into place as soon as your baby is born, and if you have never used these ideas before, it's not too late to start now.

Support your child's natural 'body clock'

We all have a natural body clock that is affected by many things, including daylight and daytime activities. It's something we tend to become more aware of when we travel and experience 'jet lag'. Children benefit from routines that help to 'switch on' their state of alertness and 'switch off' when it's time to sleep. This is particularly key for newborns, who don't understand the difference between night-time and daytime. Some ideas that have been shown to support our bodies to naturally seek sleep include:

Regular 'wake up' and 'sleep' routines

Babies under four months of age don't tend to have predictable sleep patterns. This is normal and nothing to worry about. They don't benefit from forced 'waking and sleep' schedules, but they do benefit from experiences that help them learn there is a difference between daytime and night-time. This includes getting lots of fresh air and sunlight. A twenty-minute walk first thing in the morning or sitting by an open window can work well. Offer them the experience of everyday busyness through sounds, lively chatter and textures, lights and smells during the daytime, while keeping lights dimmed and sounds to a minimum during the evenings and night-time. This helps their brain learn that daytime and night-time are different, and after a few months you will notice your baby adjust their waking and sleeping patterns to this.

Encourage movement and exercise daily

When people talk about getting babies and/or children 'tired' enough to sleep, they are not talking about missing their naps or keeping them awake later into the evening in the hope of a later wake-up. It is a paradox, but sleep breeds sleep and babies who nap well tend to sleep well. If you push past their sleepiness to a point of overtiredness, you eat into their melatonin stores (the sleepiness chemical), making falling asleep harder and it more likely that your child gives you an early wake-up call. Focus on movement and exercise. When babies and children have been inactive or lacked stimulation throughout the day, they have more difficulty falling asleep.

Babies benefit from floor-based play in different positions, including time on their tummy, rolling (with your support at first) and reaching for toys around them and above them on a play swing if you have one. Water-based activities, music, singing and lights are also helpful in attracting little ones' attention to reach and move their bodies.

Current guidelines suggest that children under five should be active for a minimum of three hours a day, spread out across their day. Movement can be structured exercise such as using a scooter, walking to the shops or trampolining, or unstructured movement that may include throwing and catching games, running around or dancing together.

From the age of five upwards children benefit from engaging in exercise for at least an hour a day. This might be through cycling, walking, playing team sports, swimming or running, with intense exercise three days a week.

Follow your child's sleepy cues

I don't know who decided that children 'need' to sleep from 7 p.m. to 7 a.m., but it's a made-up myth. Little ones have evolving sleep needs as they grow and develop, but don't waste time adding up the numbers – some children sleep more than the 'recommended' sleep time and some 'snack' on sleep throughout the day. Think of your own sleep. Are you a 'morning person' or a 'night owl'? How is this similar or different to your partner? And if you were to swap your sleep habits and force yourself to do the opposite of what you are naturally inclined towards, how would it feel? Our children are no different to us – they have their own sleep preferences and their needs are pre-wired. Some children want to sleep early, and others simply cannot. They are not trying to manipulate you; their brain is not ready to switch off yet.

Rather than get into sleep battles, notice when your child's sleepy cues show up. If you are trying to get them to bed at 7 p.m. every night and they are only dropping off at 9 p.m. after you have read them ten books, don't keep pushing on the 7 p.m. bedtime. Consider how to help their body get sleepy (i.e. follow some of the steps above) and move bedtime to a little later. You don't want to associate bedtime with 'fun awake time' with you. Daytime is for connection; night-time should feel boring, calm and unexciting. The less time they are in bed lying awake, the better. You cannot force sleep; you can only follow sleepy cues. (Note: if you are at a stage where your child's bedtime is later than you hope and they are waking any time between 6 and 7 a.m., this phase will pass. If, however, your child is sleeping in until nine or ten in the morning, it may be time to start waking them earlier, to bring their bedtime forward.)

Switch on the sleepy hormones

The sleep hormone is called melatonin, and it helps our brains and bodies prepare for sleep and drift off. It is activated by night-time, but because of electricity, blue light from screens and our permanent state of 'alertness', it doesn't harm to give melatonin a bit of a helping hand.

You can close curtains, blinds and dim the lights in the early evening and begin to bring quiet to your home. Rather than using screens, offer your child hand—eye coordination activities such as toys to grab and explore or, when they are older, drawing, puzzles, mazes and card games. There is no evidence that changing the colour of your lights will aid sleep; dimming the brightness of your home is enough to let melatonin do its work.

Create a bedtime routine you can stick to

A routine doesn't mean doing the same things, at the same time, every day. That is a schedule, and it might work for our adult lives, but it's too rigid for children because their needs change and evolve. If you have a baby, you will know exactly what this feels like when a 'schedule' that worked for you two weeks ago is thrown out the window as they become more alert and develop skills.

A routine offers predictability during the day and can bring reassurance to a child because they know what will come next, but you can be flexible on the timing and length of each step. At bedtime this may look like 1) a bath, 2) moisturizing, 3) putting on pyjamas, 4) story time, 5) a goodnight ritual, 6) lights off. There may be nights when your child chooses to have an extra-long bath, or days when you skip bathing altogether to follow their tiredness cues and jump straight into reading a book. Routines anchor and contain children in the predictability of a familiar rhythm, even if the specifics change.

Bedtime is the start of a child's longest separation from you

If your child is frequently waking up at night, it is important to remember that sleep is the biggest separation a child experiences from you every day. Separation anxiety at bedtime goes back to our hunter-gatherer days. Fear has evolved to keep us close and safe, and this shows up in our children when they are left alone in the dark. This is not a manipulation, it's a bio-logical instinct for safety; falling asleep is a vulnerable act that needs our brains and bodies to know we are safe. If you have ever stayed awake at night worrying about an interview or about missing an early flight, you will know exactly what I am talking about. When we feel under threat, sleep doesn't come easily.

You can help your child overcome anxiety at bedtime. There are no 'magic solutions' that will bring hours of uninterrupted sleep, only ways of helping your child's nervous system find a place of stillness which, over time, shrinks bedtime wobbles so sleep can come more easily. It takes time to find safety, so choose what you think may work and be gentle with your-self and your child when bedtime anxiety shows up.

Notice what feelings you bring to bedtime

If bedtime is tough or a lengthy process, it makes sense that your evenings might fill you with dread. No matter how well you think you are masking this, your tone of voice, your facial expressions and your behaviours are tell-tale signs of your emotional state. Getting into a calm and confident position will help the bedtime process, and even if your child takes ages to fall asleep, your calm will help them know that going to bed is 'not scary' and will make separation easier. Take five or ten minutes for yourself before you begin the bedtime routine and find some calm, close your eyes, do a short relaxation. I repeat a mantra: 'She will fall asleep. She always does.' Don't clock-watch; this will stress you out. Follow the routine and try some of the steps below.

Connect

If your child is scared to be left at bedtime, it is usually a communication that they want to stay close. Give one-on-one quality time in the evening, find a game that makes you both laugh, dance, get physical and get silly. Laughter is a great way to connect, and physical movement that isn't vigorous but is fun and connecting (for example, rolling them into a sausage roll with a blanket and then rolling them out, when they are old enough to roll) can be deeply regulating to a little one's nervous system and set them up for sleep more easily.

Validate their bedtime experience

Let your child know that it is okay to feel scared at night and remind them of the safety that surrounds them with concrete examples: 'I know you are scared at bedtime, but remember, I am still here and I will be here when you wake up in the morning. You are safe in your bedroom.'

Be mindful not to talk through difficult feelings too close to bedtime, as this can raise anxiety. Write any worries your child has down, put them in a notepad or a jar and talk about them in the morning.

Bring in extra comfort

Children benefit from having things in their bedroom that remind them of you. This may be a T-shirt that smells of you, photos or small objects of tokens that remind them of you. Set them up during the day and talk about them. At night, remind your child, 'This is a little bit of me that will stay with you when you sleep. Even when you cannot see me, I am always by your side.'

Have a goodnight ritual

It may be really tempting to sneak out while your child is drifting off, but it can make things much worse in the long run. It tells your child that if they start to fall asleep or look away for a moment, you might disappear. Having a goodnight ritual and keeping a boundary of when you leave can help children settle because it's connecting and predictable.

You might invite your child to put their teddies to bed and role-play the actions they are going to go through with you. This can help children feel more 'in control' of bedtime. You may want to share a little 'bedtime song' – singing can be soothing and regulating, and if your child joins you, their singing voice will also slow down their breathing and help to shrink any bedtime anxiety. You can also have a special bedtime kiss or words you always tell each other before you switch off the light. In our home that sounds like 'I love you. You are safe in your cosy bed with your Pipi bear. Even if you cannot see me, I am always with you. Sleep well.'

These small rituals have deep meaning to children. They remind them of your special bond and that it does not diminish when you are physically apart. Rituals can help children let go just a little more easily when it's time to say goodnight.

Final thoughts . . .

Your child's ability to sleep through the night is not a reflection of your parenting, it's a consequence of development and multiple factors that are part of everyday life.

Children will manage longer stretches of sleep when they are developmentally ready to do so. My best-practice suggestion is to focus on evidence around 'sleep hygiene' and reach out to your family, friends and community to support and give you a break so you can then meet your own sleep needs.

However, I have met parents who are on the edge of a mental health crisis due to sleep deprivation. For those lacking a community or financial and social resources, who are left unable to cope, 'sleep training' may be a necessity rather than a choice. Get curious about the strategies on offer and consider what is most developmentally appropriate for the age and stage of your baby. Making an informed choice about the strategies you choose may positively impact not just your quality of sleep but also your child's brain development and overall wellbeing.

CHAPTER 18

Play

Play is fun, and to children it's also how they learn, how they express feelings and talk about their experiences. How many times have you heard a little one say, 'Play with me'? When you hear this as an adult, do you understand it as 'Entertain me?' Or do you hear it from a child's perspective, and understand that it actually says:

- 'I want to say something to you.'
- 'I have something to show you.'
- 'I am confused about what happened the other day. Can you help me understand?'
- 'I miss you.'
- 'Playing with you helps me feel close to you.'

Little ones will never say, 'Hmmm . . . I have a lot on my mind. Can we sit for a chat?' They invite you to play so you can witness their inner worlds, help them process experiences and life events, and practise skills. Up to the age of eight, most learning happens when children have all their senses engaged, and play is one of the best mediums for this.

All children know how to play

There is a misunderstanding among adults that we need to 'entertain' children, that being a parent who 'plays well' means creating fun and making up exciting games. There are so many baby and child groups based around play that are structured and directive. These can teach children different skills such as following direction from an adult, listening to instruction, focus and attention. However, children benefit most from engaging in unstructured play that engages their imaginary worlds, free of the pressure of what an adult deems good play to 'look like'. Your role is to provide an enriching, welcoming and safe environment with limited distractions (including yourself) so children can suspend reality and be where their brain is most comfortable, in a 'dream-like state' of fantasy-world. If you want to make play an enriching world that a child enjoys entering on their own, even at times when your child invites you to play you need to become an observer to play, not an active actor in it, or if you are a natural entertainer, hold back at least some of the time.

Passive toys encourage better play

I don't know about you, but I always find the strangest things around our home being used as play items by my child. Recently, it's shopping tags I have put in the recycling that become 'credit cards' in her shopping game, socks that become sleeping bags for small teddies, or clothes hangers that become handles to carry and pull things. All these everyday home objects and many more can be toys to children, and they don't cost anything extra. With crawling and toddling babies, Tupperware and wooden kitchen utensils can be winning play items. These everyday objects offer sensory exploration that allow children to learn about the world while playing.

Whatever toy companies tell you, children don't need lots of battery-operated singing/dancing/light-flashing toys. These may offer some short-term visual and auditory stimulation, but long term they don't spark imaginary play and children tend to get tired of them quickly. Instead, favour 'passive toys' such as blocks, dolls, figures, pens and paper that put the focus on your child creating play.

Independent play is a slow, gradual process

For many adults, 'independent play' means having a child play by themselves. In reality, 'independent play' is a child engaging in play without adult interaction. It doesn't mean that they are in a separate room from you; it is more likely to happen when they are in close proximity to you and feel safe to dive into their imaginary worlds. On a good day, 'independent play' gives you and your child some freedom to do your own thing while sharing a physical space.

Nobody likes to feel like they're being set aside for more important things. Think of what it might be like if you came home and were looking forward to seeing your partner and they said, 'Here you go, I made you some food and that's your favourite show. I am going to sit in the other room. See you later.' Maybe, some evenings, this would be just what you wanted, but on others you might feel a little rejected. Why wouldn't they want to spend some time with you first? Children need to feel nourished by your attention and get their 'fill' before they let go. Babies up to the age of one should not be left out of sight, and you need to keep toddlers in sight too. Initially, you won't be able to step away, but you can watch them from a slightly greater distance. You might start sitting in the same room but a little further apart, until over time your child tolerates you going to the next room. It is important to tell your child that you are going and will be coming back (e.g. 'I am going to get the washing, I will be right back'). If you sneak off quietly, your child learns to keep an eye on you. Walking away without a proper goodbye makes children want to stay closer for fear they will lose you. The first few times, make sure you go for tiny amounts of time (one or two minutes) and gradually extend this to build up your child's sense of safety in separating from you.

Play is a developmental progression that takes time

Babies and children up to the age of two may not be able to play for longer than five to ten minutes on their own, and this is a normal part of development. It isn't your child being 'clingy' – they need close contact, and it's a natural instinct to want to follow you around or cry when you are out of sight. Their attachment instinct is loud. Toddlers up to the age of five may play for fifteen to twenty minutes, and this may seem brief, but their attention spans are short so it's normal to see them flit from one thing to the next. As children reach the school years you may notice their play changes to 'private play', and that wanting to be in a different room may no longer become your choice.

The insights you get to witness through your child's play are windows into their inner worlds. Just being there, listening and watching, can tell you so much about your child. Here are some ideas to guide you during play with your child.

Let your child direct play

Children flourish in play when adults witness and value it, but they can lose confidence and creative skills when adults interfere, set goals or place too much structure around play.

Play is the one place where children should have the power and control. In fantasy and through role-play is where they learn to make sense of rules, limits, boundaries, social skills and other life lessons they are learning with you. While, typically, you are leading your child forward through tasks across the day, in play it's healthy and important that your child leads you. When you encourage this, you also help your child to make sense of what it is like to tell someone else what to do. If you interject in play, give them too many instructions or take over to make the play 'better', you short-circuit play and leave your child in doubt of their own abilities. Doing this a lot may make a child need you to entertain them during play and 'independent play' may be harder to build.

This doesn't mean you can't let your child invite you into their games, which, inevitably, they will do. Let them take the lead about what you should do and say. Use curiosity to pass the act of play on to your child ('So what does Dolly want to do now?'). When your child is a little older you can role-play interactions you have with them, so, for example, Dolly may say no to some food your child offers, in the same way your child may do this at dinnertime. Watch how your child responds. Do they use the same words you give them or something different? How do they treat Dolly when she stands up to them? Does it mirror how you speak to your child or how someone else is? This type of play gives you small clues about your child's internal world in a way you won't get to experience anywhere else. Notice what it is like for you to be told what to do by your child. How comfortable is it? Does it annoy, bore or frustrate you not to do it 'your way'? This experience may help you respond with greater compassion the next time you ask your child to do something and they say, 'No', 'I don't want to,' or 'I can't'.

Play is genderless

Whatever gender your child is, there is no box for play. Colours have no gender; the idea that 'blue is for boys' and 'pink is for girls' is socially constructed. In 1983 the *New York Times* issued a gift list for babies that separated items into these two colours;

however, a review of gender-related colour coding by Del Guidice (2012) found little evidence of the pink for girls and blue for boys claim and it is now thought of as a 'scientific urban legend'. What Del Guidice's review demonstrated is that any kind of gender-related colour coding has been artificially created by fashion trends over time and has nothing to do with gender.

Accepting that anything goes in play (within safe limits) helps children to develop self-confidence, individuality and acceptance of themselves and others. When you accept your child's likes and dislikes without imposing your view, you give them a secure base from which they can explore, have fun and get creative. Wearing glitter on their face with a Spider-Man costume is not about gender, it's about fun!

It is totally okay if your child falls in line with 'social stereotypes'. You don't need to change this, and you can keep offering choices. It's healthy for little boys to play with dolls and for little girls to have trains and cars to play with. When we narrowly and quickly assign what is 'appropriate' for children based on one random attribute (their gender) we ignore the rest of them as a whole person.

If you want to build on this further with your child, consider conversations about their preferences when the opportunity arises.

- How do you know that [clothing item] is for a boy/girl?
- Who is allowed to like [toy/character]?
- What would you think of a [boy/girl] playing with/wearing that?
- Would you be surprised to know [boys/girls] like that too?

And if your worry is what to say in the moment when someone comments on your child's clothes or toys, you can set respectful boundaries that don't place judgement or shame on anyone. This may sound like 'My child chose this [jumper/toy]. It's one of their favourites. We love their individuality. Thank you for showing curiosity about their tastes.' Judgement is not personal to you or your child, it's a reflection of someone else's discomfort at witnessing freedom of expression in a way they have probably never been allowed to experience themselves.

Embrace boredom

We have been sold the lie that being busy is good for us. But here is a paradox: when children are endlessly busy, they struggle to know what to do by themselves.

Boredom doesn't need fixing or distracting. It is a feeling that connects us with what is not working or has got stuck. Boredom makes us question, 'Is there something else I could be doing?'; 'Do I need to stop and rest?'; 'What would make this better/more fun?' These are questions children need to experience to make sense of their needs. In many ways, boredom is a precursor to, and catalyst for, play.

Rather than offering suggestions when your child says, 'I am so bored,' help them embrace it. This might sound like 'Ah, you are not used to feeling bored. Yep, it's hard not to have anything to do. I can't wait to see what ideas you come up with.' Sometimes this type of response will make your child moan louder. This is your invitation to problem-solve with your child. Ask them, 'What do you think boredom is telling you about what you need? Is it a break? Is it to find some fun? Let's figure it out together.'

Our worlds are getting more fast-paced, and developing brains need slowness to consolidate learning and develop skills. See boredom as a welcome feeling in your home. You might be surprised what happens if you just let it hang around for a little while.

6

Big Topics

When you were growing up, what topics were taboo in your home; the things your parents never talked about? What message did this send to you about these topics? And if your parents never talked about them, how did you learn about them?

There are certain topics that we consider taboo in our society, including consent, sex and talking about death. If these topics were never spoken about to you in ways that felt honest and safe, it makes sense that you might find these conversations a little daunting, or even frightening. And yet you don't have to wait for your child to bring up these topics 'when they're ready' because being 'ready' might never happen.

Consent is a topic that is relatively new. My generation and the ones before didn't really teach consent – there was a sense that this knowledge was 'innate', that 'good people' would know how to show respect towards another person's body. Because hearing 'no' isn't always enough, I would like to reframe consent as a need to witness enthusiasm for mutual affection. It's the passionate 'yes' that we need to teach our children to look out for. Throughout the chapter on consent, it may be that painful emotions show up as you recognize times when consent was breached with you. I want you to listen to the urge you may have to dismiss consent as 'trivial' or only for those who are 'sensitive'. If we want to safeguard children and help them make better decisions in relationships, we need to begin embodying a culture of consent in our homes and within ourselves.

When it comes to talking about sex and death, the message you want to give your child is that they are both a part of life. Notice whether these topics bring up discomfort or fears about breaking a child's innocence or saying the wrong thing. Not talking about things doesn't protect children, it stops them from being prepared and having the tools to cope.

The truth doesn't scare children; they are more afraid of sitting alone in the unknown. One of the greatest gifts you can offer to a child is being a safe person they can talk to about anything. There are only four things you really need to hold in mind:

- All feelings are allowed
- Speak simply
- Stay honest
- And if you don't know, say so.

The message you want to send a child, no matter what they ask, is 'You can talk to me about anything. I will always listen. You are always safe with me.' Be courageous in having the conversation and give your child information that will safeguard their wellbeing long term. This can be hard, so I'm going to give you some ideas of how you can start.

Three topics that children *do* need to be protected from

The state of family finances

Talking about money within the context of financial deprivation can place a burden on children that leaves them with the threat that their family is not coping. When this happens, children are more likely to hide their needs, omit sharing when there are costs involved (e.g. paying for a school trip), and resort to lying and hiding information to protect their parents.

The care of or responsibility for siblings

You may witness times when older siblings try to tell a younger sibling what they can and cannot do or tell them off when they make a mistake. Keep a clear separation between your child's relationship with their siblings and your responsibility as a parent: 'Thank you for trying to support your brother. It is not your job to tell them off. Your job is to play and have fun together. My job is to keep an eye on both of you and keep you safe. If you think your brother might get hurt, shout and I will come.'

Avoid the parentification trap

Children should be shielded from feeling responsible for caring for their parents' emotional world and relationships. The parent–child relationship exists within a hierarchy where the adults are in the position to guide and support, and a child needs to lean on a parent for emotional, physical and practical safety. When children become an adult's confidante or the person they seek emotional support from, it blurs the relational boundaries and interrupts healthy emotional development.

CHAPTER 19

Consent

Consent is the foundation of having safe relationships with people. It's about the freedom of choice to agree to do something with someone else. All children need to learn how to protect their bodies and respect other people's, and this should be an ongoing conversation that begins in the toddler years and keeps developing as they get older.

Kwasi and Leanne are friends and they are having a great time in the playground. Leanne jumps on a free swing and says, 'Mummy! Push me!' Leanne's mummy is feeding her baby sister by the park bench while chatting to Kwasi's mother. She smiles and says, 'Kwasi, can you please give Leanne a push on the swing? I will be over there in a moment.'

Response A: Kwasi goes over to Leanne and gives her a little push on the swing. Leanne giggles.
Response B: Kwasi asks Leanne, 'Is it okay if I push you on the swing?' Leanne says, 'Yes! Push me HIGH!'

Can you see why response B in this example is the one where Kwasi requests consent? Kwasi asks Leanne if it's okay for him to push her on the swing. What makes this a true example of consent is not Kwasi's question but Leanne's unambiguous 'Yes!' and her clear description of 'how' she wants to be pushed. The difference is subtle and important. In response A,

Leanne is seen as the object of her mother's request, while in response B she is seen as the only person able to decide what happens to her body.

We need to recognize the other person's enthusiasm as a key part of consent. This is particularly true for children, whose big feelings get in the way of them being able to use their words. A child staying silent when someone says, 'Want a hug?' does not mean 'Yes, feel free to hug me.' It means they are not able to give you an enthusiastic 'yes', and that needs to be read as a 'no'.

Children need clear messages about consent, and what it feels to have it respected. I am offering you a step-by-step guide to help you get started and reflect on where you may already be embodying a culture of consent.

Explain body boundaries simply

The word 'consent' is a hard one to make sense of, even for adults. One way of talking about it is to imagine that everyone has an invisible 'body bubble' around their body. Explain to your child that no one should cross their 'body bubble' unless they clearly say it is okay to do so, and that they should never cross anyone else's without being given a clear signal.

You can empower a child to understand this concept by using words and actions to this effect. This means modelling body boundaries and reinforcing them when it matters to you. For example, I know many parents who feel 'touched out' by their child climbing all over their body. Your child wants to be physically close to you, and this is a good and healthy thing for them, but when it no longer feels good to you, recognize that you have met their physical needs across the day and now it's time for you to have your physical needs met. Set a boundary and remind your child of the 'body bubble' and you'll be teaching consent alongside getting your need for some physical space met. That might sound like 'I love being close to you, but I don't want you inside my body bubble right now. I won't let you sit on my lap, but I do want to hold hands. Come and sit beside me.'

And when it comes to other people's 'body bubbles', take active steps to help your child while they are still learning about consent. When you hear their friend say, 'No! Stop it!', get close and say to your child, 'When someone says no, we always stop what we are doing immediately. No matter what.'

When we give children the experience of consent as an everyday action, they learn what it feels like to be safe in relationships with others. Rather than becoming an intellectual exercise ('Wait . . . what happened? Should I have let them do that to me? I am not sure . . .'), they can be guided by the experiences they have had with you that tell them when something does not feel right and empower them to say, 'Stop,' walk away, and seek help as needed.

Daily care is about assent, not consent

Many parents teach their child to say, 'I am the boss of my body,' and I LOVE empowered children who say this loud and clear. And yet this can backfire when you have to do something to your child that they don't want you to do, such as getting them into a car seat or taking them to see the doctor. Little ones do not understand the consequences of not bathing for a week or running around topless in the sun without sunscreen. It is an adult's job to safeguard a child's wellbeing, and this can mean touching or holding their body to ensure their safety, even when they don't enthusiastically say yes. We call this 'assent', and to do this you can:

- Talk through what you are doing and what they can expect to happen
- Offer a child choices
- Empathize with their feelings
- Validate their experience
- Set boundaries as appropriate.

I worked with Ruby, who used to scream, 'My body is mine, and I say NO!' whenever she went to the doctor's. She had an endocrine condition that meant regular medical reviews and check-ups. It was important for Ruby to have a voice about who did what to her, and it was also important that she let the doctors care for her. So we worked on making the nuance more explicit. Because children are literal beings, they need clarity about when body autonomy is theirs and when adults need to act to protect and safeguard them. Saying this to your child might sound like 'You are the boss of your body when it comes to giving affection and when we play games. But until you are old enough, there are choices I need to make for your safety and wellbeing, like going to school and seeing the doctor.'

Ruby's parents told her that she could always say, 'Stop,' if she felt uncomfortable or unsafe in the way her body was being touched, and they would pause what they were doing to support her feelings in that moment. Specifically naming what you are doing when it is for a child's safety, like buckling up a seatbelt while acknowledging a child's feelings, can help to engage their willingness to participate – for example, saying 'I know you don't like the seatbelt. We all have to wear one when we go in the car, for our safety. I can push the buckle in, or you can do it. Which do you prefer?'

Offer choices and give a child time

Good consent gives another person the power to freely make a choice. Whenever possible, offer open questions that give your child choices:

'How do you want to say goodbye? Do you want to wave or give me a high five?'
'What can I do to help you right now? Do you want me to sit here with you, give you some space, or maybe get you a drink?'

My daughter struggles to say goodbye when she leaves anyone's house. She feels sad to leave, and saying 'goodbye' makes it real. Knowing this, I always prepare her in advance of leaving a friend's house. Twenty minutes before we are going to leave I call her over, get down close to her eye level and prepare her for what is to come. That sounds something like 'We are going home soon. I know saying goodbye feels sad; you never want to leave. It is kind to say goodbye. It shows we care about our friends. How do you want to do it today? Do you want to wave or give a high five or ask for a hug?' When she doesn't answer, I tell her I trust her to choose what feels right for her when we leave. I never pressure her, but I do model how I show gratitude to our hosts with words of appreciation and, often, hugs. She is more regularly giving a little quiet wave when we leave, and at other times being more buoyant with a 'I love coming here. See you soon!' Children watch what we do and learn from us – never forget it.

Whenever you ask something of your child, give them space to think. Pressure erodes consent, so avoid trying to speed up their response. Sit tight. Don't let other adults pressure your child either. It might feel like your child's answer is taking for ever, but children eventually make up their own minds, and if they cannot, model the behaviour you want them to learn. See these moments as opportunities to help you prepare better next time.

Create a culture of consent

Embedding a culture of consent in your home means helping a child to trust their instincts.

You can foster consent through modelling in how you speak to your child and others:

- 'Let's ask Paul if he wants a hug or just a wave at the door.'
- 'Would you like to give Nanny a hug or blow her a kiss?'

- 'Can I wash your back now? And how about your feet? And what about your bottom?' This is also a good opportunity to bring up privacy (e.g. 'Only Mummy and Daddy are allowed to wash your bottom')
- 'Do you like to be tickled? How will I know when it doesn't feel good any more? What words/signal will you use to tell me?'
- 'Do you like it when I spin you around and make you feel dizzy? How will you tell me you want me to stop if you have had enough?'
- 'How does your body feel at the top of that slide? Does it feel good?'

Pausing an activity to consider how their body feels is powerful. Try and remember to offer a 'check in' during physical play, perhaps when they seem to feel tired, bored or are no longer enjoying something. Stop in your tracks and say, 'Okay, pause the game. How are you feeling right now? Want to do more, or stop? I am feeling . . . a bit tired, but okay. We can do a few more minutes, then stop for a drink.' You are allowed to stop the game when it no longer feels good to you too.

Never ask a child to keep a secret; talk about surprising others instead

Have you ever asked your child to 'keep a secret' so you could surprise someone with a gift or some home-baked goodies? We need to teach children not to keep secrets, even the harmless ones where you want to create a 'special bond' between you and your child, because normalizing the idea of 'hiding' information from you or others can put them at risk. Secrets can be a gateway for abuse because they create barriers to honest conversation.

I have met many children who hold 'secrets' for someone. They fear becoming a 'snitch' and/or losing another person's trust. Secrets are powerful because they can become impenetrable, holding someone to ransom because the secret cannot be talked about. So the best thing you can do is never ask a child to hold a secret and be clear that there is a difference between 'secrets' and 'surprises'. That might sound like: 'Surprises are things that are happy and fun, and we always share them with someone at some point. So we might not tell Grandma what her present is, so that when she opens it, she get a surprise. Secrets are not things we keep, no matter who asks us to. If someone tells you that you will get in trouble if you tell their secret, I want you to know that is impossible. You will never get in trouble for sharing a secret because, just like surprises, they need to get revealed.'

So rather than saying, 'Let's keep Mummy's birthday card a secret. Shh . . . don't tell her,' you can say, 'Let's make Mummy's birthday card a surprise. Shh . . . don't tell her we did this until we give it to her, okay?' And to make things really clear, you can add, 'This isn't a secret. It's a surprise. We don't hold secrets. So if it slips out that we did Mummy a card, that's okay. You will not get into trouble and Mummy will still love it when she sees it on the day.'

Doing these simple steps and embedding them into your everyday inter-actions allows children to differentiate between what a safe, healthy relationship with consent sounds and feels like, as opposed to one that may be manipulative, coercive or abusive.

CHAPTER 20

Sex

Let's talk about sex. Who was the first person to talk to you about sex when you were growing up? Who told you what your body parts are called? What do you call your body parts – factual names or 'nicknames'? When I asked this question to over 170,000 people in my Instagram community – largely made up of people aged between twenty-five and forty-four – 5 per cent said their parents had first talked to them about sex, 30 per cent said they learned about it at school and around 20 per cent reported that they had learned about sex from reading magazines such as *Sugar* and hearing their friends with older siblings talk about it. Devastatingly, 45 per cent said 'no one' had talked to them about sex growing up; they had learned 'through experience' only. The generations that came before us had little if any education around sex and consent, so it's unsurprising that these conversations felt challenging or even impossible to have once they became parents. When you don't have the language or the knowledge, it's difficult to impart this to someone else.

I like to think the adults of my generation have learned, both through experience (sadly, often not good ones) and further education in adulthood, that talking about sex in the way that it was talked about to us is not fit for purpose. I also know that there are lots of 'new words' and that access to the internet has made information about sex more normalized and accessible to children and young people than it ever was for us growing up, and this can be scary and overwhelming too. It can feel like children know more than we do, and that can put us in a helpless position. I want to offer you some ideas to empower you to have these conversations with your child so that when you begin you are no longer feeling lost but instead confident about what you are saying and doing.

Talking about sex doesn't make it dirty – it makes it safe

'Sex talk' isn't something you do once and have to get right. It's an ongoing conversation. You can begin as early as you like, simply by talking about body parts in ways that are both accurate and honest, then slowly moving towards conversations around privacy, sex and pleasure when the time feels right.

Talking about sex begins in early childhood over the course of many, often small, teachable moments. Rather than thinking about 'sex' as a lecture where you sit your child down and explain 'this is what sex is', think about teaching a child about their body, sexuality, pleasure, love and healthy relationships. Overwhelmingly, adults tend to exclude the positive sides of sex and sexuality in favour of prioritizing warnings around pregnancy, sexually transmitted infections, abuse and exploitation (Ashcraft & Murray, 2016).

Adults often fear that portraying sex in a positive light may entice or encourage a child to experiment. Talking about sex and sexuality can be factual and sex-positive while embedding boundaries that teach your child to stay safe. For example, you can say, 'The day you feel ready to have sex, it is important to use a condom for your health and safety. Condoms help prevent sexually transmitted infections and unintended pregnancies.' Contrary to popular belief, national and international research overwhelmingly demonstrates the benefits of talking about sex with children. Programmes that promote abstinence only have been found to be ineffective in delaying sexual initiation, reducing the frequency of sex or number of sexual partners. Instead, giving factual and accurate information encourages young people to delay sexual initiation, reduce risk-taking behaviour and increase the use of contraception with healthier, more realistic attitudes to sex and reproduction (Fonne et al., 2014; UNESCO, 2016; Leijten et al., 2016).

Always call body parts what they are

Would you ever call a hand anything other than a hand? If your answer is no, notice what pulls you to label body parts as anything other than what they are supposed to be called, and whether you do this for the benefit of your child or to avoid your own discomfort.

Never dismiss the power of the words you use with your child. Using the correct terminology normalizes body parts as 'matter of fact' rather than 'rude' or shameful. Any care task, such as changing a nappy, getting dressed, bathing, wiping hands or face and moisturizing are opportunities to talk about body parts. The same way you label your child's arm when you put their top on or their nose when you use a tissue, you can label their penis, vulva or anus when you wipe them. This makes body parts non-threatening and care tasks collaborative.

And if you do not know the correct labels, it's never too late to learn. Here's my simplified crib sheet for you:

- The vulva is the outside part of female genitals (and includes the labia and the clitoris)
- The vagina is internal and leads to the womb – you cannot see the vagina
- A male sexual organ is called a penis

- The scrotum is the external part of the testicles
- The testicle is the internal area that holds the sperm – you cannot see testicles.

You might think, 'A friendly nickname is just as good. It never did me any harm.' If this is going through your mind, you are not alone. A recent poll with my Instagram community about labels for sexual body parts included: biscuit, cookie, penny, foof, fanny, kitty, front bottom and willy. Consider how many of these words place an additional stigma on the body of a little girl or woman. I think we can all agree that bottoms are for pooing and farting, so what imagery does a 'front bottom' give children about a girl's body parts?

Now take a moment to imagine what would happen if a child said to you, 'My uncle licked my biscuit,' or 'Grandpa touched my penny.' Would you immediately think they are referring to their vulva? Or would you dismiss this as completely harmless? Neither of these are random examples; they are based on real-life stories of sexual abuse. Sadly, this isn't a 'one-off case'; it is well documented that children who disclose sexual abuse are often misunderstood by the adults they share this with, who are often teachers, extended family and friends (Borg et al., 2014).

While it is frightening, and uncomfortable to talk about, it is a sad truth that some children are victims of sexual abuse. To safeguard children, adults have a duty to get comfortable talking about bodies in ways that are accurate, factual and devoid of stigma or shame. A powerful 'one of a kind' study in 1995 by Elliot and colleagues conducted semi-structured interviews with ninety-one sex offenders about the methods they used to select and target children. This is a difficult read, but an important one, because the findings offer lessons for those who care for the safeguarding of children. The main points of the findings were that sexual abuse occurs across every social class, cultural group and gender, and abusers are more likely to be well known to a child (i.e. family members, babysitters or professionals such as nursery staff and teachers). Children who know the proper names for their body parts are less likely targets because offenders tend to try and convince children that genitals have different names, and those who have been told the true names of anatomical parts will know this isn't true, which makes offenders more vulnerable to getting caught.

I don't know about you, but as a parent this information gives me an urge never to leave my child in the care of anyone but myself and my partner. And yet the healthy part of me knows that most adults are not perpetrators of child sexual abuse. The most powerful thing we can do as safe, caring adults is to give children factual and accurate information about their body. This reduces the risk of them becoming targets of abuse and it facilitates adults to take immediate steps to safeguard them in the horrific event that it happens.

Explain what private parts are

Children need specific language to make sense of what the private areas of their body are. A simple way of doing this is by telling your child, 'There are parts of your body that are private, and that means no one should see or touch them. The private parts of your body are those that are covered by underwear, and your mouth. No one is allowed to kiss your private parts or ask you to kiss theirs.'

Some families allow kissing on the lips with little ones, and you and those who care for your child will see and touch your child's private parts. You need to explicitly name the people who these actions are allowed with (e.g. parents, siblings, care staff), but you need to ensure that this goes alongside a body boundary that if you or anyone else ever touches your child's body in ways that feel uncomfortable or unsafe they will say, 'Stop,' move away and tell a trusted adult.

When my daughter was a baby we had a clear boundary that no one would kiss her on the lips. As she grew up and witnessed me and her father kissing, she began to want to give us a kiss on the lips, and we have used this as an opportunity to teach her body boundaries. Rather than moving our face away, we have been clear and specific about this with words: 'I don't want you to kiss me on the lips, but you can kiss me on the cheek.' Sometimes, however, we allowed her to kiss us on the lips, and I started to become aware that this may have given her some mixed messages. So, recently, I decided to actively bring up this topic on a quiet afternoon while we were playing together. I asked her some questions and our conversation went a bit like this:

Me: Hey, I have been thinking about how sometimes we kiss on the lips but sometimes I say no, because I don't want to. What do you think about that?

My child: I like kissing you on the lips.

Me: Hmmm . . . yes. What do you like about it?

My child: I don't know. Feels nice. It's what you and Papa do.

Me: Ah yes . . . so Papa and I kiss on the lips, so you want to do that with us too.

My child: Yes.

Me: And do you know that kissing on the lips is private? That I only kiss Papa and you on the lips, and no one else? And that Papa only kisses me and you on the lips, and no one else?

My child: [Silence]

Me: If you have ever kissed someone on the lips and it wasn't me or Papa, that's okay . . . you are not in trouble.

My child: I kissed a friend.

Me: Oh, okay. Do you want to tell me who?

My child: It's Violet.

Me: Thank you so much for telling me. Is there anyone else you kiss on the lips?

My child: No. Only Violet. I love her.

Me: Oh, I know you love her. She is your best friend. And kissing feels nice, and when we do it we say, 'I love you.' I get it. It makes sense. I want you to know that kissing on the lips is private. It is okay to kiss me or Papa on the lips because we are a family. But we don't kiss our friends. Have you ever seen me kiss Jane on the lips? Or Harry when he comes to visit?

My child: No.

Me: I love them very much, they are two of my best friends, but I don't kiss them on the lips because it's private. I only do that with you or Papa. Does that make sense?

My child: Yes.

Me: You can show Violet you love her in many ways, like offering a hug, or a kiss on the cheek, or even saying, 'I love you, Violet.'

Since this conversation, we have talked about 'kissing on the lips' and privacy a lot more. My child is allowed to give someone a kiss if she chooses to, and I want this to be safe and part of a larger conversation about body boundaries and consent. Of course, this conversation will evolve as we continue to talk about sex, romantic relationships and pleasure. What I hope she learns is that she can always talk to me about the things she does with her body, that she will never get into trouble for it and that I will always prioritize her safety.

When your child asks about sex

If your child has not asked yet, take a moment to imagine what feelings and thoughts may show up the first time you hear them say, 'What is sex?' Will you panic about who or where they have heard about sex from? Will you have an urge to ignore them, distract them from receiving an answer by using humour or saying something like 'You are too young to talk about that'?

Pause and, without judgement, be honest about what this brings up for you. Talking about sex with a child can feel scary and risky if you believe it may shatter their innocence. And if your goal is to support your child in staying safe and healthy, your response needs to come from a place of acceptance, openness to listen and willingness to engage in the conversation.

There is no perfect scripted answer about 'what to say' to a child. It's not about reading all the books to become 'good at sex talk'. These are ongoing conversations that are both a privilege and an opportunity. If a child openly asks a question, it means they feel safe enough to hear an answer. No child asks something without knowing or imagining something about it, so first get curious:

- What do they know?
- What have they learned? (Who from? Where?)
- What feelings do they carry from what they know/have seen/heard?
- What can you do to help fill in their knowledge gaps in age-appropriate ways?
- Do you have to take a safeguarding action to protect them (e.g. talk to teachers, set up parental protection on digital devices, etc.)?

More than getting answers, children want to be seen and heard. Knowing that you can sit with their questions, tolerate their feelings and hold space for them is enough for a first conversation. In time, you can broach the topic of sex using books and images to answer questions they have along the way.

The sex video dilemma

A mother disclosed concerns that her seven-year-old, Georgina, had watched a sex tape of her and her father having consensual sex. The mother was concerned about the impact of this on her child, but no one had talked about it. In therapy, it was clear that there was no factual understanding of what Georgina had watched. Georgina had around the same time started to hit out physically and verbally towards her mother, who saw this as a symptom of psychological harm caused by the video. To compensate for this, her parents started loosening the boundaries.

With her parents, I worked on building their confidence to sit with Georgina and talk about what she had seen, what it meant to her and how she was feeling. To begin, the parents shared a brief story with Georgina of what had happened, keeping things simple and honest: 'The other day, you used Mummy's laptop and opened a video. We are not angry with you, and you are not in trouble. We just want to understand what you saw and how you feel about it.'

Part of the work we did together was centred on helping them calm their nervous systems to move through this conversation without leaning into their fears. Some of the questions they asked included things like:

'Tell me what you watched . . . you are not in trouble.'
'Who do you think was on the video?'
'What do you think they were doing?'
'How did you feel watching it?'

These questions are markedly different from questions that place a parent's assumptions, fear or anger at the forefront, such as, 'Why did you watch that video?', 'What was it like to watch people having sex?' or 'Did you feel embarrassed?' You want to give space for a child to speak about what has happened to them and leave out your assumptions.

Georgina's parents discovered that she had not recognized the adults in the film. Instead, she had assumed that her mother had been watching a sex tape and this had left her feeling angry, because Georgina saw this as 'cheating' on her father. Georgina's parents chose not to reveal that they were the adults in the film so as to maintain their privacy. Instead, they focused on reassuring Georgina that their relationship was secure, soothed her big feelings and continued to have educational conversations about sex and consent.

Georgina was not harmed by watching a small part of a sex video because her parents took it as an opportunity to talk about things with her. They also learned to better safeguard their child, including how to set parental controls on family computers and/or limiting access to certain websites on the internet.

A sex script

Below are my words, based on my personal values as a woman who is straight and a parent. They will need adapting. Don't ever try and 'memorize' such a script. Instead, think about what you want your child to learn.

Sex is many things. It is about experiencing pleasure with your body, alone or with someone else. Sex can be words, things you might see, hear or imagine that bring up a feeling of desire. You are allowed to explore all areas of your body, including your private parts, and this is something we call masturbation that you can do in the privacy of your bedroom or the bathroom.

Sex sometimes happens with another person after you have both agreed what is and isn't okay to do to each other and what kind of touch you are happy with. This is a form of intimacy, and if you are having sex with someone who produces sperm it is important to use protection, like a condom. Sex with another person is only legal from the age of sixteen, and doing it before then is unsafe. If anyone ever asks to see, touch or kiss your genitals before you are sixteen, you need to say, 'No. That is private,' and tell me or another adult you trust. You will never get into trouble if this happens. I will always keep you safe.

Some forms of sex can lead to making babies, but most sex doesn't, and many people aren't interested in having sex at all, and that's okay too.

Remember that you don't have to wait for your child to ask questions. You can begin to introduce this topic whenever it seems appropriate, using books, a real-life event or situation, or just when your child expresses genuine curiosity.

Do create a list of 'safe adults' that your child knows they can talk to about the topic of sex or other things they may be nervous speaking with you about. Identify five people your child can call their 'safety network'; this may be extended family, godparents or friends. Don't be offended if your child chooses to talk to someone other than you; see this other person as a resource. All adults have a duty to support their child on this topic. Keep communication collaborative and ongoing with your child and those they might turn to one day.

Everyday opportunities to engage in 'sex talk'

When someone is pregnant

Reproduction is more than just 'penis-in-vagina sex'. That is a very narrow view, and one that is particularly harmful when it comes to the time when they may choose to have a baby themselves. Conception can occur in myriad ways, even if they all include a sperm and an egg. IVF, donor conceptions, adoption and surrogacy are all 'natural ways' of conceiving. All humans deserve to be honoured and treated with respect, whatever beginnings they have.

When themes around LGBTQI+ dating, love and sex come up in stories and films

Ask questions like:

'What do you think about them as a couple?'
'Who else do you know that has two mummies/two daddies?'
'How does it make you feel?'

When you can bring up topics with normality and confidence, it helps children see that all sorts of families and relationships are normal. Don't assume that your child will align with the binary and heterosexual narrative in our society; keep your heart and mind open to who they will become. Model acceptance, and let your child know that they will always be accepted by you.

When gender stereotypes show up in adverts, games, TV, books, films, etc.

Ask questions like:

'Have you noticed how the girls in [that film] who are in relationships are all with boys . . . What do you think of that?'
'Who do you think in [that film] might not be straight? Who do you think they would like?'

The idea that adults need to 'preserve children's innocence' does not align with the programmes, images and stories children come across from an early age. Some TV programmes show male and female characters kissing and in relationships. Others include same-sex characters who live together. What children see and experience is what feels normal to them. Not talking about these topics doesn't stop them being real. Open conversations around media, stories and films that show representations of all kinds of families can educate children in becoming compassionate and accepting other people.

Permission to 'pause and rewind'

When conversations don't go 'as planned', you can pause the conversation and start again. This is not a failure, it's a self-reflection. It might be when emotions take over, or when you use a word or say a sentence you know isn't quite right. At these times, simply say, 'Okay, pause. That's not what I wanted to say. Can we rewind and start again?'

If you have never done this, it might feel a little strange at first. And yet this is a great way of modelling that conversations can be imperfect, that mistakes happen and you can slow down and refocus on what is most important to continue the conversation.

Give yourself permission to talk when it feels right for you

The moment your child chooses to talk about sex will be the moment you are busy doing something important or in a context that makes you think, 'Why now?' Children find it easier to bring things up when the focus isn't on them. If you cannot give this conversation the commitment it deserves, name it, and give yourself permission to come back to it. That might sound like 'This is an important question. I want to talk to you about this, but right now/here, I can't. Can we sit and talk about this together later/another day? Your question is important and I want to answer it.'

It's okay to delay something if you don't feel ready either emotionally or practically; it's never going to be too late to have these conversations. It's having them that matters.

CHAPTER 21

Death Talk

Milo's parents contacted me for a consultation in order to share the news that their beloved cocker spaniel, Lindo, was going to die. Milo and Lindo had such a close bond that his mother did not know how to broach the news. She explained how Lindo had helped Milo tame his night fears by sleeping by the end of his bed. 'They are inseparable,' she said. 'How is Milo going to sleep at night? How can I say that his dog has been "put to sleep"? It's not right . . .'

Death is taboo in our society, and we are constantly looking for words to avoid saying 'death':

- 'They passed away.'
- 'We lost them.'
- 'They are resting in peace.'
- 'They have gone to a better place.'

These are all phrases that try and soften death, and they can be confusing to children. They may ask, 'If someone has gone and everyone is sad, why is no one going to find them?' or, more painfully, 'Where is this better place? Why can't I go with them?' Not talking with openness and honesty about death creates barriers to communication and connection that can have an immediate impact and long-term consequences for processing grief.

When death happens, as adults it can feel hard to include a child in the process. Perhaps you don't know how to talk about it, or maybe you want to protect a child from experiencing pain, or it may be that the depths of your grief leave no space to support them in theirs. The process of grieving is different for every family, and finding a story of death that feels right is unique to you. That is why I won't attempt to give you a 'script' for death, only points of reference to guide the possible conversations that may happen with your child.

There is no 'right' or 'wrong' story about death

We all carry stories about death and dying from our experiences, our family stories, our culture, our society and what we have seen in films and read in books. We don't tend to think about these stories, or even question them. They come to life when someone close to us dies. Have a think for a moment about what stories you carry about death. If you are someone who finds thinking about this topic easier in conversation with someone else, try and answer these questions with a partner, friend or family member:

- What stories about death do you know (family stories, films, books, society . . .)?
- What messages, images and words come to mind?
- In two or three sentences, how do you explain what death is?
- What do you like about this explanation?
- If you were to rewrite a new story about death, what would that sound like? What words or images would you want to include?
- What story do you want to pass on to your children about death and dying?

Milo's parents agreed that using the word 'death' was going to be more useful than using a metaphor. They also knew that Milo was a big Marvel fan and that in the last *Avengers* film he had watched Iron Man die and become flecks of gold dust. This gave them an idea of how to share a death story with Milo that would make sense to him.

Sometimes it can help to read or hear stories about death, to think about how you want to talk about it as a family. There are many books on death and dying, and I use them as resources with children and their parents in my therapy room to consider different ideas. Most books are moving and beautiful, rather than dark and depressing. It can help to see death from multiple perspectives that open up possibilities for the conversation you might have.

Preparing to talk is as important as the talking itself

Children don't need to know about death immediately. You can take minutes, hours and, when someone is unwell, months to gather your thoughts and feel ready to talk.

Choose a time and a place when your child is most able to listen and feel at ease, and where you won't be interrupted. Visualize sitting with your child and imagine what that place may represent for you both in the future. Places can become etched into your memory, with physical and emotional sensations returning when you are in them. For example, talking about death while sitting on the family sofa may feel safer than in a bedroom.

Milo's parents decided to talk to Milo about Lindo's death on a Sunday morning. Sundays were chill-out days and the parents typically pottered around while Milo played with his toys. His parents thought this would be the right time to talk as they would both be available and there would be a good amount of time before bedtime or going to school to talk about any feelings that showed up.

Children don't tend to just sit and talk; it's not developmentally aligned with how their brain works. They talk better when they have things they can play with, draw or do. If your child is younger than ten, setting up some quiet activities that aren't too exciting, such as paper and pens, or a simple sticker book alongside some snacks and a drink, can help to make them feel calm and better able to listen and digest any information you share.

If you have more than one child, it's best to talk to them together, regardless of their age. This prevents older siblings from carrying the burden of protecting younger ones and removes the possibility of younger children feeling 'left out'. My rule of thumb is to privilege language that your youngest child can make sense of, because your eldest can always ask more questions if they want to.

Developmentally appropriate responses

Little ones (under three)
Children can pick up that something serious is happening, but they cannot understand that death is permanent. They may show tearfulness, and this may match the emotional state of the adults around them rather than be a sign of distress. Keeping routines constant (i.e. predictable times for meals, sleep and playtime) can be enough. It is common for children of this age to behave and talk as if nothing has happened.

Young children (between three and five)
Children may have heard about death, but they won't understand what it means. They may imagine that a dead person will come back or is living somewhere else (e.g. 'Can we go and visit

Grandma in Heaven?'). They need reminding that the person who has died will not come back, but they can look at photos and re-member all the things they did together. It is normal to witness children creating 'death stories' in their role-play to make sense of what has happened.

Older children (six to twelve)

Children know that death is permanent but may not understand why they feel strong emotions. They may worry about death being frightening or painful and their loved one getting hurt. They also tend to worry about death happening to them or their family and may show fears of separation or at bedtime.

Sharing your 'death story'

Young children need a simple and literal story about death, one that is straightforward and has no flowery language. Avoid talking about someone being 'lost' or having 'passed away'; children often wonder why no one is looking for the person who has died. Don't say that someone has 'gone to a better place', as children can feel abandoned or angry that the person didn't think being with them was enough. And never tell a child that some-one has 'gone to sleep'. This association can make children avoid going to sleep for fear they or you won't wake up in the morning.

To adults, talking in clear, literal language may appear harsh, but to chil-dren this makes the message clear. The more words you use, the more confusing this can be, so keep it simple, remembering that this will likely be the first conversation of many.

'[The person] has died. That means their body stopped working. So we cannot see them any more, hug them, play with them or eat food with them.'

'You might see me cry because I feel sad. You don't have to worry about my tears. I am okay.'

'It is okay to feel sad, but you are allowed to feel happy or angry or scared. Anything you feel is allowed. I am here for you.'

'Nothing you have said, done or thought has made [the person] die. [The person] dying was no one's fault.'

'We are all safe and healthy. None of us is going to die any time soon.'

'Do you have questions? We can talk about this any time you like.'

These sentences may need adaptation for what is appropriate for you and your family. You can add more context or you can keep it to a few sentences, take a pause and let your child's response guide you.

There is no right or wrong, only what feels right for you and might benefit your child the most. It can help to reassure children that they are not responsible for someone's death, that they didn't do (or not do) anything to make it happen. Due to their brain development and the merging of reality and fantasy, children often find reasons to blame themselves when things go wrong. Separating death from any responsibility on their part can make a big difference.

Milo's mum: Milo, we need to talk to you about something serious. It is not an easy conversation and we want you to know that however you feel, it is okay.

Milo: [Looking up from his play] Okay.

Milo's dad: You know how we have been saying that Lindo is a little bit sick, and that's why we have to give him medicine every day?

Milo: Is he going to die?

Milo's mum: . . . Yes. Yes, he is going to die. I'm sorry, Milo.

Milo: [Starts to cry] I knew it.

Milo's father: Come here, my love. You can cry all you want. We are here for you.

Milo: It's not fair. You said the vet would make him better, and he hasn't. It's all his fault.

Milo's mum: Oh, Milo. It's no one's fault. The vet has done what he could to help Lindo. The medicine has helped him keep going for walks with you, but he isn't the jumpy, playful dog he used to be. His body is not comfortable. We must help Lindo not be in pain any more.

Milo: I don't think I can live without him!

Milo's father: Living without Lindo is going to be very hard for all of us. He is a big part of our family. We all feel sad.

It is important to affirm to children that all feelings in grief are normal and that letting them out is healthy. It can also help to connect through the emotion with your child. Sharing how you feel can help your child normalize their experience. If the feelings of grief are too strong or you think it will be too overwhelming for them to witness, speak with a supportive adult who can help your child and explain why you may need some time to be alone with your feelings. Arrange to spend time with your child when you feel a little brighter to reassure them that you are safe.

Connecting in grief

Milo's parents decided to offer Milo choices about how much he wanted to be a part of taking Lindo to the vet. Milo wanted to spend the most amount of time possible with Lindo and be the last person to give him a cuddle. While they talked, Milo drew a picture – a sunny, bright kind of picture, of a big tree surrounded by lots of colourful flowers and a squirrel. Milo explained that this was Lindo's 'happy place' because he loved the woods and chasing squirrels.

It can help children to be involved in acts of remembrance. Some ideas you may wish to consider:

Start a family ritual

Cook a meal or bake a cake at a particular time of the year, plant a perennial flower or a tree, visit a special place at significant moments across the year or have a small altar of images, amulets or scents that remind you of the person in a special area of your home.

Create a memory box

Fill a box with items about or from the person. Ask your child to add pictures, letters, drawings or items that they make or find that remind them of the person. Look in the box and at its items whenever it feels useful to do so.

Keep their presence alive

Mark the anniversary of the death by celebrating in a way that is meaningful to you (e.g. wearing the person's favourite colour).

Remembering through symbolism

There may be symbols or images that remind you of the person who has died. You can ask your child whether any images or symbols are special to them and think of ways you can have these around if it brings comfort. Many children I have worked with chose animals and plants to represent loved ones, such as birds, butterflies or flowers.

Milo's parents got in touch to let me know how things had gone. Milo had been the last person to say goodbye to Lindo and left the 'happy place' picture to go with him, 'So he feels safe when he sleeps without me,' Milo said. A few days later, they all went to the woods and had a picnic in one of Lindo's favourite spots. Despite Milo's grief, the bedtime fears did not return; Lindo's dog collar and ID tag remained at the end of his bedpost. He and his family made it a Sunday ritual to walk in the woods and be together in Lindo's 'happy place'.

When death hits a family, it can be a time of overwhelming emotions and change. It can also serve to strengthen your family bonds as you navigate grief and acts of remembrance together. Your loved one, whether it is a person or a pet, will always be part of your family story; you will always carry them and the stories you shared together with you.

How to answer children's questions about death

I am regularly asked how to answer children's questions about death. What I offer below are not scripts, they are frameworks I have put into words. I have added more than one possible answer to show you how you can approach the same question differently, depending on your family stories and values.

Will you die?/Will I die?

'Yes, we will all die sometime. Death is a part of life. Right now, you and I are safe and healthy. We are not going to die any time soon.'

'So you've been thinking about death . . . What has made you think about this? What do you think the answer is? How do you feel about that answer? Would you like to know what I think?'

Where have they gone?

'They died, which means their body stopped working. They can no longer feel, speak, walk or see us. We have decided to

remember them by going to visit [special place], and they
will always be with us in our thoughts and our memories.'
'In our faith, we have a story that people go to a place called
Heaven. This is not a real place that we can ever visit. It's an
imaginary place where we like to believe our spirits live on.'

Can they come back?

'No, they cannot. We can never see them again, but we can
look at photos, remember them and talk about them
whenever you want. Would you like to talk about them now?'
'Do you miss seeing them? Yeah, I miss them too. What do
you miss the most? Is that something you would like to
keep doing, even if it is with someone else? Who do you
want to do that with?'

Can we go and see them?

'We cannot see them because they are not alive. How do you
feel about that?'
'Yes, we can see them in photos, but not in person. Would
you like to look at photos with me?'

Are they alone? Cold? Hungry? Do they have toys they can play with? Can they see us?

'When someone dies, their body stops working, so they no
longer feel like we do. They don't get cold/hungry/lonely/
have fun/see us any more because those are things we do
when our body is working and we are alive, like you and I
are right now.'

'I love how thoughtful and caring you are. They knew you loved
them. Do you remember what their favourite [food/game/
etc.] was? Would you like to [eat/play/etc.] that with me?'

Can I send them a picture?

'You can draw or make something in their memory, and we
can talk about it together and put it in a special place. It is
nice to make things for someone you love, and you can
keep loving them for ever, even though you cannot give it
to them.'

'Would you like to make something to remember them by?
How beautiful. Here are some pens and paper. If you want,
next time we go to [their special place], we can leave it
there as an offering, or we can put it up on display on the
mantelpiece and talk about it.'

Do they know we love them/miss them?

'We loved them very much when they were alive, and they
knew this. They loved you too. You were an important part
of their life.'

'I know you loved them very much and miss them deeply. I do
too. Do you want a cuddle? Can you remember how they
used to love us showing them our love and affection?
What did they love doing with you?'

7

Family Life

No family is static. You and your children will change, grow and evolve over time. There are many life changes across the life of a child and their family: rites of passage and transitions that punctuate the passing of time as a family, such as getting a sibling; learning to separate from you to attend nursery, school or spend time with friends; becoming an adolescent; and, eventually, leaving the family home to build their own life, while remaining closely connected to you.

Change is a social, emotional and psychological process that children find tricky. Even just leaving the playground or moving from their cot to a bed can be a trigger for behaviour such as whining, tears and protests. Children do not have the cognitive or emotional capacity to manage the big emotions that accompany transitions, and this might make them stall or push back in order to avoid the change just that little bit longer. If your child is neurodivergent, they may find it hard to switch their attention from one thing to the next either because the change interrupts something they enjoy (e.g. being at home with you versus going to school) or because they have a preference for routine and predictability. In truth, life transitions are hard for everyone. It takes time to adjust to the new rhythm in your home, to learn how to relate to each other amidst the change and to adapt how you spend time together as a family.

A change always comes with an ending, and not all children want to talk about this, but many will communicate their experience through physical signs such as changes in their sleep and appetite, more irritability or tearfulness and a need for physical comfort, touch and tenderness from you. Change is a part of life, so you cannot stop it from happening, but you can prepare your child for a change, validate their feelings, provide support and skills-building and be a grounding anchor while they settle into the new aspect of their life.

CHAPTER 22

Sibling Relationships

Getting a sibling is one of the biggest transitions a child goes through, and it's both a privilege and a gift. No matter what the age gap is, or if you have twins, sibling relationships take time to build and need your compassion and understanding to flourish.

The way you think and talk about your children's relationship has power. When a child gets a sibling, they may be gaining a companion for life, but in those first years in childhood they are also losing the unique devoted relationship they had with you. When children argue, fight, physically hurt another person or say words such as 'I hate the baby. I want them to go away!', parents describe these big feelings as jealousy. I like to reframe these big feelings as something that is closer to grief. When we ask a child, with no choice of their own, to share their home, their space and their most important possession – you – they experience intense emotions. A child's greatest fear is that the baby might steal the love you had for them and keep it for themselves. The behaviours you witness are often masking difficult emotions of pain and loss, of being in a relationship with you that is now going to look different. Difference can be a good and healthy thing, and it can also be hard and take time to adjust to.

Children get along best with their siblings when parents accept that their role is not to interfere in the relationship or act as a 'referee' but to support siblings to nurture their relationship separately to their parents and help them cherish their individuality rather than be in competition with each other. In our society we tend to focus on ways to avoid conflict rather than on how you can nurture relationships. Prevention is more effective than cure, so I am going to focus on the things you can do to support your children in building a positive relationship with each other.

Cherish individual time with each of your children

Spending time together as a family is important, but so is one-to-one, focused time with each of your children. When a child spends time alone with a parent it offers them a space to be seen as an individual and reduces the effects differential treatment can have. Connection is your greatest tool. When a child feels that you could never love anyone else more than you love them, sibling rivalry melts away. Protecting regular time to be with each of your children will give them a sense that they have a special connection to you that cannot be taken away. Make the focus on quality, rather than putting a time on your relationship. Ten to fifteen minutes can be enough – just make sure you and your child enjoy it. In busy households and single-parent homes, this might only be possible once a week while one child is occupied in an activity, playdate or in the care of another safe adult.

When you witness big behaviours that you read as jealousy, remember that what lies beneath is the pain of missing out on your love and that you can do something about this. Protecting individual time for each of your children also offers them an individual space to talk, which can persuade them away from acting out jealous behaviour that hurts, upsets or harms their sibling. A child's perceived threat of losing your love is dispelled when they know that you prioritize and value spending time with them.

Don't blame the sibling

This sounds obvious, but it's something all parents do without intending to. It rolls off the tongue to say, 'I can't play with you right now, I have to change the baby's nappy,' or 'I can't take you to the park, we need to take your brother to gymnastics.' When you blame the baby or other child for why you cannot do things with your child, you inadvertently build resentment and sibling rivalry. Siblings can feel threatened by the amount of care and attention you give to the other child, so keeping language neutral can go a long way to stop this. When you have to prioritize one child over the other, connect with the child you have to leave waiting and give them a clear expectation that separates their needs from what you have to do with their sibling. It might sound like 'Yes, I would love to play with you [connection]. I need ten minutes. Why don't you set up the game and I will be back?' [neutral expectation] or 'Yes, I want to take you to the park [connection]. We can go after school tomorrow. I am sorry that today we haven't got time [expectation].'

When children protest about having to wait, remember that it is always a good opportunity to build patience. Empathize with their feelings (e.g. 'I know it's hard to wait. I'll be back') and be confident that you already do your best to prioritize each child's needs at different times. This is the tricky balance you have to find. When children are upset, it doesn't mean you have got it wrong, it just means it's hard to get enough time with you. See this as a reflection of the relationship you have with each child.

Giving your children the same treatment at all times denies their individual needs, developmental stage, and unique strengths and weaknesses (McHale et al., 2000). Children want to feel seen and be loved by you and they cannot tolerate to be 'less than' their sibling to you. You cannot split yourself in half, but you can show your children that you can meet their unique needs, including tolerating your child's disappointment when they are the one waiting for you.

Nurture sibling relationships

Building up a supply of 'good feelings' helps to protect children from conflict and disagreements. There is a 'magic ratio' in interpersonal relationships of five positive interactions to every negative one. This ratio has been found to be true for couples, teachers and students, and in peer relationships (Sabey et al., 2019). Although the research did not extend to siblings, this is a good range to aim for.

Times when children come together and enjoy each other's company are never random. It may take some 'detective work' to notice what the ingredients are that make this possible, but there are always good reasons why some places, times of day and activities bring siblings together. Consider the below:

- Is it more likely when things are following a routine or outside the mundane (e.g. on holiday, in someone else's house)?
- Is it when they see themselves as 'a team' separate to you (e.g. during structured games when they purposefully 'team up' to reach a goal, like delaying bedtime or running after an adult while playing catch)?
- Is it at particular times of day (e.g. moments of reunion or separation, such as bedtime)?
- What kind of play sparks joy between your children (e.g. creative play, quiet play, outdoor play . . .)?
- Are they better connected when you are not in sight (i.e. what is their behaviour communicating when you are around)?
- Is their connection triggered by emotion (e.g. to comfort, soothe or support)?
- Do they have their basic needs met before they can spend fun time with each other (e.g. hunger, sleep, sensory calm, having personal space)?

Focusing on conflict alone will not support children to build up their relationship. Look at your answers to these questions and think of ways you can create more opportunities for your children to build up their relationship in positive ways. This is where you will see companionship, support and enjoyment blossom in their relationship.

When conflict shows up . . .

Part of building a relationship means experiencing conflict, and sibling relationships are fertile ground to learn skills for conflict resolution. Rather than thinking of conflict as 'bad', reframe conflict as part of the process of being in relationships with others.

Depending on whether you are 'conflict confident' or 'conflict avoidant', you may find this useful or perhaps triggering. If you tend to avoid or distract from having a conflict with others, take a moment to be curious about why. Who told you conflict was bad, scary or dangerous? When you avoid speaking up about your needs, wants or wishes to avoid a conflict, does it bring you closer to the other person or further apart? Your thoughts and emotions will shape the responses you have when you witness conflict around your child.

When your children are arguing or bickering, consider what the conflict is communicating:

- Is it a bid for connection and affection (before they know how to do it in another way)?
- It is because of forced requests to share? (Do they need your protection?)
- Is there a need for personal space? (Is being in the car for an hour too much?)
- Are there basic unmet needs? (How can you pre-empt these in the future?)

- Is it rivalry? (Due to winning or losing, or does one of them not want to compete?)
- Is it a misunderstanding? (What communication skills are missing?)
- Is it teasing and winding-up? (Is it bullying or the need for assertiveness skills?)

Rather than ending the interaction, focus on the opportunity to support and grow your children's relationship with each other by focusing on their skills gaps and unmet needs. If this feels like a gargantuan task, I have two ideas to get you started:

Keep conflict separate from the relationship

Disagreements are often differences in opinion, perspective or knowledge, and not anything to do with the intrinsic value of another person. Teaching this to children means placing the highest value on the relationship, not on the argument.

- Name the behaviour, idea or thought, separate to the identity of a child.
- Offer control by asking children questions that prompt them to think of solutions. This builds problem-solving skills.
- Invite children to do something to nurture their relationship.

Instead of: 'Your brother is being mean. Of course you are upset. Come here.'
Try: 'Your brother doesn't want to play with you, and that hurts. Maybe if we find something fun for you to do, he might want to join later. What do you think?'

Instead of: 'Stop winding up your sister. Did you hear me? Leave her alone!'

Try: 'Hey, come here . . . You're not in trouble. If you want to get your sister's attention, you can just say, "Hey, let's play!" and she might be up for some fun with you.'

Children tend to use conflict as a bid for attention and connection. They haven't yet mastered the skill of openly asking someone to play or do something with them. You can support your child in getting their needs met by teaching them useful communication skills, such as saying, 'I want attention. Please can we play?' or 'I am bored. Can we do something?'

If reading this has landed a little uncomfortably with you because you have an idea that asking for attention is 'bad', think about what this means for you as an adult. When you need to vent to someone, want to have fun or feel sad and need to talk, how do you say to someone else, 'Hey, I need some attention'? Do you use your behaviour, or do you use your words? Thinking about how you communicate your needs may give you an insight into what you are modelling to your child.

Place their relationship at higher value than the conflict

Often, when disagreements show up but there is no risk of physical or emotional harm, the best thing to do as an adult is to keep a close eye but not interfere. Ground yourself for a moment and remember 'My children's relationship is their own, not mine. I trust they can find a way through this.' When you 'referee' your child's interactions, you instinctively tell them who is right and who is wrong. This only makes sibling rivalry grow. Instead, become like Switzerland and stay neutral.

When your children are fighting about 'who' gets to play with a toy or a ball, rather than jumping in to shut them down by saying something like 'If you cannot share this ball, I will take it away,' recognize that your children are learning to take another person's perspective and that you can guide them through this and teach them empathy too. It may sound more like 'He ran off with the ball? Oh, and you felt sad that he didn't want to play with you any more so you shouted . . . We only have one ball, so you're going to have to find a way of making this work for both of you . . . What do you want to do? Any ideas?'

Siblings don't just 'get on', they learn to be in a relationship with each other over time, with conscious effort that nurtures their individuality and the value of coming together. As a parent, your job is to see each of your children as unique individuals, give them individual time to feel secure in your relationship, and focus on consciously nurturing their relationship and building skills for conflict resolution.

CHAPTER 23

Family Relationships

Nurturing your adult relationship

For those parents who have the privilege of being in a parenting couple, the strength of your relationship needs nurturing too. This is built through small moments each day that provide points of connection that deepen your bond.

Think of your relationship as a jar. When you drop in a small 'token', the jar begins to fill up. Putting in a token once a month, no matter how 'big' (e.g. a night out for a nice meal), will mean it takes a long time to fill the jar. When you put in a token each day, no matter how small, these little investments amount to a lot at the end of a week, a month, a year.

Every day, you and your partner will make small bids of attention towards each other, and some might be missed. Imagine that your partner is leaning in for a kiss to say goodbye but, in your mind, you have to run to catch the bus. This could be an opportunity to add a 'token' in your relationship jar. How big the token is depends on how you choose to respond. If you move your cheek towards your partner and run off, it's a tiny token. If, instead, you give them full eye contact and lean in meaningfully to give them a kiss that says 'I see you,' it's going to be a bigger token. These little things may seem unimportant, but amidst the parenting juggle and all the tasks you have to hold in mind, strengthening your relationship should be a priority.

The more your relationship jar fills up, the more conflict protection and the greater resilience you build up for times when arguments between you or your child show up. Connection truly is your best armour.

When children witness conflict between adults

An argument is a fight using words or silence. It is normal for conflict to happen once in a while between adults, and it can be a first step to getting feelings out in the open. Witnessing an argument can make children feel 'wobbly' inside, unprotected and scared. The emotional dysregulation that children witness in the adults/parents has an effect on their sense of emotional and physical safety. Some studies have found that babies as young as six months can register their parents' distress, and children often internalize responsibility and want to fix it or stop it. This is because young children's brains haven't developed enough to understand that what happens between two people is separate to them.

When 'destructive conflict' is around, children may also show behavioural and physical symptoms of distress, including more irritability and aggression, sleep difficulties, headaches, stomach aches, or frequent bouts of pain and illness.

Destructive fighting might look like:

- Verbal aggression: name-calling, insults and threats of abandonment
- Physical aggression: hitting, pushing and aggressive physical contact (e.g. throwing or breaking objects)

- Silence: avoidance, walking out, sulking or withdrawing
- Capitulation: giving in, which might look like a solution but isn't a true one.

Destructive fighting is a form of abuse, and if you experience or witness this around a child, seek support from either a healthcare professional or the police in cases where aggression is present.

When children witness conflict, you have the power to transform this into a learning opportunity. Here are some simple steps to guide you, with the essential ingredients of what helps a child's nervous system regain safety after they have witnessed an argument between two loved adults:

1. **Tell the story**

   To help children understand what has happened, share a simple story of the conflict. 'Daddy and I had an argument. We sometimes don't agree about things, and it is important we talk about it, but we got angry and it was wrong of us to shout like that.'

2. **Reassure**

   Offer reassurance about your family's safety and security with words, physical touch and closeness. 'It is not your fault – the argument was not about you. Even though we fight, we are still a family.'

3. **Bring back safety through repair**

   Adults often repair behind closed doors. ALWAYS repair in front of your child, even if you made up while they were sleeping. Say sorry, give each other a hug. Model to your child what repair looks like and show them that you are okay in a way that is explicit and obvious. Getting on with

> your day as if nothing has happened will keep your child's nervous system on high alert in case the conflict has been paused but isn't finished.
>
> 4. **Validate your child's experience**
>   Offer a safe space for them to talk about their feelings and anything that worried or scared them at the time. 'That felt scary. You really don't like it when I shout at your daddy. I get that. It's not okay. Is there anything else that scared you? I am listening.'
>
> Remember: for children to experience AND witness repair is more important than what the fight itself was about.

Separation

Changes in the family dynamic can take many forms and can involve separation for periods of time. The term 'separation anxiety' gives the impression that there is a problem if you feel anxious when you leave the safety of someone's side. But humans are interdependent, and meaningful connection with others is a human need that brings us comfort, safety and a sense of belonging that extends way past the childhood years. So when children struggle to separate, this isn't a 'problem behaviour', it's a natural part of the process of letting go. One of the consequences of developing object permanence, at around eight months of age, is that children become scared when you go out of sight. Whenever you separate from your child, I want you to remember that to be missed is to be loved. Don't be afraid to get closer before you let go; connection before a separation is also for you.

Taylor had to move schools in September due to a house move. His family had moved house before and this change had been met with excitement from Taylor about all the new things he would do and the new friends he was going to make. This time, though, Taylor was very angry, and he met any attempt to discuss things with his parents with anger or non-committal grunting. I didn't attempt to change his views; instead, I tried to understand what feelings lay beneath his grunts. Taylor let me know that he didn't want to 'say goodbye', that he 'loved his friends' and that moving schools would be 'horrible'.

Help your child prepare for the change

Taylor's parents wanted him 'on board' with the change of school. They struggled with his moping around the home and the angry 'tweenager' they saw in him. The parents had offered to show Taylor photos and videos of the school online and share with him all the extracurricular activities he might want to join in with, but he showed no interest in any of it. This created frustration in his parents and made Taylor push back harder. Taylor wanted his parents to sit with his feelings, to recognize that he did not want to move schools and that saying goodbye to his friends was going to be painful. Before thinking about the new school, Taylor was going through a period of grief for the things he would miss and lose.

Children can take time to understand changes. They benefit from honest facts and, whenever possible, photos, videos or a 'taster' of what the change might be like, for example spending a day with a friend who has a new baby sibling, going to the open day of a school or taking your child to a house viewing. Getting to see and understand what lies ahead can help children make sense of the questions they want to ask and the feelings they may want to share with you.

It's important to be mindful of the expectations you hold about your child looking forward to the 'new'. Children tend to move through experiences at their own pace and with their own unique feelings, and this may not align with yours. Focus on offering preparation with respect towards your child's feelings and when they are ready to learn more about the changes.

Connection before separation gives your child an anchor

Rituals can help with separations, as they have a regulatory effect on our emotions and increase social connection (Hobson et al., 2018). For them to work, you need to make sure the steps are simple and actionable in the moment. When a change is more permanent, either because of a house move, school change or welcoming a new member of the family, it can help to punctuate endings through 'ceremonies' of celebration and goodbye.

This may be things like having a party and celebration for yourselves as a family (e.g. if a new baby is coming) or with friends and people in your community if you are moving away, sharing certificates and notes of gratitude with those that matter to you, planting seeds in a special place to come back to and see them grow, or making concrete plans to see and be with people who matter to you, even if you now live a little further away (even if it is a different country). Giving a concrete end to the way things were can provide closure and allow greater space for the new things that are to come.

Taylor ended up planning a big celebration with all his friends, to play five-a-side football and then have pizza in the park. Taylor was particularly sad and worried that his friends would forget him and that he would miss out on time with them. So his parents agreed that he could invite each of his friends on a different week for a sleepover in the summer once they had settled into their new home. Taylor prepared invitations to give out at his party to make sure that his friends didn't forget the date and he had something to look forward to in the first few weeks of his big change.

When separation is between you and your child, you might use a special word or sentence, a gesture, kiss or hug that tells your child it is nearly time to say goodbye. When it's time to leave, avoid sneaking away while your child is distracted; this is more likely to make your child keep a close eye on you at all times for fear you may disappear. Instead, hold on to the confident courage that tells you your child is going to be safe when you leave, and tolerate witnessing their sadness when you go. To your child, that may sound like 'You are going to be with Lorna. She will keep you safe and has paints and blocks for you to play with. After your snack I will be back to pick you up.'

The love button

Love is an abstract concept to children. They benefit from literal, concrete things they can see and feel to help them understand the idea of 'missing' each other when you are apart.

This tool works well for nursery or school separations, or if you are staying away from your child overnight. It may work best with little ones up to the age of around six or seven, before their brain begins to make sense of abstract concepts. Older children may prefer to carry a 'token of your love' such as a matching bracelet, or carry something of yours with them throughout the day (e.g. a small token, a scarf, a keyring).

1. Draw a heart on the inside of your wrist and one on your child's. Some children like to draw this on you, and some prefer a different symbol. Make it your own and get creative. You can use stick-on tattoos or sew a special button on their cuff and a similar one on yours.
2. Tell them the symbol is a 'love button' and that it keeps you connected. It is a visual representation of the love that connects you.

3. Whenever they miss you, tell them they can look at or press their 'love button' and know you will be thinking of them too.

The 'love button' creates a visual representation of your connection – that thing adults call love. It's not just for your child; separating can be hard for you too, and this little emblem that connects you to your child may bring you comfort throughout your day.

CHAPTER 24

Adolescence

When your child becomes an adolescent

Adolescence is the beginning of a becoming an adult-child, with greater independence and separation from you, their parent. This critical moment in development involves psychological, social and physical changes that will transform your child into someone who looks, thinks and identifies differently to who they were in childhood. All the skills you have learned in relationship with your child up to this point will be a useful toolkit to help you navigate what is to come. To give you a little boost in preparation for this stage, I am offering you three more ideas that I hope will serve as a useful guide.

Get to know your child again

This might sound odd, but when your child becomes an adolescent it's an opportunity for you to get to know them. This means showing an interest in their likes and dislikes, getting to know their friends and using curiosity and connection to influence them.

Research shows that adolescents are motivated more by what their peers think than by any adult around them. Knoll et al. (2015) invited 563 people aged between eight and fifty-nine to rate the riskiness of everyday situations such as crossing a street while texting, cycling without a helmet, driving without a seatbelt and climbing on a roof. The scenarios were presented via audio, alongside a visual image for context. Everyone who participated was shown 'risk ratings' made by other adults or adolescents. Everyone was influenced by seeing someone else's opinion, but children and adults were highly influenced by the risk ratings of adults, whereas twelve- to fourteen-year-olds only changed their ratings to match that of other adolescents, regardless of whether this was underestimating or overestimating a risk.

The primary goal of adolescence is to 'fit in' and find a sense of belonging within a peer group. This study clearly demonstrates that forcing your ideas or opinions on an adolescent is unlikely to work. Instead, if you want to be a positive influence on your child, you have to meet them in a developmentally appropriate way, by becoming interested and curious about the things they are exploring or doing. This can help you become a safe sounding board to guide them. When an adolescent feels that you are interested in them, it makes it more likely they will be willing to share their thoughts, opinions and feelings with you – while maintaining some privacy – which is a normal part of growing up.

Offer unwavering acceptance

More than anything, adolescents want to feel valued for who they are – and who doesn't want that? Showing them acceptance, interest and respect is key to keeping your connection growing and being a positive influence on them.

Setting clear boundaries is important, but rather than giving structured choices as you may have done in childhood, you now have to adapt to relating to your child in a more grown-up way. This means getting vulnerable enough to share your concerns honestly and openly while truly listening to their point of view.

Max recently turned fifteen, and his parents were adjusting to his push for freedom. His mother was scared of letting him go out to house parties because Max had told her there was sometimes alcohol there. We talked about their relationship and how strong it must be for Max to be so honest about the alcohol, which he had shared willingly and without pressure. We also talked about trust and whether his parents believed him when he said he wanted to go to be with his friends but had no intention of drinking at the party. Given their close bond, Max's parents negotiated with him that he was allowed to go out up to 10.30 p.m. and that they would be collecting him in the car. Max was responsible for keeping an eye on the clock and seeing his parents' text to meet them outside. His parents also set a clear boundary that if Max ever did any underage drinking it would break their trust and they would be less willing to let him go out.

As parents, it's so normal to feel scared in situations like this and get pulled into saying no immediately, to safeguard your child. After all, no matter what age your child is, they are still your child. Remember that 'no' can shut down their brain and escalate into conflict. It can help to slow things down by either using 'yes' as a boundary, or 'maybe' to give you time to talk and think before giving an answer.

When you shut down your child's voice too firmly or too soon, you are likely to create barriers to communication, and this makes it less likely they will want to talk about their world and experiences with you. This will interfere with your relationship and put you in a blind spot about how to safeguard and protect your child – when you are out of the loop about their life, you do not know what risks they or their friends might be taking.

Show them you value them

Be intentional about making your home a place that doesn't function in the same way without your adolescent, because they are a core member of it. You might hate it, you might be bad at it, and it might make you uncomfortable, but regularly joining in with your adolescent child in something they love can have a big impact. What am I talking about? I mean getting out of your comfort zone to engage in an activity they enjoy that you may not, or that you may be terrible at. For example, if your adolescent is into video games, ask them if they can teach you how to play so you can join them. Ask if you can watch the latest TV series or reality show, or whatever else they are into. You might find this cringey, but if you don't know what they are watching, you miss out on conversations with your child about the things they learn from TV, and you may also miss out on doing or watching things you didn't know you enjoyed.

Adolescents need to belong with their peers, and they need to find a new way of belonging in your home with you too. It might be that they are 'a fixer' and can help fix things around your home, like changing a lightbulb or working out why the remote-control car has stopped working. Perhaps they are a 'thinker' who likes to research and understand information, so they can help research hotels or holidays for your next family trip. Maybe they are 'creative' and can plan or decorate for birthdays or yearly festivities such as Christmas. Think about who your child is and give them opportunities to take responsibility for parts of your family home that can help them shine. This cements their role in your family and lets them know they are valued members of your 'family tribe', now and always.

Adolescence is an important chapter in a child's life, one that sets them up to go into the world as a young adult with a brain a lot closer to maturity. You are likely to get things wrong in this part of your child's life, as you will have done when they were younger. Give yourself permission to get things wrong, and try again. Mismatched interactions can bring you closer to understanding this new relationship you are creating, and that will guide you into becoming the parent of an adult-child.

CHAPTER 25

Adult Repair

Being a parent is messy work and, because we are human, we will get it wrong. No matter what toolkits you carry and how hard you work at being gentle, validating and collaborative, it's likely that one day your child will say, 'You could have done [X] differently.' It is also likely that in becoming a parent you begin to recognize things in your own childhood that could have been different. This isn't about placing blame, it's about having conversations of repair that can bring you closer together. These conversations are an invitation to understand your relationship with one another, and that can bring you closer together if you approach it with an open heart and willingness to accept difference. Three ideas to hold in mind:

Listen

If it is your adult-child bringing something up, allow them to feel understood and heard by you. Don't interject or correct them; only they know what it felt like to be the child parented by you. The more open to listening to your child's story you are, the better this conversation will flow.

If you are the one bringing up the conversation with your own parent, pay attention to what they say back. If it sounds like a conversation is possible, keep talking. If their defences are coming up, they are getting angry or denying your experience, set a boundary. You don't have to engage in conflict; you can choose to step away by gently backtracking. This may sound like 'I don't want to hurt you, I just want to talk. I can tell now is not a good time to talk about this so maybe we can talk another time.'

Show empathy and compassion – for you and for them

Focus on validating your adult-child's experience. Instead of 'Well, that is unfair. I wasn't around because I was working so I could get you the things you need. You sound very ungrateful,' try to connect with their emotion. Just like in childhood, see beneath their words to understand your child's experience: 'I didn't know you felt so abandoned and held on to this for years. I guess I did not show you how much I missed being with you and our family when I went away for work. That's on me. I am sorry.'

If you are the one sharing the experiences that made you feel sad, hurt or in pain, know that whatever your parent says, your lived experience was real and no one can take that away from you. If your parent is not able to empathize with it now, it's likely that hearing your experience makes them feel shame or guilt. Give your parents compassion – it can take time for someone to find the courage to self-reflect and understand that they did their best and that their mistakes were part of the process.

Set boundaries

In some cases, an adult-child may feel such pain that they can't help but attack. You always have the right to set boundaries to protect yourself and do so respectfully: 'I won't let you shout at me. I am happy to talk to you about this another time, but now I need you to go.'

Similarly, if you notice yourself getting fired up, or beginning to shout and become dysregulated, take a pause. Self-regulate. And set a boundary that says, 'This conversation is too important for me to argue about. Let's talk when we are both calmer.'

It is never too late to have a conversation to repair. I don't believe in placing blame on our parents, because we are all flawed humans. I do believe in finding forgiveness for whatever was experienced in your childhood and setting firm boundaries that keep you and those you love protected, whether that be restricting contact or having no contact whatsoever, ensuring you only meet in safe places, or setting limits on how long you spend with someone. Only you know what is right for you and your family.

New Beginnings

Getting to the end of this book is no small feat. It takes commitment and courage to pick up a book on parenting, let alone one that might dispel many of the things you learned growing up or have been told are 'right' by society. To me, as a clinical psychologist, it says a lot about the dedication you have towards your child and the relationship you wish to have with them.

My one hope with this book is that it offers you reassurance that your instincts to lean in to hold, love, soothe, validate and listen to your child are the right ones. They are not 'soft' or enabling of bad behaviour but are developmentally appropriate strategies that support you to learn more effectively and create tighter bonds of trust in your relationship. This will then allow you to be a positive influence for your child during their childhood years and beyond.

In reality, there is no book that is ever going to be able to connect with your whole experience as a parent. You are the expert in your child, and they are the expert of what they feel, see and want. I trust you to make the right choices for your child as you lean in to get to know them and understand them, and that you will take the tools that are most useful to you from this book and drop any that aren't a good fit.

Parenting is messy and imperfect, no matter how hard you work at it. You will make mistakes. See these moments as possibilities for growth, change and repair. Forgive yourself for not knowing then what you know now. Change is always possible, and it is never too late to do something different if you think it may be useful for you or your child.

The words on these pages are meaningless unless you choose to bring them to life. That is why I have a deep gratitude to you for taking the time to read them. I hope they remind you that you are already a good parent and that doing your best truly is enough. If it offers you ideas and small tweaks you can add to your everyday life to shrink power battles, alter the atmosphere in your home or give you a slight shift in perspective that you find useful, then that is credit to you – not this book. You are the one putting in the hours of work caring for and loving a child (or several) every day. I have huge admiration for all parents who can see that parenting is a job *and* a gift. And you are the greatest gift of all to your child. I am honoured if anything I have shared in this book becomes a tiny part of this crazy parenting journey we are on.

With love – from me to you.

Further Reading

If you are interested in reading the research that is discussed in this book or want to learn more on a particular topic, here is a list of curated resources for you to read with your child.

FOUNDATIONS

Carroll J. E., Gruenewald T. L., Taylor S. E., et al. (2013). Childhood abuse, parental warmth, and adult multisystem biological risk in the Coronary Artery Risk Development in Young Adults study. *Proceedings of the National Academy of Sciences (PNAS)*, 110 (42): 17149–17153.

Cesario, J., Johnson, D. J., & Eisthen, H. L. (2020). Your Brain Is Not an Onion With a Tiny Reptile Inside. *Current Directions in Psychological Science*, 29(3): 255–260.

Dixon, S. V., Graber, J. A., & Brooks-Gunn, J. (2008). The roles of respect for parental authority and parenting practices in parent-child conflict among African American, Latino, and European American families. *Journal of Family Psychology*, 22(1): 1–10.

Eadie P., Bavin E. L., Bretherton L., et al. (2021). Predictors in infancy for language and academic outcomes at 11 years. *Pediatrics* 147(2): 1–12.

Feldman R., Rosenthal Z., & Eidelman A. (2014). Maternal-Preterm Skin-to-Skin Contact Enhances Child Physiological Organization and Cognitive Control Across the First 10 Years of Life. *Biological Psychiatry*, 75(1): 56–64.

Luby J. L., Barch D. M., Belden A. et al. (2012). Maternal support in early childhood predicts larger hippocampal volumes at school age. *Proceedings of the National Academy of Sciences (PNAS)*, 109(8): 2854–2859.

Young, E. S., Simpson, J. A., Griskevicius, V., Huelsnitz, C. & Fleck, C. (2019) Childhood attachment and adult personality: A life history perspective. *Self and Identity*, 18(1): 22–38.

Zhang, W., Wei, X., Ji, L. et al. (2017). Reconsidering Parenting in Chinese Culture: Subtypes, Stability, and Change of Maternal Parenting Style During Early Adolescence. *Journal of Youth and Adolescence*, 46: 1117–1136.

Further Reading

Boswell, S., *Understanding Your Baby (The Tavistock Clinic)* (Jessica Kingsley, 2004).

Gerhardt, S., *Why Love Matters: How affection shapes a baby's brain* (Routledge; 2nd Edition, 2014).

Lapointe, V., *Parenting Right From The Start: Laying a Healthy Foundation in the Baby and Toddler Years* (LifeTree, 2019).

Roy, D., *Executive Functioning Workbook for Kids: A Fun Adventure with Bora the Space Cat to Learn How to Plan, Prioritize, and Set Goals for Everyday Life* (Edchieve LLC, 2022).

FEELINGS

Durston, S., Davidson, M. C., Tottenham, N., et al. (2006). A shift from diffuse to focal cortical activity with development. *Developmental Science*, 9(1), 1–8.

Ekman, P. (1970). Universal facial expressions of emotion. *California Mental Health Research Digest*, 8(4), 151–158.

Lebowitz E. R., Marin C., Martino A., et al. (2020). Parent-Based Treatment as Efficacious as Cognitive-Behavioral Therapy for Childhood Anxiety:

A Randomized Noninferiority Study of Supportive Parenting for Anxious Childhood Emotions. *Journal of the American Academy of Child and Adolescent Psychiatry,* 59(3), 362–372.

Morris, A. S., Silk, J. S., Morris, M. D. S., et al. (2011). The influence of mother–child emotion regulation strategies on children's expression of anger and sadness. *Developmental Psychology,* 47(1), 213–225.

Plutchik R. (1982) A psychoevolutionary theory of emotions. *Social Science Information,* 21(4–5), 529–53.

Silvers, J. A., Insel, C., Powers, A. et al. (2017). The transition from childhood to adolescence is marked by a general decrease in amygdala reactivity and an affect-specific ventral-to-dorsal shift in medial prefrontal recruitment. *Developmental Cognitive Neuroscience,* 25: 128–137.

Thomassin, K., & Seddon, J. A. (2019). Implicit attitudes about gender and emotion are associated with mothers' but not fathers' emotion socialization. *Canadian Journal of Behavioural Science / Revue canadienne des sciences du comportement,* 51(4), 254–260.

White, M., & Epston, D. (1990). *Narrative Means To Therapeutic Ends.* (W. W. Norton, 1990).

Yin, B., Teng, T., Tong, L. et al. (2021). Efficacy and acceptability of parent-only group cognitive behavioral intervention for treatment of anxiety disorder in children and adolescents: a meta-analysis of randomized controlled trials. *BMC Psychiatry,* 21(29).

Further Reading

Brown, B., *Atlas of the Heart: Mapping Meaningful Connection and the Language of Human Experience* (Vermilion, 2021).

Feldman-Barret, L., *How Emotions Are Made: The Secret Life of the Brain* (Macmillan press, 2017).

Hepburn, E., *A Toolkit for Your Emotions: 45 Ways to Feel Better* (Greenfinch, 2023).

Ironside, V., *The Huge Bag of Worries* (Hodder Children's Books, 2011).

The School of Life, *An Emotional Menagerie: Feelings from A to Z* (The School of Life Press, 2020).

Stewart, L., *Happy, Healthy Minds: A Children's Guide to Emotional Well-being* (The School of Life Press, 2020).

LOSING CONTROL

Bryson, T. P. & Siegel, D., *The Whole-Brain Child: 12 Proven Strategies to Nurture Your Child's Developing Mind* (Robinson, 2012).

Music, G., *Nurturing Natures* (Routledge, 2016).

Peters, S., *My Hidden Chimp* (Studio Press, 2018).

DISCIPLINE

Blake, P. R. & Harris, P. L. (2009). Children's understanding of ownership transfers, *Cognitive Development*, 24(2): 133–145.

Blake, P. R. (2010). *The cognitive development of ownership: How children learn to recognize and respect private property.* Harvard University ProQuest Dissertations Publishing.

Emmons, R. A. & McCullogh, M. E. (2003). Counting Blessings Versus Burdens: An Experimental Investigation of Gratitude and Subjective Well-Being in Daily Life. *Journal of personality and social psychology*, 84(2): 377–389.

Larzelere, R. E., Knowles, S. J., Henry. C. S. & Ritchie, K. L. (2018). Immediate and Long-Term Effectiveness of Disciplinary Tactics by Type of Toddler Noncompliance, *Parenting*, 18(3), 141–171.

Siegel, D. J., & Bryson, T. P. *The Yes Brain: How to Cultivate Courage, Curiosity, and Resilience in Your Child.* First edition (Bantam, 2018).

Wu, Z., Zhang, Z., Guo, R., & Gros-Louis, J. (2017). Motivation counts: Autonomous But Not Obligated Sharing Promotes Happiness in Preschoolers. *Frontiers in Psychology*, 8: 867.

Further Reading

Cooper, A., *Reflective Parenting: A Guide to Understanding What's Going on in Your Child's Mind* (Routledge, 2015).

Faber, A. & Mazlish, E., *How to Talk So Kids Will Listen and Listen So Kids Will Talk* (Piccadilly Press, 2012).

Greene, R. S., *The Explosive Child: A New Approach for Understanding and Parenting Easily Frustrated, Chronically Inflexible Children* (Harper Paperbacks, 2021).

SKILLS FOR LIVING

Brazelton, T. B. (1962). A child-oriented approach to toilet training. Pediatrics, 29, 121–128.

Colten, H. R. & Altevogt, B. M. (2006). *Sleep Disorders and Sleep Deprivation: An Unmet Public Health Problem.* Institute of Medicine and Research, Washington DC.

Del Giudice, M. (2012). The Twentieth Century Reversal of Pink-Blue Gender Coding: A Scientific Urban Legend? *Archives of Sexual Behavior,* 41(6), 1321–1323.

Douglas P. S. & Hill P. S. (2013). Behavioral sleep interventions in the first six months of life do not improve outcomes for mothers or infants: a systematic review. *Journal of Developmental & Behavioural Pediatrics,* 34(7), 497–507.

Ferber R., *Solve Your Child's Sleep Problems: New, Revised, and Expanded Edition.* (Fireside, 2006).

Further Reading

Fisher J. O. & Birch L. L. (1999). Restricting access to palatable foods affects children's behavioral response, food selection, and intake. *American Journal of Clinical Nutrition* 69(6), 1264–1272.

Haines J., Haycraft E., Lytle L., et al. (2019). Nurturing Children's Healthy Eating: Position statement. *Appetite,* 1(137), 124–133.

Hall, W. A., Hutton, E., Brant, R. F. et al. (2015). A randomized controlled trial of an intervention for infants' behavioral sleep problems. *BMC Pediatrics,* 15: 181.

Institute of Medicine (2006). *Sleep Disorders and Sleep Deprivation: An Unmet Public Health Problem.* Washington, DC: The National Academies Press.

Ramos K. D. & Young Clarke D. M. (2006) Parenting advice books about child sleep: cosleeping and crying it out. *Sleep,* 29(12), 1616–1623.

Reuter, A., Silfverdal, S-A., Lindblom, K., Hjern, A. (2020). A systematic review of prevention and treatment of infant behavioural sleep problems. *Acta Paediatrica,* 109(9): 1717–1732.

Rollins B. Y., Loken E., Savage J. S. & Birch L. L. (2014). Effects of restriction on children's intake differ by child temperament, food reinforcement, and parent's chronic use of restriction. *Appetite,* 73, 31–39.

Rosier, J. G., & Cassels, T. (2021). From "Crying Expands the Lungs" to "You're Going to Spoil That Baby": How the Cry-It-Out Method Became Authoritative Knowledge. *Journal of Family Issues,* 42(7), 1516–1535.

Satter, E. (1990) The Feeding Relationship: Problems and Interventions. *Journal of Pediatrics,* 117, 181–189.

Wolke, D., Meyer, R., Ohrt, B. and Riegel, K. (1995). The Incidence of Sleeping Problems in Preterm and Fullterm Infants Discharged from Neonatal Special Care Units: An Epidemiological Longitudinal Study. *Journal of Child Psychology and Psychiatry,* 36(2), 203–225.

Further Reading

Brown, S., *Play: How It Shapes the Brain, Opens the Imagination, and Invigorates the Soul* (J. P Tarcher/Penguin Putnam, 2010).

Hookway, L., *Still Awake: Responsive Sleep Tools for Toddlers to Tweens* (Pinter & Martin, 1st Edition, 2021).

Russell, C., *The PlayHOORAY! Handbook: 100 Fun Activities for Busy Parents and Little Kids Who Want to Play* (Seven Dials, 2021).

Stirling-Reed, C., *How to Wean Your Baby: the step-by-step plan to help your baby love broccoli as much as their cake* (Vermilion, 2021).

Thomas, L., *Just Eat It* (Pan Macmillan, 2019).

BIG TOPICS

Ashcraft A. M., Murray P. J. (2017). Talking to Parents About Adolescent Sexuality. *Pediatric Clinics of North America*, 64(2), 305–320.

Borg, K., Snowdon, C. & Hodes, D. (2014). Child sexual abuse: recognition and response when there is a suspicion or allegation. *Paediatrics and Child Health*, 24(12), 536–543.

Elliot, M. (1995). Child sexual abuse prevention: What offenders tell us. *Child Abuse & Neglect*, 19(5), 579–594.

Fonner, V. A., Armstrong, K. S., Kennedy, C. E., O'Reilly, K. R., & Sweat, M. D. (2014). School based sex education and HIV prevention in low- and middle-income countries: a systematic review and meta-analysis. *PLoS One*, 9(3).

Gardner, F., Montgomery, P. & Knerr, W. (2015). Transporting evidence-based parenting programs for child problem behavior (Age 3–10) between countries: Systematic review and meta-analysis. *Journal of Clinical Child and Adolescent Psychology*, 45(6), 749–762.

Leijten, P., Melendez-Torres, G. J., Knerr, W. & Gardner, F. (2016). Transported Versus Homegrown Parenting Interventions for Reducing Disruptive Child Behavior: A Multilevel MetaRegression Study. *Journal of the American Academy of Child and Adolescent Psychiatry*, 55(7), 610–61.

Lois Tonkin TTC, Cert Counselling (NZ) (1996) Growing around grief—another way of looking at grief and recovery, *Bereavement Care*, 15(1).

UNESCO (2016). *Review of the evidence on sexuality education. Report to inform the update of the UNESCO International Technical Guidance on Sexuality Education.* Montgomery, P. & Knerr, W. University of Oxford Centre for Evidence-Based Intervention.

Further Reading

Fredman, G., *Death Talk: Conversations with Children and Families* (Routledge, 1997).

Greener, R., *Making a baby: An inclusive guide to how every family begins* (Nosy Crow, 2021).

Gurney, K., *Mind the Gap: The Truth about Desire and How to Futureproof Your Sex Life* (Headline Home, 2020).

Hancock, J., *Can We Talk about Consent?* (Frances Lincoln Children's Books, 2021).

Karst, P., *The Invisible String* (Little Brown Young Readers, 2018).

Silverberg, C., *Sex Is a Funny Word: A Book about Bodies, Feelings and YOU* (Seven Stories Press, 2015).

Teckentrup, B., *The Memory Tree* (Orchard Books, 2014).

FAMILY LIFE

Hobson, N. M., Schroeder, J., Risen, J. L., Xygalatas, D., & Inzlicht, M. (2018). The Psychology of Rituals: An Integrative Review and Process-Based Framework. *Personality and Social Psychology Review*, 22(3), 260–284.

Knoll, L. J., Magis-Weinberg, L., Speekenbrink, M., & Blakemore, S-J. (2015). Social Influence on Risk Perception During Adolescence. *Psychological Science*, 26(5), 583–592.

McHale, M. S., Updegraff, K. A., Jackson-Newsom., J, Tucker, C. J. & Crouter, A. C. (2000). When does parental differential treatment have negative implications for siblings? *Social Development*, 9(2): 149–172.

Sabey, C. V., Charlton, C. & Charlton, S. R. (2019). The "magic" positive-to-negative interaction ratio: Benefits, applications, cautions and recommendations. *Journal of Emotional and Behavioral Disorders*, 27(3), 154–164.

Further Reading

Markham, L., *Calm Parents, Happy Siblings: How to stop the fighting and raise friends for life* (Vermilion, 2015).

Perry, P., *The Book You Wish Your Parents Had Read (and Your Children Will Be Glad That You Did)* (Penguin Life, 2020).

Samuel, J., *Every Family Has a Story: How We Inherit Love and Loss* (Penguin Life, 2022).

Siegel, D. J., *Brainstorm: The Power and Purpose of the Teenage Brain* (Scribe: UK edition, 2014).

Gratitude

This book would never have been written if it wasn't for the support, guidance and love I received throughout this process.

Writing this book would not have been possible without the enthusiastic support, love and commitment of my husband, Chris, who cared for our child, our home and my wellbeing while I hid away with my laptop for days on end. You are my greatest cheerleader and you helped me believe I could do this even when I didn't think it was possible. Thank you for always making me laugh through hardship (even when it's completely inappropriate!).

To my daughters, L and E, who inspire me daily to be a better version of myself. Thank you for loving me the way you do and choosing me to be your mama. You are my greatest achievements; I am so proud to be a part of your life story.

Never on earth would I have contemplated writing a book if it wasn't for Francesca Zampi and Carly Cook who saw 'something' in me. I hope this book does their vision justice. Thank you for your support day and night and for being my trusted and safe sounding boards when I get wobbly (I am not always worried, I am often just confused . . .). Your warmth and enthusiasm are contagious, and you make me believe in myself in ways I never thought possible. I love you both dearly and feel privileged to have had your incredible minds and warm hearts by my side throughout.

To my editor, Kate Fox, and the team at Transworld and Penguin Random House, I am grateful for your passion that helped me condense two books' worth of writing into this one! In a market saturated by books on parenting, thank you for believing in a new author like me to communicate the science of child and family psychology.

Gratitude

Thank you to Emma Hepburn, who offered me regular nudges of support, giggles, and wisdom about the ups and downs of writing a book as a clinical psychologist. I so valued your company throughout this process.

And to my circle of silent and loud cheerleaders: my friends, my parents, my brother and my village of local mums – thank you for your words of encouragement and practical help given to me and my family. I won't list your names because you know who you are (and if you don't, don't worry – I will make sure to remind you frequently).

In a world where social media gets a terrible rap, it is a rare gem to find a space that is supportive, kind and passionate about children's wellbeing. I am grateful to all of you who have chosen to join my Instagram community, listen to my podcasts, and/or have joined the Confident Parent Course. Thank you for all you do for your children every day, I feel honoured if any of the work I share helps to empower you in parenting your children.

And finally, I want to express gratitude for every child and family I have had the privilege to support in the NHS and in my private practice. You have all touched my life in more ways than you will ever know, and I have learnt more from you than any textbook or course could ever teach me. I feel honoured to have walked alongside you through a part of your life journey.

Picture Acknowledgements

Diagram on p. 78 by Dan Prescott at Couper Street Type Co.
Diagram on p. 98 by Hannah Dale at Global Creative Learning.

About the Author

Dr Martha Deiros Collado is a clinical psychologist trained in health psychology and family systems theory and practice. She has spent nearly two decades of her life learning, critically understanding and making sense of psychological models of therapy, and health science. Most importantly, she applies her learnings every day in her therapy room, having met with thousands of families over the course of her more than sixteen-year career working in paediatric medical teams within the NHS. She manages to deftly mix scientific knowledge with practical application.

Notes

Notes

Notes

Notes

Notes

Notes

Notes

Notes